S0-ABD-883

The Complete Multi-Engine Pilot

Second Edition

Bob Gardner

Foreword by Barry Schiff

Aviation Supplies & Academics, Inc.
Newcastle, Washington

ASA-MPT-2

The Complete Multi-Engine Pilot, Second Edition
Bob Gardner

Aviation Supplies & Academics, Inc.
7005 132nd Place SE
Newcastle, WA 98059-3153

©1995–2001
Aviation Supplies & Academics, Inc.
All rights reserved. Published 1999. Second Printing 2001
(First edition published 1995.)

None of the material in this manual supersedes any operational documents or procedures issued by the Federal Aviation Administration, aircraft and avionics manufacturers, flight schools, or the operators of the aircraft.

Cover photo © Jim Larsen

Original artwork by Richard Bringloe
Photo and illustration credits: p. 1-7 photo by Tonya Rutan, used by permission (courtesy Scaled Composites); p. 2-1, photo courtesy Chuck Pepka; p. 2-5, courtesy Avco Lycoming Flyer; p. 2-9 & 2-16, pp. 3-2, 3-4–3-8, 3-13–3-20, courtesy Beech Aircraft Corporation; p. 5-1, Jim Larsen; pp. 5-3, 5-4, 6-2, 7-3, courtesy Beech Aircraft Corporation. *Note:* All illustrations from the Beechcraft Duchess Manual are for educational purposes only and are not to be used for the operation of any aircraft.

Printed in Canada

04   03   02   01   9   8   7   6   5   4   3   2

ISBN 1-56027-448-4
ASA-MPT-2

Library of Congress Cataloging-in-Publication Data:

Gardner, Robert E., 1928–
   The complete multi-engine pilot / by Bob Gardner ;
   original artwork by Richard Bringloe.
      p.   cm.   (The complete pilot series)
   Includes index.
   ISBN 1-56027-124-8
   1. Multi-engine flying. I. Title. II. Series.
TL711.T85G37 1995
629.132'52—dc20   95-48922
                                        CIP

Contents

Acknowledgement

As an aviation educator, I have amassed quite a collection of books, magazines, audio tapes and videotapes. I have subscribed to just about every aviation publication available during the past 20 years, and I can't visit a pilot supply store without buying at least one book. My library includes a wide variety of federal publications available to the public and some that I have scrounged from friends in the FAA.

I must admit, then, that the methods and procedures discussed in this book are not new, unique or original; with the exception of the zero sideslip theory, there is nothing new in the aerodynamics of multi-engine flight and the handling of emergencies. This text is a synthesis of the ideas of many authors as I have absorbed them over the years, molded and shaped by my own experience as a pilot and instructor. My thanks to all of the pilot-authors whose words and thoughts have contributed to this book.

In addition, a new appendix added in this second edition offers a chance for readers to take a look at what the FAA has provided in multi-engine training materials.

I am fortunate that Les Berven, the FAA engineer whose research on zero sideslip forced changes in multi-engine training, is based right here in Seattle. Mr. Berven has checked the text to be sure that it accurately reflects his findings and has contributed invaluable information based on his experience as a test pilot and engineer.

Bob Gardner

Foreword

In 1956, I was working my way through college by flying part-time for the Acme Meat Company in Los Angeles. As the chief-and-only pilot for Acme, my job was to fly cattle buyers around the Southwest in a 260-hp Navion. At that time, it was the largest, most-powerful airplane I had ever flown.

But then one day, my employer, Paul Blackman, advised that he was planning to replace the single-engine airplane with a Riley-converted Twin Navion, and I would soon be getting my multi-engine rating. Upon hearing this wonderful news, I hopped in my Volkswagen "Beetle" and sped to Pan American Navigation Service in Van Nuys, California, which at that time was the world's largest publisher and supplier of aviation books.

"I'd like a book about multi-engine flying," I told the sales clerk.

"Well, son. There is no such thing. You'll learn everything you need to know from your instructor."

And so it went. I never had the advantage of a well-written textbook such as you are now holding. In those days, the "secrets" of learning to fly a multi-engine airplane were handed down from one pilot to the next. Needless to say, there were as many misconceptions passed along as there were pearls of wisdom.

My instructor was Paul Bell. He advised that there was little difference between a single and a twin when both engines operate as advertised. "The problems," he cautioned, "are encountered when an engine fails. It requires sound training and diligent adherence to procedures to keep the airplane flying straight ahead and coaxing needed performance from the crippled craft."

While sitting together at the airport coffee shop, he grabbed a napkin from the dispenser and prepared the following list:

1. Control the airplane.

2. Maximize power.

3. Minimize drag.

4. Trim for maximum performance.

5. "This," he said with a grin, "is all you need to know."

Gee, I thought, this doesn't seem very complicated. But as I soon learned, the brevity of that short list belies the amount of skill and knowledge needed to comply with its mandates. As I proceeded with my training, I kept praying that a textbook would suddenly appear to answer the myriad questions that arose. No such luck.

Although this book is a bit late to satisfy my needs of 1956, you are fortunate that it is available now to provide valuable guidance and assistance. By following Bob Gardner's sage and enlightening advice, and studying the principles he so eloquently discusses (and simplifies!), the challenging task of becoming a proficient and knowledgeable multi-engine pilot will become easier and more understandable.

So I leave you now in Bob Gardner's capable hands and wish you the best of luck and lots of fun in your multi-engine endeavors.

Barry Schiff
TWA Captain, Retired
Los Angeles, California

Introduction to Twins

Art Blanster's six-passenger single-engine airplane is sleek, fast, and equipped with the latest in navigation equipment, but it is uncomfortably close to its maximum gross takeoff weight when he loads it with his business associates and the equipment they need to make a sales demonstration in a distant city. A multi-engine airplane will give Art the load-carrying capability that he needs. Adding "Multi-Engine Land" to his certificate is a business necessity.

Paula Forsham's flying club has six singles and a twin, and she is checked out in every one of the single-engine airplanes. Six months ago, a vacuum pump failure in one of them resulted in a descent through clouds using needle, ball, and airspeed, and just last week a broken alternator belt caused a total electrical failure. Paula is aware that a twin's redundant vacuum and electrical systems will tip the odds in her favor.

Pat Manley is 21 and has already logged 1,400 hours in single-engine airplanes as an instructor and charter pilot. He wants to put a multi-engine Airline Transport Pilot certificate in his wallet when he turns 23, and he knows that the more twin time he has in his log, the better his chances with a commuter or major airline will be. For Pat, getting a twin rating is a smart career move.

Each of these pilots accepts the fact that getting a multi-engine rating will involve additional costs, but they all feel the advantages outweigh the cost factor. Each pilot will rationalize the decision to upgrade in his or her own way, but there is no denying that

having Multi-Engine Land added to a pilot's certificate provides the extra pride of accomplishment that goes with stepping up to a higher skill level. Paula, Pat, and Art are ready to take on a new challenge—are you?

Multi-Engine Training

The FAA does not require you to log a minimum number of hours of instruction before the multi-engine checkride. The flight check is a demonstration of proficiency, and your instructor will sign the recommendation form when he or she feels you are ready. During training, you will probably spend an hour or two doing airwork such as slow flight, approaches to stalls, and steep turns, to develop a sense of how an airplane with more of its mass off-center behaves. Pattern work will consist of normal takeoffs and landings as well as short- and soft-field takeoffs and landings. Then the emphasis will shift to emergencies, both at altitude and close to the surface.

You can hone some of the required skills in a good multi-engine simulator, at a considerable reduction in cost and total time. My definition of a "good" multi-engine ground training device (FAA-speak for what light-plane folks call simulators) is one that replicates the changes in control pressures that occur when an engine fails—most pilot reactions to emergency situations are based on rudder pressure. However, a PC-based device such as ASA's "On Top" is useful for learning emergency procedures based on instrument indications alone, practicing IFR procedures based on instrument indications alone, as well as practicing IFR procedures with more complex systems and higher airspeeds.

Although skill levels of pilots and instructors vary, figure that five hours is a questionable short course, and that twenty hours of airplane time is overkill. Ground-training device time will shorten the amount of airplane time required.

No FAA Knowledge Exam is required for the multi-engine rating, but you can expect to be grilled on your trainer's performance numbers and operational systems by your instructor, by the examiner who gives you the checkride, and by anyone from whom you rent a similar twin. Thorough knowledge of any multi-engine airplane's systems is required.

This is an outline of what you are getting into, as far as flying goes. Now let's talk about this book.

Isn't it true that almost all of your one-on-one education as a pilot took place before you received your Private Pilot certificate, when new information and experiences were a part of every flight lesson? Except for being checked out in different singles, have you had many opportunities to sit down with an instructor and go over how the aeronautical facts of life you learned as a student apply to larger, more powerful airplanes? As a multi-engine pilot, your safety and that of your passengers will depend on your full understanding of the aerodynamic laws that govern flight in a twin when one engine is not delivering power. This book is intended to serve as that one-on-one talk.

Yes, there are dual systems, but they offer more variables than you have been exposed to in single-engine airplanes. You need a thorough grasp of how these systems work, what they can do for you, and how they are affected by an engine failure. This book will dig more deeply into systems than did your basic texts.

What will the examiner look for on your checkride? To what new experiences will your multi-engine instructor expose you? What new elements of flight planning will a multi-engine airplane require? We'll go through each of these subjects together, with the goal of making you a knowledgeable multi-engine pilot.

Other than having an extra engine, how does a twin differ from the airplanes you have been flying? We'll discuss that first, with special attention to operating systems, then we will look into the planning considerations. From there, we will go into a normal take-off and climb, cruise considerations, approach planning, and the landing. All-engine and engine-out procedures are discussed in each section. We'll discuss the FAA Practical Test Standards for the multi-engine rating and talk about how to prepare for each area of operation and task.

From the earliest hours of your private pilot training you were asked, "Where would you put it if the engine failed?" Your job was to find a suitable landing site within gliding distance, and you didn't have to fight to control the airplane on the way down. When one engine quits on a twin, however, control is your paramount concern. That is why your training—and this book—will concentrate heavily on what to do if an engine fails, why the failure causes control problems, and how following the correct procedures will make the airplane easier to control.

There will be review questions at the end of each chapter. They are meant for confirming your understanding, not for preparing for a Knowledge Exam.

The Multi-Engine Instructor Rating

A flight instructor with a multi-engine rating on his or her pilot certificate can add a multi-engine rating to his or her flight instructor certificate by taking a checkride with an FAA operations inspector or designated examiner. No minimum training time is required, and there is no knowledge examination. However, the applicant must have logged at least 15 hours as pilot-in-command in the category and class of aircraft involved (multi-engine land or multi-engine sea).

Additionally, before training a pilot in a specific make and model of multi-engine airplane, an MEI must have logged 5 hours as pilot-in-command in that make and model. That is, if you get your MEI in a Duchess you must log 5 hours of Seneca II time before giving multi-engine instruction in a Seneca II.

This is not a nit-picky requirement—manufacturers make changes in systems and procedures between models, and you cannot assume that what worked with twin A will work with twin B.

Caveat

As a flight instructor I tend to talk most of the time, and I like to present the same information in a variety of contexts to assure understanding; if I repeat information in more than one chapter, that is my reason.

The Concept of Multi-Engine Flying

Why does a multi-engine airplane need two engines? Because it won't fly on one, that's why. To expand on this statement, the significant factor is "pounds per horsepower," which relates to the amount of weight a given engine can haul into the air at sea level on a standard day. If you want to lift more pounds, you must either install a larger engine or add an engine, and there are practical limits as to just how big a single-engine can be for a given airframe. Big engines require lots of room and a plentiful source of cooling air, which translates into a large cowling with equally large frontal area. That, in turn, adds drag, and pretty soon you defeat the original purpose. Often, the best solution is a second engine.

Why Two Engines?

The Piper Seneca (Figure 1-1) is an excellent example of a manufacturer adding a second engine to an existing airframe. Its ancestor, the Cherokee Six, with a single 300-horsepower engine, is able to carry seven people and has capacious baggage compartments. The Seneca I (the original, non-turbocharged model) was a Cherokee Six airframe with two engines. It didn't offer much in the way of additional useful load, but it did provide two-engine safety. Other examples of singles that became twins when they grew up are the Twin Comanche and the Baron.

The gain that is achieved by adding an engine is in excess horsepower. Every airplane derives its ability to climb from excess horsepower; excess, that is, to the amount of power required to sustain level

Figure 1-1. Piper Seneca II

flight. You typically choose a cruise power setting which keeps power in reserve, ready for use when called upon, instead of pushing all of the levers full forward. Those extra horses would, if summoned to action, provide either greater level flight speed or climb capability. As you climb to higher altitudes, and the power output of the engines decreases, the ability to climb also decreases. When rate of climb has decreased to 100 feet per minute, the airplane has reached its service ceiling.

Figure 1-2 on the next page illustrates how total drag varies with airspeed. Its components are induced drag, which is greatest at low speed and diminishes as speed increases, and parasite drag, which is negligible at low speed but increases with the square of airspeed. The minimum total drag point (the bottom of the curve) is very close to the single-engine best rate-of-climb speed, which is achieved, in this illustration, at 40% power.

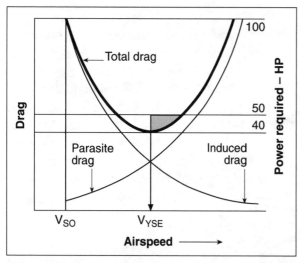

Figure 1-2. Drag vs. airspeed

As you can see, there is plenty of excess power to the right of the minimum drag point as long as both engines are running. When the power of one engine is not available, however, only the power in the shaded portion of the graph is available. High density altitude or a "good" engine which, for one reason or another, is not putting out full rated power, will cause the shaded area to shrink.

During the first hour or so of multi-engine training, you and your instructor can perform an experiment that will prove how the excess horsepower pays off. Trim your aircraft to maintain level flight at its best rate-of-climb speed and record the power setting; then, without touching the throttle or trim wheel, pull back on the control yoke and wait. For a few moments, the kinetic energy of the airplane's forward motion will allow it to climb—but it won't last. Because the increased angle of attack adds to induced drag, the airspeed will slowly decrease and the airplane will begin to descend. After a few oscillations, it will stabilize at the original altitude. You have established the minimum power required to maintain altitude. Now go back to the original situation (trimmed for level flight at V_Y) and add power; the aircraft will climb as a result of power in excess of that required to sustain level flight. It should be apparent that if an engine fails, erasing one-half of the total power, there will be little excess power available for climbing.

To prove how the loss of excess power hurts performance, repeat your earlier experiment, but this time trim to maintain the single-engine best rate-of-climb speed (V_{YSE}, or the blue line on the airspeed indicator) in level flight. Pull one throttle back to zero thrust (about 12 inches of manifold pressure is a good approximation) and do whatever is necessary to the remaining engine to avoid losing altitude. You will find that the "good" engine is producing 75% power or more, and that pushing it up to maximum power may result in a very modest rate of climb. The effect of the loss of power in excess of that necessary for level flight will be obvious. Indeed, depending on density altitude and weight, your airplane might not climb at all. File that away in your memory bank for later reference.

This is the concept of multi-engine flight—add a second engine, and as long as both are humming the same tune, you will have copious amounts of excess horsepower to convert into cruising speed or climb capability if temperature, pressure altitude, and weight are within reasonable limits. That's the good news.

The bad news is that your multi-engine flight training will place disproportionate emphasis on engine failures—disproportionate, that is, to the chance that you would ever experience a total power loss on one engine. All instructors know that placing emphasis on the negative aspects of a subject is a poor teaching technique, and it is with reluctance that they devote more time to the hazards of multi-engine flight than to its positive aspects. What they know, and what you should read into their instruction and into this text, is that multi-engine airplanes can be controlled when only one engine is running if the pilot knows what to do, how to do it, and why it is being done—and has the presence of mind to do the right thing when the situation demands it. When your friends show you statistics on multi-engine accidents, point out that there are no statistics on how many twins experienced problems but landed without incident.

When both engines are purring in sweet harmony, a twin doesn't fly any differently than any sleek single-engine retractable. If the single-engine of that retractable quits, however, the failure does not create control problems. You have little choice but to find the safest, least expensive spot to put it down. A second engine provides you with options, depending on where you are when the failure occurs. Some wags have said that it takes you to the scene of the accident. Realistically, once you have gained control of the airplane after an engine failure, the odds are very much in your favor.

The FAA doesn't require that a multi-engine airplane weighing less than 6,000 pounds be able to climb or even maintain altitude on one engine; its only requirement is that the plane be controllable as it gradually sinks earthward. When you hear the phrase "light twin," remember that 6,000-pound limit. However, almost all light twins are able to climb at least minimally on one engine. The Champion Lancer, a fabric-covered, fixed-gear twin, is known for its inability to maintain altitude when one of its little engines quits. Airplanes heavier than 6,000 pounds (or which stall at a speed higher than 61 knots) must demonstrate the ability to climb on one engine at 5,000 feet above sea level, and that means either more horsepower or turbocharging.

Beginning Your Multi-Engine Training

When you first learned to fly, your relationship with your instructor was clear-cut; the instructor took over control of the airplane whenever a situation began to deteriorate. You were a novice, your instructor was a professional, and "I've got it!" was your signal to let go of everything. When you begin your multi-engine instruction, the situation will change. You are now an experienced pilot, and until your instructor decides it is time to begin failing engines, he or she will place responsibility for normal operations in your hands. Unfortunately, the airplane doesn't know this comfortable situation exists, and it may decide to test the reactions of the entire front-seat crew. From the first takeoff, then, there should be complete understanding of who is in charge of the airplane if something out of the ordinary occurs. There have been many incidents in which each pilot thought the other was in control, and just as many in which both pilots were trying to fly the airplane at the same time.

Instructional flight has the highest rate of accidents after engine failure, and for good reason. One proficient pilot can handle an engine-out emergency alone, and a crew of two with specific emergency duties assigned can handle a failed engine without it turning into an accident. With an instructor and multi-engine student occupying the front seats, however, confusion can result. The instructor wants to see how far into a situation the student can go without losing control, and the student feels that the instructor will bail him or her out before things get dicey.

Each occupant of a pilot seat should have a clear understanding of his or her responsibilities as the throttles are pushed forward. By now I hope that you are asking, "What is so different about having one of the engines fail on a multi-engine airplane?" The answer lies in some aerodynamic laws you are already aware of.

What Happens When an Engine Fails

When you practiced steep turns as a student pilot, you learned that if one wing is moving faster than the other, the lift imbalance will cause the airplane to roll toward the slower wing; you called it "overbanking tendency" then. You also learned about P-factor, the force created by the descending propeller blade that causes left-turning tendency in single-engine airplanes. Your instructor admonished you to use rudder when rolling into a turn to offset the drag created by a downward-deflected aileron. All of these elements will be present as we consider the effect of engine failure.

Basically, when an engine fails on a twin, its wing is no longer being pulled forward and the opposite wing begins to move faster; the resulting yaw develops a rolling moment toward the dead engine. P-factor comes into play as the pilot increases the pitch attitude to avoid losing altitude. Finally, the windmilling propeller on the ailing engine creates drag of much greater magnitude than a deflected aileron. Put all of these reactions together, and you can visualize why the airplane rolls and turns toward the failed engine, and why, if the pilot does not act quickly and correctly, the airplane might hit the ground in a steep bank or inverted. It doesn't have to happen, and your training will give you confidence in your ability to handle such an emergency if your skills are kept sharp. In later chapters, we will go into detail about what to do and why you do it.

Multi-Engine Aerodynamics

Figure 1-3 shows the forces at work when both engines are operating. There is no imbalance in either thrust or lift. The propellers on both engines rotate clockwise as seen from the cockpit, so the descending blades on the right side of the propeller discs are doing most of the work. However, note that the left engine's descending blade is much closer to the centerline of the fuselage than is the descending blade on the right engine. If the right engine fails, the yawing force exerted by the left engine's P-factor will be relatively small, as indicated by the little arrow. If the left engine fails, however, the force exerted by the right engine's descending blade will be farther from the centerline and the yawing force will be much greater; the large arrow emphasizes the difference. The left engine is called the critical engine; its failure would create the most control problems for the pilot.

The propellers on twins certificated overseas usually rotate counterclockwise as seen from the pilot seat, so the situation is reversed—for those airplanes, the right engine is the critical engine.

Many modern multi-engine airplanes have counter-rotating propellers—the right engine's propeller rotates counterclockwise, so that the descending blades of both engines are equidistant from the centerline and P-factor cancels out. There is no critical engine. This reduces, but does not eliminate, the problems associated with controlling the airplane on one engine.

To illustrate how an engine failure causes a yaw and roll toward the dead engine, first look at the top of Figure 1-4 in which the thrust developed by the engines is represented by airplane tugs. (Since airplane tugs can't get much traction when airborne, the airplane in the illustration is on the ramp and cannot be banked.) The forces on the wings are balanced, and the airplane moves forward in a straight line. However, if one tug loses a wheel and stops pulling, the force of the other tug pulling its wing forward will cause the airplane to turn toward the dead tug. If a third tug rushes to the rescue and pushes on the good tug side of the fuselage near the tail, the turning motion can be arrested. Imagine all of this activity taking place in the dead of winter with the ramp covered with ice; the airplane will continue to move

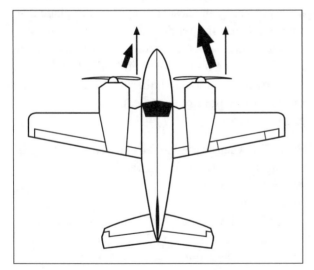

Figure 1-3. *Yaw force due to P-factor*

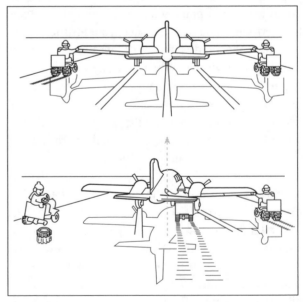

Figure 1-4. *Zero sideslip without banking*

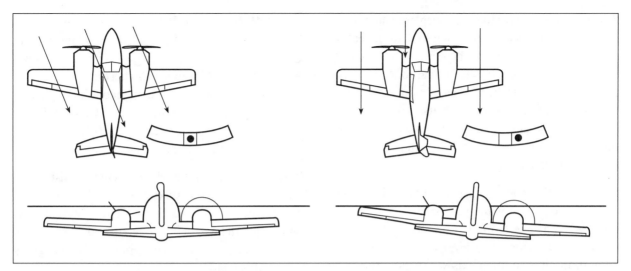

Figure 1-5. Horizontal component of lift provides force to correct sideslip

straight down the taxiway, although its nose is pointed to the right of the direction of travel. This is the result of the force exerted by the tug on the right wing, and the push on the tail's right side provided by the third tug's driver.

Replace the two wing-tip tugs with engine thrust and the fuselage tug with a fully deflected rudder, and you can see why an airplane with one engine inoperative and its wings level is slipping toward the dead engine. The relative wind blows against the side of the fuselage and the resultant drag increase is significant. There is no way to bring the relative wind into alignment with the centerline of the fuselage as long as the wings are level.

Get the airplane airborne, however, and a new stabilizing force becomes available: the horizontal component of lift that is developed when the wings are banked. On the left side of Figure 1-5, control surface deflection replaces the forces exerted by the tugs in Figure 1-4, and the resultant motion is indicated by the arrows. When the wings are level, a vertical lift vector is developed, and the magnitude of that vector is equal to the weight of the airplane. As you begin to roll the airplane, the vertical lift vector shrinks (and you must increase the angle of attack to maintain altitude), and a horizontal lift component is developed which increases in proportion to the angle of bank. At a 90-degree bank angle, there would be no vertical lift vector and the airplane would fall out of the sky.

So much for reviewing turn dynamics. By banking toward the good engine (Figure 1-5, right side) you can develop a horizontal lift vector that will, in effect, provide a correcting force so the airplane will fly forward without any appreciable degree of sideslip. You could, theoretically, bank steeply enough that the horizontal component of force would make rudder deflection unnecessary. Of course, at liftoff and initial climb speeds, it is not possible to maintain altitude if you bank that steeply. Note the position of the ball on each side of Figure 1-5. With the wings level and the airplane slipping toward the dead engine, trimming the ball into the center is the wrong answer. FAA experiments have shown that a pilot can lose control of the airplane at airspeeds as much as 15 knots higher than the minimum control speed marked on the airspeed indicator if the wings are level with the ball centered. Minimum control speed (V_{MC}) will be discussed in detail in Chapter 3.

To achieve the book V_{MC} figure, you must establish a bank angle of *at least* 5 degrees toward the good engine and let the ball move about one-half diameter toward the good engine. In this situation, the ball acts as a bank indicator, not a slip/skid indicator. A 5-degree bank duplicates the conditions under which the manufacturer determined V_{MC}, and its intent is to help you regain control after an engine failure. The 5-degree figure does not apply in real life, however. Bank as much as you have to in order to avoid loss of control. As bank angle approaches 10 degrees, climb performance is adversely affected, though, so when you have the airplane under control, you can reduce the bank angle until the ball is deflected halfway out of the center for best performance. That lays the theoretical foundation for the actions you will take in an engine-out emergency. In later chapters, we will discuss just what you should do if an engine fails during takeoff and initial climb, during cruise, or during the descent and approach to land.

Figure 1-6 illustrates the use of a yaw string, taped to the nose of the airplane and free to stream with the relative wind. The string streams toward the good engine side with the wings level, and becomes aligned with the longitudinal axis when the airplane is banked into the good engine, graphically illustrating zero sideslip.

The last few paragraphs have talked about bank angle. Go back to Page 1-5 and note the words "fully deflected rudder." Never fail to push the rudder on the good engine side all the way to the firewall; if you don't stop the nose from yawing toward the dead engine it will be impossible to control the resulting roll.

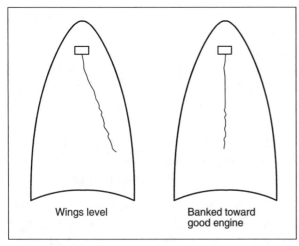

Wings level   Banked toward good engine

Figure 1-6. Yaw string

Centerline Thrust

The obvious answer to the problems presented by off-center thrust is to place the engines on the airplane's centerline. This is just what Cessna did with the 336/337 Skymaster, which made its debut in 1964. The in-line twin served in Vietnam as the U. S. Air Force O-2. They were last produced in 1980, having failed to excite enough interest to sustain production.

The certificate of a pilot who takes the Multi-Engine Land practical test in a Skymaster will be endorsed "For Centerline Thrust Only." The newly minted twin pilot will have to be trained in and take another checkride in an airplane with wing-mounted engines to have this restriction removed.

From the pilot's perspective, a Skymaster with both engines running flies like a very capable single-engine airplane. Performance suffers drastically when either engine fails, of course, but the airplane climbs better with only the rear engine running than it does on the front engine alone. This is because the discharge airflow from the front engine is energized as it passes through the rotating rear propeller and hugs the fuselage. With the rear engine feathered, discharge air from the front propeller detaches from the fuselage, creating drag and reducing climb performance.

Unlike most other twins, retracting the landing gear is not an immediate-action checklist item when an engine fails. Putting the gear switch in the "retract" position causes the gear doors (which are closed when the gear is down) to open while the gear is in transit, exposing large drag-producing openings.

Skymaster pilots start the rear engine first, and let its instrument indications stabilize before starting the front engine. If the rear engine should shut down after the front engine is started, the pilot has nothing but instrument indications to rely on as a warning; there have been incidents/accidents when the pilot took off on the front engine only, unaware that the rear engine had failed.

The Boomerang

Burt Rutan, designer of the Voyager, the in-line twin that circled the globe nonstop, has turned his talents to eliminating the problems of off-center thrust. Figure 1-7 is a picture of his Boomerang, which has two engines — one mounted on the fuselage and the other on the wing. The two engines are not the same type — one develops more horsepower than the other. If either engine fails, there is no yaw toward the failed engine. Rutan plans to put the airplane into production, but it will be several years before a reader of this text will have an opportunity to fly one.

Photo by Tonya Rutan

Figure 1-7. The Boomerang

Chapter 1
Review Questions

1. What distinguishes a "light" twin from a "heavy" twin?

   A—A light twin weighs less than 6,000 pounds.
   B—A light twin's V_{SO} is less than 61 knots.
   C—Both A and B.

2. On a conventional twin, when an engine fails the airplane yaws toward

   A—the good engine.
   B—the critical engine.
   C—the failed engine.

3. If an airplane weighs less than 6,000 pounds and has a V_{SO} of less than 60 knots, the manufacturer must demonstrate that the airplane is able to climb at least _____ feet per minute on a standard day at sea level with one propeller feathered.

   A—50
   B—100
   C—There is no minimum climb requirement.

4. If an airplane cannot climb with one propeller feathered, the reason is that

   A—drag is greater than lift.
   B—drag is greater than thrust.
   C—lift is greater than thrust.

5. Which statement concerning drag is true?

   A—Parasitic drag is greatest at low speed.
   B—Parasitic drag increases as speed increases.
   C—The airplane is most efficient when parasitic and induced drag are equal.

6. In a high-power, low-speed situation such as initial climb, a propeller's descending blade

   A—creates more torque than the ascending blade.
   B—creates more thrust than the ascending blade.
   C—is further from the centerline than the ascending blade.

7. The propeller of a failed engine creates the least drag when it is

   A—feathered.
   B—windmilling.
   C—stopped.

8. On an airplane with counter-rotating propellers, the _____ engine is the critical engine.

   A—right
   B—left
   C—Neither; there is no critical engine.

9. A pilot whose multi-engine rating is limited to centerline thrust cannot act as pilot-in-command of an airplane with wing-mounted engines. (true, false)

10. When an engine fails on a twin-engine airplane, how much climb performance is lost?

    A—80 percent
    B—50 percent
    C—20 percent

Multi-Engine Airplane Systems

2

As the pilot of a multi-engine airplane, you will have more systems to learn and understand than you ever had to contend with in a single-engine airplane, because of duplication. (*See* redundant systems in Figure 2-1.) It's great to have two alternators sharing the electrical load, but not quite so great when one alternator is out of action because its engine has failed and you have to throw the correct switches and pull the proper breakers to keep from overloading the sole survivor. And it's great to have lots of fuel to feed the engines—but not quite so great when a pump fails and you must know how to get fuel to the engines without that pump. But don't despair; all that

is necessary is a little study and some judicious questioning of a friendly mechanic. Let's start by discussing systems that are unique to twins.

Propeller Feathering

If you have flown an airplane with a constant-speed propeller, you know the propeller hub contains a governor that keeps the propeller's rotational speed constant by varying the pitch of the blades. The terms "pitch" and "blade angle" are used interchangeably, although they describe different things. The pitch of a propeller blade, expressed in inches, is the theoreti-

Figure 2-1. The redundant systems of the twin aircraft are reflected in the cockpit instrumentation.

cal distance that the propeller moves forward through the air during one revolution (without slippage). Blade angle is the angle between the chord of the propeller blade and the plane of rotation. Because changes in blade angle cause changes in pitch, little confusion results from interchanging the two terms.

The most efficient angle of attack for a propeller is 2 to 4 degrees, and the actual blade angle necessary to maintain this small angle of attack varies with the forward speed of the airplane. Figure 2-2 illustrates the forces involved. The forward velocity vector is shortened and lengthened as the airplane loses or gains airspeed; the governor wants to keep the blade angle constant. If the angle of attack "a" is to stay within the efficient range, the blade angle "b" must be reduced (higher RPM) when forward velocity slows, and increased (lower RPM) when forward velocity accelerates. This is the function of the governor.

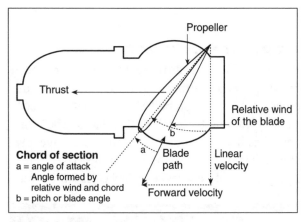

Figure 2-2. *Propeller forces*

In the prop hub of some single-engine airplanes, the governor uses oil from the engine's lubricating system to force the propeller blades toward the low pitch (high RPM) position, and if oil pressure is lost due to engine stoppage, the blades are automatically moved to a high pitch or low RPM setting by counterweights (*see* Figure 2-3). Other governing systems use oil pressure to move the blades to the high pitch (low RPM) setting and, if oil pressure is lost, the blades are moved to the high RPM position by centrifugal twisting force. (Some texts identify the high pitch and low pitch settings as coarse pitch and fine pitch.) Proper operation of the governing system depends on a supply of warm engine oil to the governor, which explains why you exercise the propel-

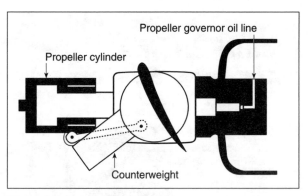

Figure 2-3. *Pitch mechanism*

ler during the pretakeoff runup—that action moves cold, thick oil out of the governor's oil lines and replaces it with warm oil from the engine sump. Pull the prop control back almost to the feather detent three times. The first time, confirm that the RPM decreases and then returns to normal as you push the control forward again. The second time, check for a rise in manifold pressure as the RPM drops, and the third time, look for a slight drop in oil pressure followed by an increase as the RPM comes back up.

To know what to expect in the event of engine failure in a single-engine airplane with a controllable-pitch propeller, then, you must know what happens to propeller pitch when the engine stops running—one system goes to high RPM and the other goes to low RPM. In contrast, the system used by most manufacturers of propellers for multi-engine airplanes uses engine sump oil to drive the propellers toward flat pitch, and engine failure causes the blades to move toward the feathered position. The force opposing the oil pressure is either a charge of compressed dry air or nitrogen, or a system of springs and counterweights, or both. In gas-charged systems, loss of gas pressure means no feathering force. Exercising the propellers is part of the pretakeoff checklist for twins, of course, but there is an additional checklist item: the feathering check.

In the event of engine failure, the propeller blades must be rotated until they are edge-on to the direction of travel (feathered), to create minimum drag. When you move the prop control past the feather detent, governor oil pressure is released, and the air or nitrogen charge (or centrifugal force acting on the counterweights) forces the blade to the feathered position. The engine must work harder to rotate the propeller when the blades begin to move toward the 90-degree position, and this is reflected in increased manifold pressure. To prove that the feathering system works (without overloading the engine), pull the prop control back into the feather detent just long enough for the hum of rotation to change to a whop-whop-whop and move it smoothly forward again. It is much easier to do than it is to describe. If the propeller is sluggish and slow to move toward feather, scratch the trip; you never want to be airborne in a twin if you can't feather the prop on a sick engine.

"If loss of oil pressure causes the prop to feather, why doesn't it feather when I shut down the engine on the ramp?" Good question. There are internal centrifugal latches that keep the propeller from feathering when it spins down to 600-800 RPM, that's why. That's also why you can't wait forever to feather the propeller on a failed engine; if you let the RPM get low enough, you won't be able to feather the propeller at all. On the other hand, if an engine fails in cruising flight, the airplane's forward motion through the air will keep its propeller windmilling at well above those RPM figures while you troubleshoot.

The Piper Seminole (Figure 2-4) is the only multi-engine trainer in production as this is written. Most training takes place in airplanes which have been in production for years. Many stalwart twin trainers are still turning out students after 40 years. I mention this because it is entirely possible that you will take your training in an airplane that doesn't use the prop governor system described above. Don't worry; study and understand the system you are using, and be ready to learn new systems as you move up in class.

Accumulators

As you read the emergency procedures section of the Pilot's Operating Handbook for the twin you are flying, you may find two unfeathering procedures, one for airplanes with an unfeathering accumulator and one for those without. Basically, an accumulator (Figure 2-5) is a receptacle or tank in which oil is stored under pressure, to be released into the propeller hub when the prop control is moved out of the feather detent. It is a one-shot deal, so if the engine doesn't start on the first try, the procedure reverts to the no-accumulator method. The goal in unfeathering

Figure 2-4. *Piper Seminole*

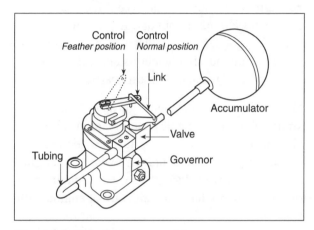

Figure 2-5. *Unfeathering accumulator*

is to put oil pressure (from either the accumulator or the lubricating system) to work, twisting the blades toward a positive angle of attack. The Beechcraft Duchess book calls for the prop control to be pushed full forward if accumulators are installed, and moved just forward of the feather detent if they are not.

Without an accumulator, you will have to get oil moving up to the prop governor by using the starter or by putting the airplane into a slight dive (or both) to get the blades windmilling. As the prop begins to move on its own, it rotates the crankshaft, which in turn rotates the engine and, via the accessory case, the oil pump. Oil pressure from the pump forces the blades toward their cruise position, spinning them faster and causing the oil pump to deliver greater pressure. Kind of a backwards process. Once the prop is spinning, all that is required is fuel and ignition, and you're back in business. It's similar to starting a stick-shift car by pushing it. Keep the power settings low on the recently revived engine until its temperatures have stabilized—air has been rushing past the engine while the prop was feathered, cooling the engine rapidly. You wouldn't want to run a marathon right after being brought back to life, would you? Neither would the engine.

Air Starts

Some airplanes simply won't start in the air without using the starter; no amount of diving will cause the blades to windmill. The Twin Otter is an excellent example. If you are training in such an airplane and the engine balks at restarting, you're on your way home with an engine out and its propeller feathered—not good. Never feather an engine in training if there is any question about its ability to air start, unless there is a suitable airport nearby.

Air starts are hard on the engines, and the Beech Aircraft Corporation notes that numerous air starts without accumulators can shorten the life of engine mounts. You'll understand why when the engine vibrates excessively during an air start. Your instructor will probably have you air start an engine with its prop feathered only once during your training. It is not a skill you will need very often, because it is usually wiser to land at the nearest suitable airport and troubleshoot the problem. It doesn't help the engines to cycle between operating temperatures and cold iron, either. A shutdown and restart is required by the Multi-Engine Practical Test Standard, though, and you don't want to do your first one with the examiner in the right seat.

Propeller Synchronizers

The subject of propeller synchronization will be introduced about one minute into your first multi-engine takeoff and climb, when you or your instructor make the first power change. Unless the two propellers are rotating at exactly the same number of revolutions per minute (RPM), you will hear and feel a low-frequency throbbing sound caused by the difference in rotational speed. Set one prop (usually the right) to the desired RPM and then smoothly adjust the left prop control until the beat frequency between the two props gradually slows and then blends into a single tone. It will become second na-

ture to you after a few power changes, or your instructor will go crazy. Setting the friction lock on the power quadrant should keep things in tune between power changes.

When you move up into more sophisticated twins, you may encounter an automatic propeller synchronizer or synchrophaser. This device will keep the props in sync for you, but you must sync them manually before throwing the PROPSYNC switch. The automatic synchronizer system uses the right propeller as the master, and, if it senses a difference in speed between itself and the left prop, an error signal is sent to the left prop governor, driving it into agreement with the master. You must turn the synchrophaser off when making a power change, and turn it back and re-sync the props at the new power setting.

Prop sync must be off for takeoff and landing, and in the event of engine failure…(if the right prop is spinning down to a stop, you don't want the left one to follow it, do you?)

Heat Consciousness

Excessive heat is your engine's enemy. In fact, it is the enemy of all of the hoses and wires crammed into the nacelle with the engine. If your twin's engines are normally aspirated, the heat developed will gradually decrease as you climb to altitude, in part because of decreasing ambient temperature, and because the engine's power output decreases with altitude. Turbocharged engines operate at or near full power all the way to cruise altitude, so heat management is a real concern.

Your primary source of temperature information is the cylinder head temperature gauge. Oil temperature is a secondary indicator, because the oil carries heat away from the cylinder head. Increasing oil temperature is an early indicator of trouble, however.

You have three basic tools with which to control cylinder head temperatures: power reduction, cowl flaps, and mixture control. Pulling back the throttle means a change from your flight-planned airspeed, while opening the cowl flaps means added drag with some decrease in airspeed. Enriching the mixture exacts a dollar cost and eats into your fuel reserve. You must decide which method meets your needs, but you cannot ignore high cylinder head temperatures.

There are very few twins that are not equipped with exhaust gas temperature (EGT) gauges. These devices get their input from thermocouples exposed to the exhaust stream. Engine exhaust reaches its highest temperature when the fuel-air mixture is slightly richer than the best economy setting. Figure 2-6, from the Avco Lycoming Flyer, illustrates the relationships involved.

Although you should read the instructions for the EGT system for your particular airplane, the general rule is to set the desired percentage of power using handbook figures, and then lean until the EGT gauge reaches its peak temperature indication (some systems will have a maximum temperature beyond which you will not lean, no matter what! Lycoming says that for almost all of its engines, 1,650°F is the limit). When you have noted the peak temperature, pushing the mixture control in until the temperature has dropped 50 degrees will put the engine at its best power setting. As you can see from the chart, the fuel consumption line slants upward as the EGT line slants downward—it is in your best interest to operate your engines on the hot side of the maximum power range.

Cooling the mixture by richening is called operating on the fuel side of peak. Some engines can be operated on the lean, or air side of peak, for best economy. Always observe the engine manufacturer's recommendations—but keep in mind that those recommendations may be 30 or 40 years old; get the latest information from your mechanic or from the engine manufacturer. The peak temperature limitation is based on metallurgical factors, because extended exposure to high temperatures will weaken portions of the exhaust system. You are hurting your engine's efficiency if you don't lean the mixture by reference to the EGT, but you must do it intelligently, by the book. This is another area where what you do in one airplane does not necessarily apply in a different model.

The better EGT gauging systems have probes for each cylinder, allowing you to compare the exhaust temperatures. If one cylinder is running hotter than the others, the chances are a clogged fuel injector is forcing that cylinder to operate on the lean side of

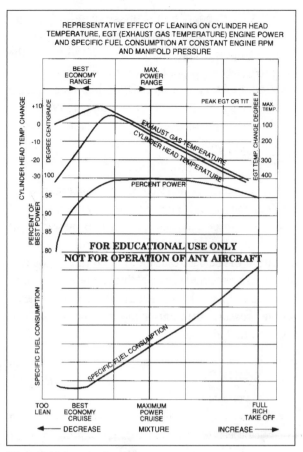

Figure 2-6. Leaning by exhaust gas temperature gauge

peak. Single-probe installations rely on a probe in what the manufacturer has identified as the hottest cylinder, and the rest of the cylinders have to accept whatever you decide is best for the hot one. There have been so many advances in electronic engine monitoring devices in the past few years, and their cost is so low compared to engine repairs, that installing this equipment offers a great cost/benefit ratio.

A Review of Fuel Injection

Your multi-engine trainer may very well have carbureted engines, just like your single-engine trainer, and in that case you already know the starting and operating procedures. On the other hand, this may be your first exposure to fuel injection, and a brief discussion of the differences is in order.

In the familiar carbureted engine, fuel is drawn into the carburetor by the vacuum created by the downward movement of the pistons during the intake stroke, mixed with air in the carburetor, and distributed to the cylinders by the intake manifold. Figure 2-7 shows how the throttle controls airflow — it illustrates an updraft carburetor, so airflow is from the bottom up. The temperature drop in the throat of the carburetor raises the hazard of carburetor ice, and the effectiveness of the fuel-air mixture delivery is a function of the intake plumbing. Getting equal charges into each of the cylinders is a difficult design problem.

A fuel-injected engine eliminates the uncertainty and imprecision in the delivery system by squirting precisely measured amounts of fuel into the intake of each cylinder. It obviously eliminates carburetor ice by virtue of the fact that there is no mixing of fuel and air in a restricted passage (throat) and thus no temperature drop. Fuel is metered to the cylinders based on the pressure differential between the impact (intake) air and air pressure at the venturi.

Just because there is no temperature drop caused by cooling of a fuel-air mixture, don't assume the danger of induction system icing is gone. An internal combustion engine must breathe air, and it will lose power if the flow of intake air is impeded in any way. The intake air filter can be clogged in many ways, and for the instrument pilot, wet snow is a frequent cause. No matter what the reason, if the manifold pressure begins to drop without any change in throttle position, your engine is gasping for air. Alternate air doors, either manual or automatic, allow air to be taken from inside the cowling, bypassing the filter. There may be a slight power loss when on alternate air, just as there is when you fly with full or partial carburetor heat.

A fuel injection system allows more precise control of fuel flow by providing a fuel flow gauge for each engine. These gauges are usually calibrated in gal-

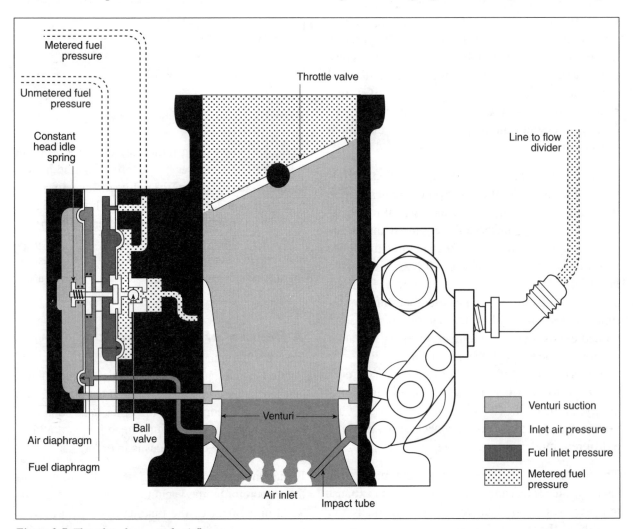

Figure 2-7. Throttle valve controls airflow

lons or pounds per hour, but they are really reading fuel pressure. An unexpected increase in fuel flow according to the gauge (above that called for by the handbook for a given power setting), is probably evidence of fuel injector fouling.

If you train for the multi-engine rating in a typical light twin, it will probably have no induction ice protection at all. Few trainers are equipped to venture into anything more challenging than soft IFR, and their greatest protection against icing is most likely limited to carburetor heat.

Fuel Systems

If you are looking for an aircraft system which, if misunderstood, can cause real, life-threatening problems, look no farther than the fuel system. Systems vary from the simple on-off-crossfeed found in many modern twins, to systems with tank, pump, switch, and gauge combinations that defy understanding. A good example is shown in Figure 2-8, the fuel selector of an older Beech Baron. (The label-maker placarding was mandated by an Airworthiness Directive.) As you can see, this airplane has a main tank and an auxiliary tank in each wing. However, there is only one fuel gauge on the instrument panel for each wing. A switch allows the pilot to select whether that gauge indicates the fuel remaining in the main tank or the auxiliary tank. Feed the engines from the mains while the gauges are switched to the "auxiliary" position and you are in for a surprise.

You can see the potential for problems if the pilot has not studied the system and become familiar with its operation.

Unlike an airliner, a light twin has no provision for moving fuel from one tank to another. You do have crossfeed capability, however, which makes it possible for an engine to use fuel from tanks on the opposite side of the airplane in case of engine failure. If you have to shut down the left engine, the right engine can burn fuel from the left main or auxiliary tanks. There is no "one size fits all" crossfeed procedure, and you must know and understand the system for the airplane you fly. It might cost a few dollars, but practicing crossfeeding on the ground might pay off in an emergency—pilots have shut down one engine and then starved the other engine for fuel by mishandling the fuel selector.

It is good operating practice to land as soon as practicable if you have to shut down an engine. Crossfeeding lets you maintain lateral balance; if you fail to crossfeed, the off-center weight might cause a lateral imbalance that could cause real problems on landing, especially if there is a crosswind. It's hard to bank to the right to offset a right crosswind when the left-side fuel tanks are full and the right-side fuel tanks are empty.

Figure 2-9, on the next page, is the fuel system of an older Cessna 310. As you can see, the wing auxiliary tanks and the wing locker tanks are optional, meaning they may or may not exist in a given air-

Figure 2-8. BE-55 fuel selector

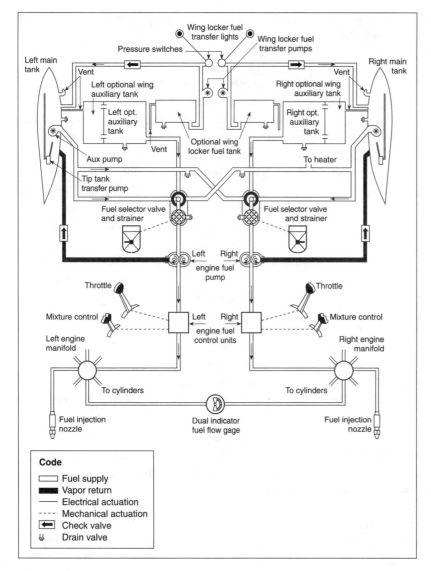

Figure 2-9. *Cessna 310 fuel system*

plane. Some 310s have both auxiliary tanks but only one wing locker tank. I mention this not to make you an expert on 310 fuel systems, but to point out the possibilities that exist when you move up into multi-engine airplanes.

Some Continental systems have a vapor return line from the engine to the main fuel tank, and a small percentage of fuel returns with the vapor. It is necessary to burn fuel from the main tanks for 30 minutes or so to make room in the tank for the vapor/fuel return when you switch to the auxiliary tank. Switch to the auxes too soon, and the return fuel will be pumped overboard after it has refilled the mains.

There will be a description of the fuel system in the owner's manual, but it won't answer questions such as "Are there any tanks with submerged pumps that

should not be run dry?" That kind of answer must come from an instructor/pilot with encyclopedic knowledge of that airplane's systems or from a mechanic who works on that airplane.

As a general rule, it is not a good idea to run any airplane fuel tank dry; this is especially true in the case of a fuel injected or turbocharged engine (which would be fuel injected). A fuel pump is designed to move fluid, not air, and if one loses its prime because a tank is dry, it may take an unsettling amount of time before it is able to draw fuel from another tank.

As you will learn later in this chapter, a turbocharger is spun by exhaust gases; if running a tank dry shuts off the supply of exhaust gas, the turbocharger may "roll back" and cause its engine to quit for lack of intake air pressure. If the airplane is pressurized, running a tank dry can result in loss of pressurization.

Electrical Systems

When comparing the systems of a twin with those of a single-engine airplane, the distribution of electricity opens a whole new world of complexity.

One of the reasons people buy and fly twins is the redundancy of systems, and an alternator on each side certainly meets that requirement. Instead of depending on a 60-amp alternator to feed juice to the radio stack, lights, and other systems, you will have two such devices. Twice as much available power! You can go down to the radio store and order one of everything—just be sure the total electrical load you place on each alternator is no more than 80% of its rated output.

The Duchess electrical distribution system in Figure 2-10 is typical of most twins. Just as is the case with your car's system, there is one "hot" wire from the alternator; the fuselage (or car body) completes the circuit. Follow the output of the left alternator with me. The little arrowhead symbol represents a diode, a device that will conduct electricity in only one direction. The loadmeter (ammeter) shunt is a part of the instrument on the panel which tells you how much current the alternator is supplying, so the electricity passes right through it. Follow the line up the page and you see what is called the left alternator bus. A bus is no more than a terminal board that allows the current from the alternator to be fed to hungry devices. The little arcs with slashes through them are combination circuit breaker/switches; you can tell from their labels that they are switches you would use frequently. Further up the page, the arcs have little tabs on their tops, representing circuit breakers that can be pulled manually; they protect devices that you do not turn off and on as a normal procedure.

The heavy black line at the top runs over to a circuit breaker called the left bus isolation breaker. It provides a means of disconnecting the left alternator

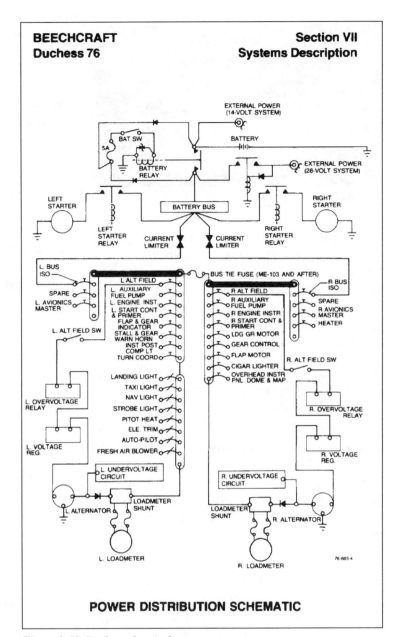

POWER DISTRIBUTION SCHEMATIC

Figure 2-10. Duchess electrical system

from the battery, so that in the event of alternator failure the battery will not be discharged through it.

Follow the output of the right alternator in the same fashion, and you will see that power from each alternator goes to certain devices that are on its bus. The bus tie fuse, between the heavy black lines, connects the systems together and allows the left alternator to provide power to the landing gear motor (for example) if the right alternator fails.

Note that each bus has a circuit breaker labeled ALT FIELD and that current flows through that breaker, through the ALT FIELD SWITCH to the overvolt-

1983 Beechcraft Duchess

age relay and voltage regulator, and back to the alternator. Unlike a generator, an alternator requires field excitation before it can produce electricity. The voltage regulator controls the alternator output by controlling the field current. The OVERVOLTAGE and UNDERVOLTAGE devices warn you of these conditions through lights on the panel.

Assume that a single warning light has come on; you check the associated loadmeter and it reads zero. That alternator is out of business and the other one is carrying the entire electrical load. Your first action would be to turn off the alternator switch, even though you know the alternator is dead. Reason? Electrical problems can be intermittent, and the "failed" alternator might come back on the line unexpectedly. Your next action is to reduce the electrical load to a level which a single alternator can handle comfortably.

At this point, I would encourage you to make up a load-shedding schedule to be kept at hand in the cockpit. It should contain a list of just how many amperes each device draws, taken from placards or technical manuals, and a list of the essential items. For example, you may be able to get along with only one nav-comm and the transponder, without cabin or instrument lighting. Things that are heated by resistance (like your toaster) are power eaters. You may have to get along without your resistance-heated pitot tube and propeller deice if you are down to a single alternator. If you keep too many devices turned on, the current drain of extending the gear may turn the cockpit into a black, silent hole. You should think ahead about those things.

Now assume a total electrical failure—follow through on the diagram. Obviously, there will be no ALTERNATOR OUT lights. The flashlight you always keep on a string around your neck shows both loadmeters reading zero. First, turn off both alternator switches—you don't know which one caused the total failure. Next, turn the battery switch OFF. Why let the energy in the battery leak away while you are troubleshooting? By turning off the battery, you are saving it for what may be a last-minute burst of juice to get the gear down. (Consider using the emergency extension system.) Pull both bus isolation circuit breakers; now one can't influence the other. Remove ALL electrical loads. Now turn on both alternator switches. Begin turning on essential items, pausing between each piece of equipment to see if it was the culprit that shut the system down. Watch the loadmeters; when you turn on the faulty device, the loadmeter reading will increase rapidly. Shut that device off again. Land as soon as practicable and have the electrical system checked.

Electrical systems can have some puzzling anomalies. For example, the continuous-duty fuel pumps in some Cessna 310 main tanks share a circuit breaker with the landing lights, so a problem in the light wiring can seriously affect your fuel management ability. If all of the electrically operated engine instruments are served by one circuit breaker, a fault in one instrument can wipe out the whole instrument cluster. Cultivate a friendly relationship with your mechanic; take him or her out to lunch and ask some "what if" questions.

Turbocharging

Ten years ago, a pilot moving up into a turbocharged multi-engine airplane had a whole new power management system to become familiar with, because there were very few turbocharged singles. Today, you can rent airplanes with inflatable engines at almost every airport. I am going to assume your first exposure to turbocharging will be in a twin, so here is a brief overview.

When you sip a soft drink through a straw, you are "aspirating" the fluid. Normally-aspirated engines suck air into their intake manifolds. Pilots of airplanes with carbureted engines know they run out of

throttle at about 7,000 feet, because, although the descending pistons are doing their best to pull in a full load of air on the intake stroke, there's not much air available. Continuing the climb results in a gradual loss of power. This is about what would happen if some practical joker had poked holes in your straw—you would have trouble aspirating.

Complex airplanes, with fuel-injected engines and constant-speed propellers, evidence the gradual reduction in air density by losing about an inch of manifold pressure for every 1,000 feet of climb. Unless there is some means of pumping the cylinders full of air at sea-level pressure or better, a climb to altitude means a loss of engine power.

A turbocharger is that pump. Exhaust gases pass through the blades of a turbine as they exit the airplane, causing it to spin at high speed. A compressor, mounted on the same shaft as the turbine, compresses intake air and feeds it to the cylinders. The amount of "boost," or pressure above that available without turbocharging, is a function of compressor rotational speed and, because of the direct connection to the turbine, of turbine speed. Turbine speed is controlled, either manually or automatically, by a waste gate that controls the amount of exhaust diverted to the turbine blades. Figure 2-11, on the next page, is a schematic diagram of a typical turbocharger system.

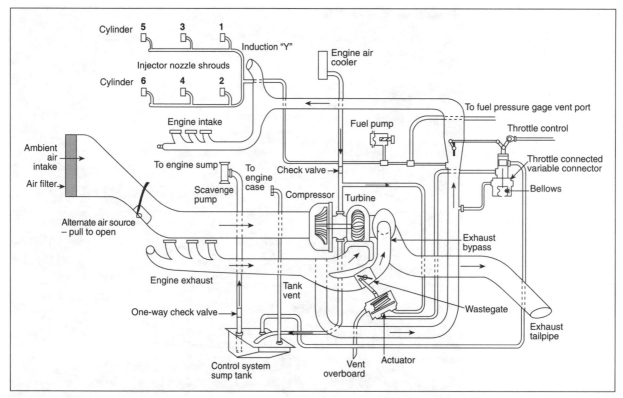

Figure 2-11. *Typical turbocharger system*

When the waste gate is fully open, the exhaust gases bypass the turbine, and the engine is essentially normally aspirated. The turbocharger is out of the picture. As the waste gate is closed, however, increasing amounts of exhaust gas go to the turbine blades, causing it to spin more rapidly. When the waste gate is fully closed, all exhaust gases pass through the turbine, and the maximum amount of boost is provided to the engine. The altitude at which the waste gate is fully closed is called the critical altitude. If you continue to climb above that altitude, the manifold pressure will gradually decrease. Don't look on that as a limitation: the critical altitude is usually in the mid to high teens, while service ceilings for turbocharged airplanes are in the upper twenties.

With a manual system (usually, but not always, an aftermarket add-on), you take off with the waste gate fully open and climb normally until the throttle is fully forward, then slowly close the waste gate while watching the manifold pressure gauge. The manufacturer's performance charts tell you what combinations of manifold pressure and propeller speed are approved at different altitudes.

As you descend into denser air, your first priority is to gradually open the waste gate until it is fully open, then use the throttle normally. Misuse of the manual control can result in overboosting, one of the worst errors of powerplant management a pilot can commit. If the waste gate is left closed as the airplane descends, the compressor will pack the denser air into the cylinders at pressures they were not designed to withstand. You can imagine the effect on the engine of applying takeoff power with the waste gate closed. The engine manufacturer may require the engine to be torn down and inspected if it is overboosted.

Some cabin-class twins boast an automatic controller which senses changes in density altitude and adjusts the waste gate accordingly. Control systems vary too widely to be discussed here. Many include a fixed waste gate, which limits the amount of manifold pressure the compressor can deliver by allowing all exhaust gas over a preset value to bypass the turbine. These systems are mechanically simple, at the price of lower critical altitudes. More sophisticated systems react to density altitude, ram air pressure, throttle position, or mixture, and they require a lot of skill in adjusting the engine controls, while delivering more performance. Automatic systems are not foolproof, however.

A sticking waste gate can cause the same problems as a forgotten manual waste gate. You must monitor the manifold pressures at all times, but especially on takeoff—a stuck waste gate will cause the airplane to head for the runway lights just as quickly as a failed engine.

Many pilots think turbocharged engines are beefed up to handle the higher pressures. Not so. Consider a piston in a normally-aspirated engine. On the intake stroke, it is pulled down by the crankshaft, creating a vacuum in the cylinder. No force is applied to the top of the piston. As the crankshaft continues to turn, the piston rises to compress the fuel-air mixture, causing increasing pressure on the top of the piston until—bang!—the mixture is ignited and the piston is forced downward in the power stroke. At the bottom of the power stroke, the piston reverses direction and moves upward to push the exhaust gases through an open valve. How's that for widely varying forces?

Now consider a piston in a turbocharged engine. On the intake stroke, it is pushed down by pressure from the compressor. During the compression and power strokes, pressure is applied to the top of the piston, and on the exhaust stroke, the piston must force the gases through a waste gate and turbine wheel. Wouldn't you say that the pressures are more consistent in the turbocharged engine? That's why aftermarket blowers can be bolted onto aircraft—and automobile—engines. Of course, an engine and turbocharger combination designed to operate together will be more efficient and have fewer unexpected problems.

Heat Management

The real killer in the world of turbocharging is heat. The life of hoses and wires is shortened when they are baked. As the pilot of a turbocharged twin, you must be temperature conscious, balancing operational requirements against the need to keep the cylinder head temperatures within the normal range. The power output of a normally-aspirated engine decreases as altitude increases, so heat generation during full power operation is limited to the initial climb. However, a turbocharged engine operates at nearly full power all the way to altitude, where the cooling ability of the air is diminished by reduced air density. The best source of cooling is a richer fuel mixture, so turbo'd engines are expensive to operate.

Many heavy twins are equipped with intercoolers—heat exchangers through which the compressed air must pass on its way from the turbocharger to the intake manifold. By lowering the temperature of the air entering the intake manifold, it reduces the amount of fuel needed for cooling. It fools the engine into thinking it is flying on a cooler day, and when the temperature is colder than standard, you can get the same effective horsepower with lower power settings. In addition to the EGT, which measures the temperature of the gas passing through the turbine blades, intercooled engines may have instrumentation to measure the temperature of the air at the outlet of the intercooler. If you fly an airplane such as a turbocharged Twin Comanche, and can see the turbocharger in the left nacelle glowing white-hot at night, you will understand why chopping the throttle to begin a descent leads to metallurgical death for the turbocharger. If the ATC system allows you to plan a gradual descent, a reduction of two or three inches of manifold pressure every two minutes or so will allow more gradual cooling.

Pressurization

Turbochargers have the capacity to produce copious amounts of compressed air, and an excellent place to put excess air to work is in the cabin, as a pressurization system. The air will have to be cooled, of course, and some sort of safety valve must be provided to keep the airplane from inflating to the bursting point.

Those are the basics of a cabin pressurization system. The airframe must be designed to withstand the pressure differential that will exist when passengers can breathe normally at 25,000 feet while the outside air pressure is about 5.5 pounds per square inch. Two airplanes with similar powerplants may have differing operational ceilings, because their relative abilities to withstand internal pressures differ.

There are two primary methods of controlling cabin pressure—fixed schedule and variable schedule. The latter is the most desirable, but you are pretty much stuck with the system approved for your airplane.

With a fixed-schedule system, the cabin is unpressurized until the airplane reaches an altitude preset by the manufacturer; at that point the outflow valve closes and the cabin altitude remains at the preset altitude until the design maximum differential pressure is reached. After that, the cabin and airplane climb together as the controller maintains the differential at its maximum value. This should not be a problem for general aviation piston-powered airplanes, because with a cabin altitude of 8,000 feet, the airplane can be as high as 27,500 feet (airline cabin altitudes range from 6,000 to 8,000 feet).

A variable-schedule system lets the pilot select the final altitude and the cabin climb rate. It is desirable to set the final altitude for climb 1,000 feet above the selected cruise altitude—if you file for 15,000 feet, set the controller to 16,000 feet. This ensures that the maximum differential will not be reached and the outflow will not be popping open and closed every minute or so with the resulting passenger discomfort. If ATC assigns a higher altitude, reset the altitude select window. For descent, set the altitude select to an altitude 500 feet above the destination airport's elevation—this will ensure the cabin depressurizes

before landing (a squat switch will depressurize the cabin when the wheels touch down, so you really don't want any pressure difference at that time).

For passenger comfort, set the cabin-rate selector to 500 fpm or less for the climb to altitude. The descent setting requires a little planning, because you are probably not going to descend the airplane at less than 500 fpm. Adjust the cabin-rate knob for a descent of about 300 fpm shortly before you start down, and monitor the airplane and cabin altitudes to be sure the airplane is always higher than the cabin. If ATC stops your descent, the cabin will continue to descend until the maximum differential pressure is reached. This should not present a problem for your passengers. Just don't let the airplane catch up with the cabin until you are at pattern or approach altitude.

In Figure 2-12, the Piper Aerostar system, the outflow valve is called the pressure regulator valve. The outflow valve provides the "leak" that keeps the cabin altitude at the desired level. Too much pressure and the valve opens, too little pressure and it closes. You control the desired pressure with panel controls as discussed above.

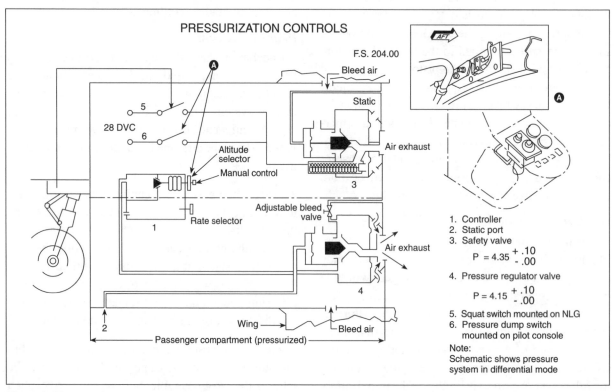

Figure 2-12. *Typical pressurization system*

The cabin safety valve is set to open at a pressure just a little less than the designed pressure differential, as you can tell from the ratings in Figure 2-12. If the outflow valve sticks closed (have you been allowing your passengers to smoke?) and cabin pressure rises toward the danger point, the safety valve will open and save the day. None of this will do your passengers' ears any good, which is a good reason to (1) prohibit smoking or (2) service and clean the outflow valve regularly.

Because passenger comfort is involved, you should have a thorough understanding of your airplane's pressurization system.

Figure 2-13. *Partenavia*

Landing Gear Extension Systems

Very few twins have their wheels welded in place—the Twin Otter, Partenavia (Figure 2-13), and Champion Lancer come immediately to mind. Most twins have fold-up landing gear, and you should become familiar with the system in the airplane you train in (you'll be asked about the gear system on the oral). Then be sure to check the handbook on any other twin you fly. Gear retraction and emergency extension systems vary widely, even between airplane models from the same manufacturer.

The system most commonly used is electro-hydraulic—an electric motor operates a hydraulic pump, which provides the muscle. You must be sure the hydraulic reservoir contains fluid during the preflight, and you should also place the location of the gear pump motor circuit breaker in your memory bank. The emergency extension procedure will probably require you to pull that circuit breaker before taking any further action. You don't want a sudden electrical glitch to turn the motor on when you are involved in pumping or cranking the gear down. Some electro-hydraulic systems allow you to hang out the gear by dumping the hydraulic pressure in an emergency; the Beech Duchess and Piper Seminole are good examples.

Does the system rely on hydraulic pressure to keep the wheels in their wells, or does it have mechanical uplocks? You'll find out by reading the POH on the airplane or by hearing the hydraulic pump run for a few seconds during the starting procedure. Gear doors and flaps have been known to sag a little when the airplane sits idle, and that quick burst of hydraulic pump operation puts them back where they belong. An electrical failure in a system without uplocks may result in the landing gear slowly extending itself when you don't particularly want it to.

The next most common method of extension is all-electric, and once again you should commit the location of circuit breakers to memory. The gear will only fail to extend at night, according to Murphy's Law, and you will have your hands full even without digging through your flight case for a flashlight.

A gear system that relies solely on electrical power will be an additional concern if you lose an engine (and its associated alternator) or experience a total electrical failure and are living on the battery, because gear motors soak up prodigious amounts of juice. It might be wiser (again, depending on how other aircraft systems operate) to extend the gear manually and reserve the rapidly failing battery for other uses. With an all-electric system, if the motor jams you may be unable to extend the landing gear.

If you write Apache or Aztec in your logbook under "Model," the job of lowering the wheels is performed entirely by hydraulics. Depending on the vintage of the airplane, there may be only one engine with a hydraulic pump—the left one. If this is the case and that engine should fail, count on doing a lot of hand pumping. If the engine is totally gone, be sure that the gear has fully retracted before you pull the prop control into the feather detent. That single pump is also used to operate the flaps in older Aztecs and Apaches, and if you operate the gear and flap levers simultaneously, both the gear and flaps will move with agonizing slowness. If a plumbing failure has left a puddle of red, sticky hydraulic fluid somewhere, there is a carbon dioxide "last chance" system to blow the gear down. When you pull the ring on the CO_2 bottle, the gas rushes into the gear extension plumbing and forces the gear into the down-and-locked position.

If your multi-engine trainer is the first retractable you have ever flown, there is an idiosyncrasy of fold-up airplanes you should be aware of: the gear-down indicator lights may have already been dimmed to a feeble glow when you turned the panel lights on. This can be disconcerting if you are flying during daylight hours and the last person to use the airplane left the panel lights on. Many a crash-fire-rescue truck has rolled toward the runway, lights flashing and siren blaring, because a pilot turned on the panel lights, extended the gear, and saw nothing when looking for three green lights. The same embarrassing situation can arise if the "gear down" indicator light (or lights—many airplanes have three) has had a bulb burn out. Swapping bulbs is always part of the troubleshooting procedure.

Environmental System

The environmental system in a multi-engine airplane will demand more of your attention than the cabin heat and ventilation system in a single, because of the extended endurance of a twin. Four or more hours in an airplane without an operating heater will discourage the most enthusiastic light twin passenger. Single-engine airplanes get their cabin heat directly from the engine compartment, massaged and modified for comfort. In a single, a heater muff surrounds a portion of the exhaust system, and the red-hot exhaust heats the air in the muff. As long as the engine is operating, heat will be available (barring a problem in the ductwork). If you want or need another reason to get your multi-engine rating, many carbon-monoxide-related accidents in single-engine airplanes have been traced to leaks between the exhaust system and the heated air being fed to the cabin.

Trying to move heat from a nacelle-mounted engine to the fuselage through ductwork without unacceptable losses is virtually impossible, so twins have gasoline-fired heaters located somewhere in the fuselage where you can't get at them in flight; the Duchess heater is in the nose compartment (Figure 2-14). It works pretty much like any internal combustion device in that fuel and air are mixed in a tightly sealed chamber and ignited by a spark plug. Figure 2-15 represents a generic heater. The fuel comes from one of the tanks, combustion air is forced into the chamber by a fan, and the spark plug—well, it's a spark plug. Outside ventilating air passes around and over the firebox, is heated, and goes on its way to the cabin to warm you and your passengers. A thermostatic switch shuts off the fuel when the temperature reaches the comfort level that you have set.

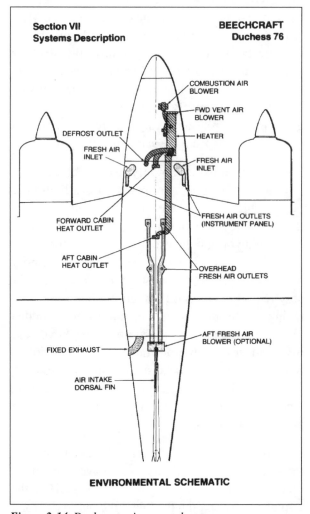

Figure 2-14. Duchess environmental system

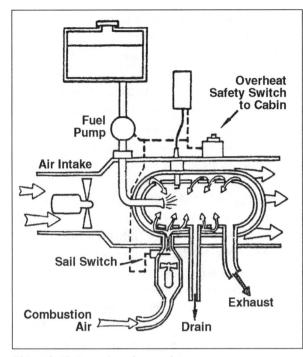

Figure 2-15. Typical combustion heater

It is a simple system, easy to use and hard to mess up. There are two major safety devices: the heater will shut off automatically if the supply of combustion air is interrupted or if the system reaches a preset maximum temperature. The overtemperature safety switch is located on the heater body where you can't get at it—if there is a malfunction and the breaker pops, you will have to land to reset it. The various blowers are protected by circuit breakers in the cockpit.

Combustion products are piped overboard. You can search out the location of the heater by looking for a short exhaust stack poking through the fuselage (with a dirty streak behind it). Nearby, you will find a little fuel drain tube that gets rid of unburned fuel. Make sure it isn't bent or obstructed.

Which tank feeds the heater? If it's the right tank, and if you have shut down the right engine, do you really want to place the right fuel selector in the OFF position? If you crossfeed the right engine from the left tank, will the heater still work? If each wing has more than one tank, will the auxiliary or nacelle tank feed the heater? These are the types of questions you must ask yourself as you study the fuel and environmental systems. You must also include fuel for the heater in your preflight planning.

The heater not only contributes to the comfort of pilot and passengers, but it may also affect the accuracy of the air-driven gyroscopic instruments. On many twins, the tiny gyroscopes that make the attitude and heading indicators work are powered by air from the passenger cabin, sucked over their paddle wheels by a vacuum pump. If cabin air falls below 40°F, the gyros will not operate properly. Pressure systems, which blow rather than suck, do not use cabin air.

Vacuum System

From your first introduction to flight instruments as a student pilot, you have heard the attitude and heading indicators referred to as the vacuum instruments, and it's time to set the record straight. The pumps mounted on the accessory pads of your airplane engines are not necessarily vacuum pumps—they might be pressure pumps, depending on the airframe manufacturer. They might be dry pumps, self-lubricated by the graphite of which the pump vanes are manufactured; or wet pumps, lubricated by engine oil. As you scan the flight instruments, you may never know the difference.

Some mechanics feel that the service life of dry pumps is shorter than that of wet pumps, but all you need to know is that all such pumps have finite lives and sooner or later you will lose a pump in flight. The nice thing about twins is that when it happens, you have a backup. Every twin has a shuttle valve in the line to the gyroscopic instruments from the pumps. When you start the right engine, the shuttle valve slides over to allow air (huffed or puffed) from its pump to operate the instruments. When you start the left engine, the shuttle valve centers so that each pump does its little bit for the cause. When either an engine or its associated pump fails, the shuttle valve moves over so the remaining pump can shoulder the entire load.

Question: what happens when the shuttle valve sticks and air from the good engine is blocked? The answer is you don't have any motive power for the gyro instruments. Even two vacuum pumps can't beat Murphy's Law. Unless your Pilot's Operating Handbook is absolutely adamant about always starting a specific engine first, make a practice of alternating your engine starts. That will not only make any shuttle valve problems apparent, but will aid in detecting other impending failures that have been masked by the noise of the engine you habitually start first.

Each air-driven instrument incorporates its own air filter, and these are backed up by a central air filter. These filters should be changed at regular inspections, but may be overlooked. If you do much hard IFR flying, check the airframe logs to see how long it has been since the filters were replaced.

Ice Protection System

A few steps up the financial ladder, you might train in a Cessna 310, a Seneca, a Baron, or a similar light twin. Airplanes in that class are used for hard IFR and may even have some deice or anti-ice capability. Regardless of the type of airplane you train in, your goal is to move up into more sophisticated, more capable equipment, without stopping until you have a column in your log headed "turbine," so a discussion of ice protection is called for.

First, let's dispose of the certification requirements. Very few non-transport category airplanes are certificated for flight into known moderate or severe icing conditions. Your airplane may have boots on the wings, booted propellers, and a hot windshield, but there will still be a notice that "Flight into known icing conditions is prohibited" in the Approved Flight Manual. The installed equipment is intended to buy time to find an escape route, and should not give you a false sense of security. When you get into Part 135 Commuter operations, ice protection equipment and procedural requirements are quite stringent.

On normally-aspirated and turbocharged twins, wing boots are pneumatically inflated to break off ice that is allowed to accumulate on the leading edges. Be sure you know where the inflation air is coming from. Two engines does mean two vacuum pumps, but if one of those engines quits, the remaining pump will be called on to both run the vacuum instruments and blow up the boots. If it is not up to the task, you will have one engine, no deicing boots, and no vacuum-driven gyro instruments.

Back in the 1930s, when airplane manufacturers first began to install deicing equipment, the inflatable tubes on wing boots were of large diameter and the pumps available in those days didn't put out much pressure. They inflated and deflated slowly — slowly enough that ice could accrete between inflation cycles or while the tubes were inflated. The recommended procedure was to wait until at least one-half inch of ice had built up before activating the boots, because if they were inflated too soon an "ice bridge" would form and the boots would become useless. Times and equipment have changed, but the same procedure has been drummed into the minds of thousands of pilots. Modern deicing boots have small diameter tubes which are inflated by high-pressure air from turbochargers, and their inflation and deflation times are measured in seconds. Airframe and boot manufacturers agree there is no evidence of such a thing as "ice bridging." Although they agree that thicker ice cracks off more readily than a thin ice coating, they say waiting for a specific thickness — which is difficult to gauge anyway — is not a valid procedure. As we move into the new century, the word is to activate the boots as soon as ice accretion is noted, and never to use an autopilot when ice is collecting on your airplane.

When ice has spread past the rear edge of the boots to adhere to the metal surface of the wing, a "fence" of ice may remain when the boots shed their coating. This abrupt edge will catch even more ice, so watch for it; just a few moments in icing conditions can cause serious disruption of airflow over the wing. Wing boots require an extra measure of care during fueling. Conscientious line personnel will use rubber pads to avoid scarring the boots. A tiny hole in something that must be inflated in order to operate properly is bad news.

Structural ice will add drag to your airplane, and ice around the engine air intakes will reduce the amount of air available for the engine to breathe. Those factors alone mean decreased airspeed. Should you struggle along, accepting the lower speed, while attempting to maintain altitude? Absolutely not. You must sacrifice altitude to maintain a small angle of attack; if you increase angle of attack to maintain altitude, ice will begin to collect on the bottom of the wing. Some manufacturers dictate a minimum air-

Figure 2-16. *Deiced C-414*

speed in icing to avoid this. Beech says 130 knots is minimum for Travel Airs and Barons, while 140 knots is minimum for other Beech twins. The National Transportation Safety Board has asked all manufacturers to include minimum safe speed in icing.

The ice collection efficiency of a surface is inversely proportional to its radius. If the wing's leading edge has a four inch radius and a propeller blade has a radius of one-half inch, what looks like a trace of ice on the wing will mean a load of ice on the propeller. Hot props have electrically heated boots covering the inner one third of the blade; the outer portions of the blades flex enough in normal operation to shed most ice, but you might have to cycle ice-laden props occasionally to hasten the process.

The usual hot prop arrangement is made up of two heating elements on each blade, with a timing device to apply power to the heating elements in a cyclic pattern. You can watch this action on the associated ammeter. If an inoperative heating element causes ice to be retained on one blade, you will experience severe vibration until it is thrown off. You will notice that many twins have plastic or metal shields on their fuselages in line with the propellers to reduce damage by ice slung from them.

When you compare the leading edges of the wing and the horizontal stabilizer, the difference in radius tells you that a little bit of ice on the leading edge of the wing means considerably more is being collected by the horizontal stabilizer, back where you can't see it. Ice in that location may cause the tail feathers to stall when you are on short final (or in the landing flare). If ice on the wing leads you to believe there is

ice on the horizontal stabilizer, do not use flaps. The downwash from extended flaps will cause the stabilizer to stall and the airplane will pitch down without enough altitude to recover. A good rule of thumb is that there is three times as much ice on the horizontal stabilizer as there is on the wing. Under those conditions, you become a test pilot; none of the numbers in the operating manual are valid when you are flying an iced-up airplane. The well-equipped Cessna 414 in Figure 2-16 has boots on the propeller, wing, vertical fin and, although you can't see them, on the horizontal stabilizer.

An electrically heated windshield, or a heated panel that will keep a portion of the windshield ice-free, will avoid a situation where the airplane is clear of clouds, but you are still IFR in the cockpit. Do not delude yourself into thinking that heat from the defroster will melt a hole in the ice you picked up at 15,000 feet when you attempt to land at an airport with a surface temperature below freezing. There's not enough heat available and too much surface to dissipate it. Pilots have landed by peeking out through the side windows, but it wasn't a pleasant experience. Many twins use an external electrically heated panel (*see* Figure 2-17 on the next page) on the pilot's side of the windshield. The heat radiated by this panel will provide a reasonable amount of visibility, although it shouldn't be expected to clear much more area than it covers — about 6 by 9 inches. These panels can be removed when there is no possibility of icing.

Electrically heated windows are a more expensive, but very effective, solution to the windshield ice problem. A grid of fine wire is embedded in the wind-

Figure 2-17. *External deice panel*

shield itself, and when current flows through the grid, it clears the entire field of view. Never use electric windshield heat on the ground; without a considerable flow of air over the windshield surface to carry away the heat, the windshield may be softened. And if you are flying a pressurized airplane, you don't want anything bad to happen to the windshield.

You may find heated fuel vents on some airplanes. A vent clogged by ice means that fuel flow to the engine can stop, and collapse of the fuel tank or bladder is a possibility. A heated static port (or two) will keep structural ice from affecting the pitot-static instruments.

Emergency Exit System

An airplane with two wing-mounted engines differs from a single-engine airplane in another important respect: it must have an emergency exit. Some manufacturers provide window exits, some provide extra doors; few provide both. While you are giving your passengers the required preflight briefing on seatbelts, you might add a few words on how to get out of the aircraft if a sudden stop puts you temporarily out of commission. Before the briefing, though, be sure you can find the exit; some of them are pretty well hidden by paint and putty (the Piper Seneca is a notable exception). A conscientious mechanic will not sign-off a thorough annual inspection without exercising the emergency exits.

Autopilots

Most twins have some kind of autopilot, even if its capability is limited to keeping the wings level while the pilot reads charts or approach plates. It is impossible to cover the details of autopilot operation in this text because there are so many variables—one manufacturer may take "wings level" information from the turn coordinator, while another might use an output from the attitude indicator.

Every airplane with an autopilot or flight director installed must have a supplement in the Approved Flight Manual containing operating instructions and a preflight test procedure. Pilots tend to use only the airframe manufacturer's checklist without reference to the back of the book—this is a mistake. At the very least, the manufacturer's checklist should be modified to include the autopilot test. Would you willingly take off with someone in the right seat who might take over the controls without warning? Of course not. That's why a preflight test of the autopilot is essential.

If your autopilot takes its wings-level information from an electrically-powered turn coordinator, failure of vacuum-operated gyro instruments should be a non-event—but that is little comfort if you think the autopilot is driven by the attitude indicator.

When the autopilot is flying the airplane, you must not make any control inputs. If altitude varies due to convective activity, correct this with the autopilot's climb/descend mode, not by overriding the autopilot wih control pressure. When an autopilot senses back pressure, for example, it adds nose-down trim. If the pilot reacts with even more back pressure, the autopilot will continue to fight back. Then, if the autopilot is disengaged either on purpose or automatically, the airplane will nose over in response to the nose-down trim. A major failing of all current autopilot systems is they bite before they bark—an alarm will sound when it disengages, but there is no warning when the autopilot has reached its limits in either pitch or bank and is ready to disengage.

Flight Directors

A flight director is not an autopilot. It is a form of computer that takes information from various sensors and presents it to the pilot by visual cues. The flight director knows when it is time to roll out of a turn, intercept a radial, glide slope, or localizer long before it becomes obvious to the pilot. A standard VOR indicator might show the needle to the left, moving imperceptibly toward the center, while the flight director would already be commanding a right turn—a pilot without a flight director, seeing the "raw data" needle to the left, might turn farther left to speed up the intercept and end up flying through the radial or localizer. If you are flying with a flight director you must follow its commands and ignore any other needle indications on the panel.

There are two forms of flight director displays: the familiar cross-needles, and command bars. With the command bar display, the pilot simply snugs the delta (which represents the airplane) into the "v" formed by the command bars and does whatever it takes to keep it there. In my opinion, the command bar display is easier to interpret than the cross-needles.

Although a flight director is not an autopilot, you can connect the autopilot to the flight director and let it do the flying. Some pilots insist on hand-flying a flight director, but most take advantage of the autopilot. There is no question that an autopilot/flight director combination can fly more smoothly than a pilot hand-flying the airplane. Here again it is essential that you study all of the material in the AFM relating to the flight management system—it is really easy to push the wrong button and get behind the airplane while trying to correct your error.

When an icing encounter is anticipated, the autopilot should be turned off. You need the tactile feedback afforded by handling the controls yourself. If you select "altitude hold," the system will maintain altitude while the airplane slows due to ice accumulation—if you are not alert, it will trim the airplane into a stall. Similarly, the autopilot/flight director will struggle to keep the wings level when ice creates a wing-heavy condition; when the system reaches the limit of its authority and disengages, the airplane can be in an unrecoverable roll. If the flight manual for the airplane you are flying contains different advice, take a look at when it was written—a lot has been learned about airframe icing since 1994.

You should know every means of disengaging the autopilot if it decides to take over, even if that means shutting off the airplane's master switch. You can overpower the autopilot, but causing clutches to slip is not the best practice; kill the autopilot and take over manually in the event of a malfunction.

Electric Trim

It is much more convenient to control elevator trim with a thumb-operated switch on the control yoke than to reach for a trim wheel. Many light singles and twins and all airplanes with autopilots have electric elevator trim. You need to know two things about your electric trim system: how to disable it if it "runs away," and whether or not the use of electric trim causes the autopilot to disengage.

Runaway trim is frightening, whether it goes nose up or nose down. The system can be overpowered manually, but when the malfunction occurs it is startling, and a pilot might allow the airplane to get into an extreme pitch-up or pitch-down attitude before reacting. Know which circuit breaker controls the electric trim; even better, turn off the master switch while you are looking for the correct breaker.

With most autopilot/electric trim situations, pushing the trim button forward or aft will activate the trim without affecting the autopilot, while pushing down on the trim button will cause the autopilot to disengage. If you didn't intend to disengage the autopilot, this can lead to loss of heading or altitude. Know what you are doing when you activate the trim button; read the autopilot supplement in the back of the flight manual.

Oxygen

The FAA requires the use of supplemental oxygen by pilots for all flight time in excess of 30 minutes at cabin altitudes between 12,500 feet MSL and 14,000 feet MSL, and full-time oxygen use above 14,000 feet MSL (14 CFR 91.211). At cabin altitudes in excess of 15,000 feet MSL, all occupants must be supplied with supplemental oxygen. In an unpressurized airplane, of course, cabin altitude and airplane altitude are the same.

There are two common methods of oxygen delivery, the familiar mask which covers nose and mouth, and cannulas—tubes that feed oxygen directly into the nostrils. You have probably seen persons with respiratory problems carrying oxygen tanks and wearing cannulas. Cannulas are approved for use at cabin altitudes of 18,000 feel MSL and below; above that altitude, masks must be worn. It is easier to use a microphone when wearing nasal cannulas, but oxygen masks with internal microphones are available.

Your responsibility as a pilot is to ensure that oxygen is available for yourself and any passengers, should flight at those altitudes be required. This could mean a portable system or a permanently installed oxygen system, and you must know how to operate either one. You must also ensure your passengers know how to use their masks or cannulas, preferably by a demonstration before takeoff. Oxygen lines terminate in bayonet fittings—the kind that must be inserted against spring tension and turned 90° to lock—before oxygen will flow. Uninformed passengers will just stick the connector in the outlet and expect oxygen to flow.

The duration of your oxygen supply is determined by flow rate and the number of persons using oxygen. Whether you are using a portable or a built-in system, you will be provided with a table of durations for different numbers of users.

You will always have a control that allows oxygen to flow from the tank to the masks or cannulas. There will be a method of controlling flow to the dispensing devices, but methods vary and it is up to you to know how your system works. The pilot usually gets more oxygen than occupants of the other seats, so check to be sure that you are wearing a pilot mask if this is the situation with your system. Show your passengers how to check the flow of oxygen to their masks or cannulas—if flow is obstructed, they will fall asleep before they notice anything wrong.

Be sure that your female passengers do not wear lipstick when using oxygen—severe burns are possible if the oils in the cosmetics ignite. Keep oils and greases of every kind away from the oxygen system, and have it serviced by a knowledgeable technician. Of course, smoking is prohibited when oxygen is being used.

Supplemental oxygen use is recommended at cabin altitudes above 5,000 feet at night to improve visual acuity, but a whiff of oxygen will clear your head at any time.

Summary

You have to study and understand the systems in the airplane you are flying—knowledge gained from flying a similar model or a model from a different year is almost useless, because manufacturers can and often do change systems and modify procedures. The FAA requires commuter pilots to receive "differences training" when they fly more than one model or type of aircraft. Should you do less for your passengers?

Chapter 2
Review Questions

1. The majority of accidents/incidents involving multi-engine airplanes is attributed to

   A—mechanical failure.
   B—fuel exhaustion/starvation.
   C—inclement weather.

2. Either alternator on a twin can handle 100% of the electrical load if the other alternator fails. (true, false)

3. A twin with fuel-injected engines can develop ice in the induction system. (true, false)

4. Propellers on piston-engine twins are driven toward the feathered position by

   A—the governor in the propeller hub.
   B—the engine oil pump.
   C—gas pressure or a combination of springs and counterweights.

5. A turbocharger's compressor is driven by

   A—relative wind.
   B—exhaust gases.
   C—intake air.

6. If oil pressure to the propeller hub is lost, the propeller will

   A—move toward the feathered position.
   B—overspeed.
   C—stop.

7. How does an unfeathering accumulator work?

   _____

8. The cylinder head heat gauge is nearing the red line. What remedies are available?

   A—Close the cowl flaps.
   B—Lean the mixture further.
   C—Reduce power.

9. You skip the feather check during the pretakeoff checks. Unknown to you, the nitrogen gas in the prop hub has leaked out. What can happen?

   A—Prop will not feather if needed.
   B—Prop governor will not work.
   C—Prop will overspeed.

10. To comply with the regulations, an airplane's fuel gauge must read accurately when

    A—the tanks are completely full.
    B—the tanks are completely empty.
    C—throughout their range.

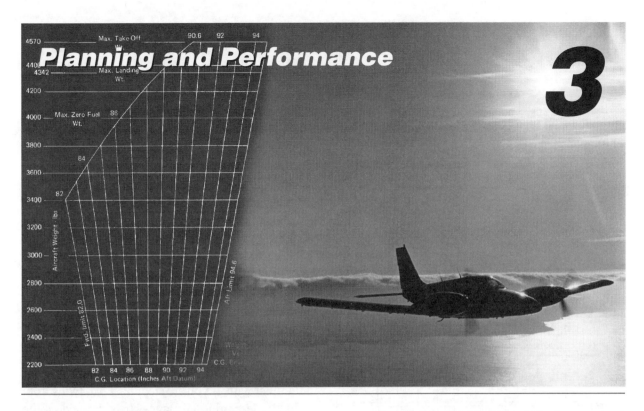

Planning and Performance

Weight and Balance Calculations

Preflight calculation of takeoff weight and center of gravity location is essential for the safe operation of any airplane, but the consequences of failing to perform this simple task before launching into the sky in a twin can be disastrous.

The manufacturer's test pilot made sure the center of gravity was within the design envelope before determining the speed at which directional control is lost when an engine fails. To get book performance, you can do no less.

There is more to the question of loading than a simple addition of weights to stay within a maximum gross weight figure. As you move from one model of multi-engine airplane to another, or when you first sit beside a forest of knobs, you should calculate that airplane's power loading. That figure, the result of dividing the maximum gross weight by the total horsepower available, tells you how many pounds of airplane each horse must lift to make the airplane fly. A few years ago, the magazine *Business and Commercial Aviation* analyzed twin-engine fatal accident statistics and noted an increase in accidents when power loading exceeded 10 pounds per horse-power. For example, the Beechcraft Duchess manual lists a gross takeoff weight of 3,900 pounds to be hoisted on the shoulders of 360 horses, a burden of 10.8 pounds per steed. To stay on the right side of *B & CA*'s statistical curve, Duchess pilots would have to limit their loads to less than 3,600 pounds. This is a calculation (and weight adjustment) you can and should perform for any twin you fly.

Every graph in the takeoff distance and climb performance section of the Pilot's Operating Handbook includes weight as a variable, and you cannot predict your twin's performance without considering its effect. If the takeoff weight of your airplane and the density altitude combine to make the two-engine climb rate marginal, the climb rate will disappear on one engine. Limiting airplane weight is the only answer. Figure 3-1 on the next page is a graphic method of determining a safe takeoff weight. Although one of the reasons for moving up into twins is their weight-carrying ability, you might consider never taking off at maximum weight, especially at high density altitudes.

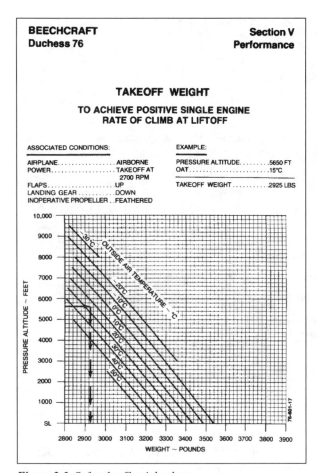

TAKEOFF WEIGHT

**TO ACHIEVE POSITIVE SINGLE ENGINE
RATE OF CLIMB AT LIFTOFF**

ASSOCIATED CONDITIONS:

AIRPLANE.................AIRBORNE	
POWER..................TAKEOFF AT	
2700 RPM	
FLAPS...................UP	
LANDING GEAR..........DOWN	
INOPERATIVE PROPELLER ..FEATHERED	

EXAMPLE:

PRESSURE ALTITUDE.........5650 FT
OAT.......................15°C

TAKEOFF WEIGHT..........2925 LBS

Figure 3-1. Safe takeoff weight chart

These are the consequences of overloading:

- Increased takeoff speed.
- Increased takeoff runway length.
- Reduced rate of climb.
- Maximum altitude capability reduced; power loading increased.
- Reduced operational range; more fuel required to carry the load.
- Less maneuverability.
- Less controllability (greater angle of attack to maintain altitude; increased induced drag).
- Higher stall speed (greater angle of attack required to carry the load).
- Higher approach speed because of increased stall speed.
- Longer landing distance (more energy to be dissipated through friction and brake heating).

One final word on loading: leave some room for ice if the possibility of running into the cold stuff exists. If you are trundling along at cruise altitude and fly into the freezer compartment, structural ice will add weight to the airplane faster than fuel consumption can reduce it.

Any airplane will fly better, faster, and farther when lightly loaded than when grossed out, yet there is one plus to being heavily laden in a twin: a lower minimum control speed. That may seem odd, but these are the aerodynamic facts: banking toward the good engine causes the horizontal component of lift to offset the yawing tendency, and the magnitude of that component varies directly with weight. At light weights, you will have to bank a little further into the good engine to develop enough force to arrest the turning tendency, or you will lose directional control at a higher airspeed.

Zero-Fuel Weight

The term "zero-fuel weight" may be one you are unfamiliar with, if you are stepping up to twins from light single-engine airplanes. It is defined as the maximum weight of the airplane without any fuel in the wings. You will usually find this limitation in the form of a placard near the fuel selectors saying something like "All weight in excess of 3,600 pounds must be in the form of fuel." That makes 3,600 pounds the zero-fuel weight.

In flight, the weight of the fuselage is supported by the wings—there's nothing new about that. The wings must also support their own weight, of course, and almost all of that weight will be fuel at takeoff time. With the total weight divided between the wings and the fuselage, all is well. The problem comes when too much weight is concentrated at the center of the spar, where the people and baggage usually congregate, and fuel burn reduces the weight in the wings. Under those conditions, if you have not observed the zero-fuel weight limitation, you are placing undue stress on the wing structure. Add a little turbulence to bounce the fuselage up and down on the center of the wing, and the result may be disastrous.

You have been calculating weight and balance since student pilot days, so the weight and balance solution should look familiar, except for the shape of the envelope. Figure 3-2, "CG Range and Weight"

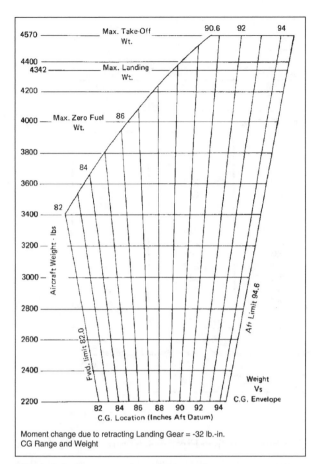

Figure 3-2. Seneca weight and CG envelope

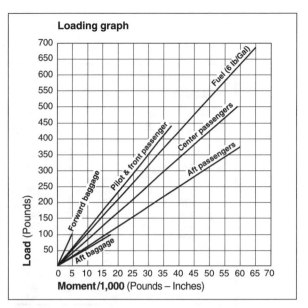

Figure 3-3. Seneca loading graph

taken from the Seneca II manual, illustrates the typical shape of the operating envelope for a light twin. Note the zero fuel line and the line for maximum landing weight.

Let's try a sample problem to see how it works.

Basic empty weight .... 3,136 lbs

Pilot and front passenger .... 380 lbs

Passengers, center seats .... 250 lbs
  (forward facing)

Baggage forward .... 50 lbs

Baggage aft .... 45 lbs

Fuel .... 360 lbs

Total weight .... 4,221 lbs

Using the weights listed above with Figure 3-3, the loading graph, and getting the empty weight moment from the airplane's manual, you will get these results:

Basic empty airplane moment .... 272.2 lb.-in.

Front seat .... 32.5 lb.-in.

Center seat .... 29.5 lb.-in.

Forward baggage .... 1.1 lb.-in.

Aft baggage .... 8.1 lb.-in.

Fuel .... 3.7 lb.-in.

Total moment .... 347.1 lb.-in.

Dividing the total moment by the total weight in the time-honored manner results in a center of gravity location of .082232, which doesn't make much sense until you look back at the loading graph and note that the moments are given as Moment/1,000. Push the decimal point three places to the right, and the center of gravity is a more reasonable 82.23 inches aft of datum.

Plot the intersection of 82 (can you find a pencil sharp enough to plot 82.23?) and 4,221 on Figure 3-2 and you will see that the airplane is nose-heavy. Move those center-seat passengers to the rear or put a case of oil in the rear seat area. I would move the forward baggage to the aft baggage compartment, if it would fit.

OCCUPANTS

WEIGHT	FRONT SEATS			3RD AND 4TH SEATS	
	*FWD POS.		*AFT POS.	STD. BENCH	OPTIONAL
	††ARM **104	†ARM **105	ARM **112	ARM **142	ARM **144
	MOMENT/100				
120	125	126	134	170	173
130	135	137	146	185	187
140	146	147	157	199	202
150	156	158	168	213	216
160	166	168	179	227	230
170	177	179	190	241	245
180	187	189	202	256	259
190	198	200	213	270	274
200	208	210	224	284	288
210	218	220	235	298	302
220	228	231	246	312	317
230	239	241	258	327	331
240	250	252	269	341	346
250	260	262	280	355	360

† Effective ME-1 thru ME-20
†† Effective ME-21 and after
* Reclining seat with back in full-up position
** Values computed from a C.G. criterion based on a 170 pound male. Differences in physical characteristics can cause variation in center of gravity location.

Figure 3-4. Duchess passenger loading

The Beechcraft Duchess weight and balance presentation makes you work a little harder, because the weight versus moment data is not presented graphically. Still, it will not challenge a $4.00 four-function calculator.

Our Duchess sample problem will be an instructional flight: student, instructor, and two loaded flight bags.

Basic empty weight .... 2,545 lbs

Front seat passengers .... 375 lbs

Baggage .... 25 lbs

Fuel .... 600 lbs

Total weight .... 3,545 lbs

For moment numbers, look first to the Occupants list, Figure 3-4. There is no listing for 375 pounds, so you'll have to interpolate. In the column marked "Arm 104," find a moment of 208 for the 200-pound pilot. Again, there is no listing for 175, so this requires interpolation. Add the moments for 170 and 180 and divide by two to get the moment for 175 pounds: 182. That makes the front seat moment 208 + 182 or 390.

The baggage list, Figure 3-5, has nothing for 25 pounds, so let's interpolate again. A conservative number would be 42 inch/pounds. The fuel number from Figure 3-6 is easy: 702. The moment for the empty airplane is listed in the Pilot's Operating Handbook as 2,775. Putting all those numbers together makes the total moment 3,909, and Beech has a tabulation of moment limits versus weight (Figure 3-7) for you to use in determining whether the loading is safe or not. According to the table, at a weight of 3,550 pounds the forward moment limit is 3,850 and the aft limit is 4,171. The sample problem moment of 3,909 falls within these limits and you can safely launch on your cross-country flight.

Figure 3-8, on Page 3-6, makes it possible for you to plot the total weight and total moment on an envelope, which gives you a better picture of where your loading lies in relation to the forward and aft CG limits.

Section VI BEECHCRAFT
Wt & Bal/Equip List Duchess 76

USEFUL LOAD WEIGHTS AND MOMENTS

BAGGAGE
ARM 167

WEIGHT	MOMENT/100
10	17
20	33
30	50
40	67
50	84
60	100
70	117
80	134
90	150
100	167
110	184
120	200
130	217
140	234
150	251
160	267
170	284
180	301
190	317
200	334

Figure 3-5. *Baggage weight and moment*

BEECHCRAFT Section VI
Duchess 76 Wt & Bal/Equip List

USEFUL LOAD WEIGHTS AND MOMENTS
USABLE FUEL
ARM 117.0

GALLONS	WEIGHT LBS	MOMENT/100
10	60	70
20	120	140
30	180	211
40	240	281
50	300	351
60	360	421
70	420	491
80	480	562
90	540	632
100	600	702

Figure 3-6. *Fuel weight and moment*

BEECHCRAFT Section VI
Duchess 76 Wt & Bal/Equip List

MOMENT LIMITS vs WEIGHT

WEIGHT POUNDS	MOMENT/100 FWD LIMIT	MOMENT/100 AFT LIMIT	WEIGHT POUNDS	MOMENT/100 FWD LIMIT	MOMENT/100 AFT LIMIT
2300	2452	2703	3125	3331	3672
2325	2479	2732	3150	3358	3701
2350	2505	2761	3175	3385	3731
2375	2532	2791	3200	3411	3760
2400	2558	2820			
2425	2585	2849	3225	3438	3789
2450	2612	2879	3250	3465	3819
2475	2638	2908	3275	3496	3848
2500	2665	2938	3300	3528	3878
2525	2692	2967	3325	3560	3907
2550	2718	2996	3350	3592	3936
2575	2745	3026	3375	3624	3966
2600	2772	3055	3400	3656	3995
2625	2798	3084	3425	3688	4024
2650	2825	3114	3450	3720	4054
2675	2852	3143	3475	3753	4083
2700	2878	3173	3500	3785	4113
2725	2905	3202	3525	3817	4142
2750	2932	3231	3550	3850	4171
2775	2958	3261	3575	3882	4201
2800	2985	3290	3600	3915	4230
2825	3012	3319	3625	3948	4259
2850	3038	3349	3650	3981	4289
2875	3065	3378	3675	4014	4318
2900	3091	3408	3700	4047	4348
2925	3118	3437	3725	4080	4377
2950	3145	3466	3750	4113	4406
2975	3171	3496	3775	4146	4436
3000	3198	3525	3800	4179	4465
3025	3225	3554	3825	4213	4494
3050	3251	3584	3850	4246	4524
3075	3278	3613	3875	4280	4553
3100	3305	3643	3900	4313	4583

Figure 3-7. *Duchess moment limits and weight*

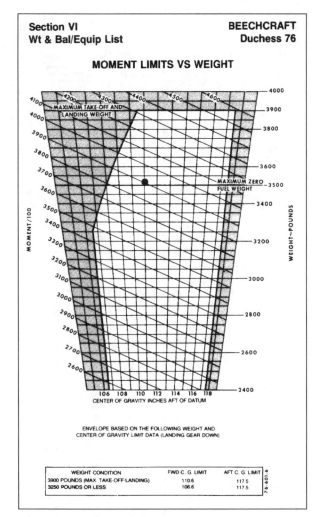

MOMENT LIMITS VS WEIGHT

ENVELOPE BASED ON THE FOLLOWING WEIGHT AND
CENTER OF GRAVITY LIMIT DATA (LANDING GEAR DOWN)

WEIGHT CONDITION	FWD C. G. LIMIT	AFT C. G. LIMIT
3900 POUNDS (MAX. TAKE-OFF/LANDING)	110.6	117.5
3250 POUNDS OR LESS	106.6	117.5

Figure 3-8. Weight and balance envelope

Lateral Balance

As the pilot of a single-engine airplane, you manage your fuel consumption to avoid having one wing heavier than the other, and you will follow the same policy in a twin. However, the consequences of off-center weight can be much greater in a twin if the engine on the heavy wing fails, because it will require more aileron deflection to raise the heavy wing, and more rudder to offset both the drag of the windmilling propeller and the adverse aileron drag. Of course, if the engine opposite the heavy wing fails, the extra weight will help you control the situation. Unless your crystal ball can tell you which engine is vulnerable, you had better keep the load balanced from side to side.

Some fuel systems have within them the potential for a hazardous lateral imbalance situation. In these systems, the failure of a pump or valve may make it impossible for you to use fuel in one wing or to cross-feed it to the other wing. This may not seem too threatening at cruise altitude, but having one wing heavier than the other can really complicate a cross-wind landing. If either engine should fail, you may have control problems on final approach. If a fuel transfer problem develops, the wisest course is to land at the nearest suitable airport before an imbalance can develop.

Performance Planning

Performance is what it is all about. When you move up into multi-engine airplanes, you experience gains in climb performance, cruise speed, and load-carrying capability. However, those gains are only realized when both fans are turning. A twin with only half of its power available loses out to a high-performance single in all categories. Now just a darn minute, I can hear you saying, are you trying to tell me that a Chieftain with only one of those 350-horse engines running can't outperform a turbocharged 210 with its 310 horsepower? That's exactly what I am saying, and the reason is that although a twin loses 50% of its available power with an engine out, it loses 80-90% of its performance. Look back at Figure 1-2 for confirmation.

The crippled twin's performance suffers dramatically for a variety of reasons. First, a portion of the lift developed by a wing with a nacelle-mounted engine is derived from the air being blown over it by the propeller. When that source of airflow disappears and is replaced by turbulent airflow behind the windmilling propeller, you are worse off than you would be if there was only a single-engine mounted on the airplane's centerline. When a failed engine's propeller is windmilling, lift over that portion of the wing directly behind the propeller disc is reduced considerably, and that wing's stall speed increases.

Second, a multi-engine airplane both rolls and yaws when an engine fails, presenting more surface area to the relative wind and thereby increasing drag. Less power, less lift due to the reduction in airflow over the nacelle, more drag (until the offending propeller is feathered)—all of these elements erode performance. The immediate actions required by the manufacturer's engine-out checklist are designed to restore as much lift as possible, decrease drag, and add whatever power is needed for you to maintain control of the airplane's attitude.

The purpose of an airplane engine is to pull the wing forward through the air (the fuselage goes along for the ride). Think of the engine as an air pump, in which air is mixed with fuel, set on fire, and pumped overboard. In the process, every power stroke contributes its energy toward rotating the propeller. When the fire goes out, however, the propeller blades are rotated by the airplane's forward motion and the action is reversed. The propeller drives the pistons up and down in their cylinders against the pressure of the air trapped in them, plus the load of all the accessories. This is why the windmilling propeller creates drag, acting almost as a flat circular plate with a diameter equal to that of the propeller disc. To eliminate that flat-plate drag, the windmilling propeller must be stopped by rotating its blades to the feathered position.

Graphs from the Pilot's Operating Handbook will help explain the loss of climb performance with an engine feathered. Using Figures 3-9 and 3-10, you can readily compare the two-engine climb rate with the single-engine climb rate under the same conditions.

OAT .... +20°C
Pressure altitude .... 2,000 feet
Weight .... 3,600 pounds

If you haven't used this kind of performance graph before, it might be a good idea to run through an example problem. You will see a lot of these graphs in twin manuals. If you were preparing for an FAA knowledge examination, I would suggest that you equip yourself with a transparent overlay, a pair of dividers, and several sharp pencils. Since we're instead preparing for the flight portion of this skill, a practical approach is in order.

Using Figure 3-9, the first step is to enter density altitude, which is a combination of temperature and pressure altitude. Find the +20 number along the baseline and follow the vertical line upward to its intersection with the 2,000-foot pressure altitude line; that combination defines the density altitude. Draw a horizontal line over to the reference line, or do it my way—the density altitude point is just over 18 squares down from the top.

Here's where your keen eye and sense of proportion come into play. Draw or eyeball a line that closely parallels one of the upward slanting lines in the

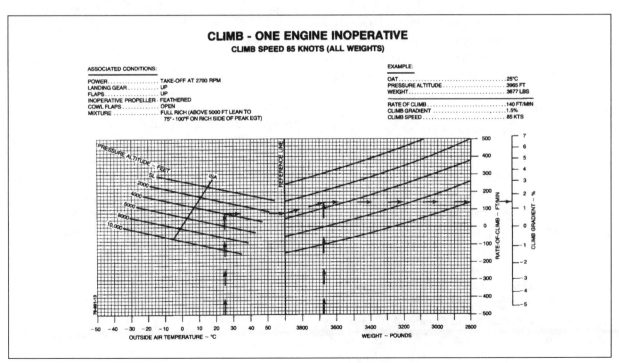

Figure 3-9. Single-engine climb performance

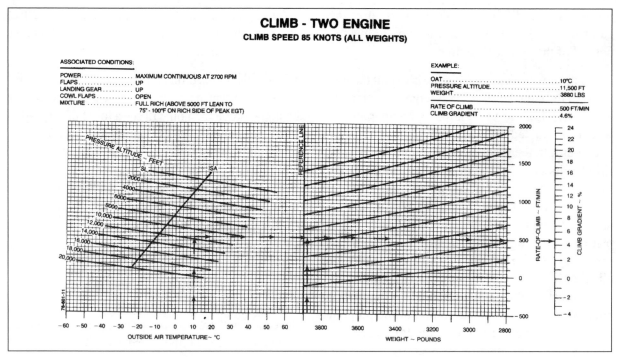

CLIMB - TWO ENGINE
CLIMB SPEED 85 KNOTS (ALL WEIGHTS)

ASSOCIATED CONDITIONS:

POWER . . . . MAXIMUM CONTINUOUS AT 2700 RPM
FLAPS . . . . UP
LANDING GEAR . . . . UP
COWL FLAPS . . . . OPEN
MIXTURE . . . . FULL RICH (ABOVE 5000 FT LEAN TO
                                                75° - 100°F ON RICH SIDE OF PEAK EGT)

EXAMPLE:

OAT . . . . 10°C
PRESSURE ALTITUDE . . . . 11,500 FT
WEIGHT . . . . 3880 LBS

RATE OF CLIMB . . . . 500 FT/MIN
CLIMB GRADIENT 4.6%

Figure 3-10. All-engine climb performance

weight area until it intersects with a vertical line drawn up from 3,600 pounds. Now draw a straight horizontal line from that point to the right margin to determine the rate of climb.

A sharp eye and a sharp pencil working together make the climb rate with both engines running about 1,300 feet per minute. Now apply those same conditions to the second graph, the climb with one engine inoperative. The sharpest eye and pencil can't improve on a climb rate of 200 feet per minute, only 15% of the two-engine climb rate. When one of the engines fails, 85% of the climb performance disappears.

To get even this meager amount of performance, it is essential that you reduce drag to a minimum; by applying full power to the good engine, you have done as much as you can on the thrust side of the equation. The landing gear and flaps are obvious drag items, and the windmilling propeller must be feathered to eliminate its drag. With the airplane under control, banking so the ball is deflected one-half ball width toward the good engine will establish zero sideslip and eliminate the drag caused by slipping toward the dead engine—one ball width while gaining control, one-half ball width for best performance after you are in charge again. Figure 3-11 shows how the drag items listed above affect vertical speed.

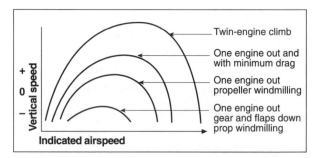

Figure 3-11. Configurations vs. vertical speed

Airspeed control is essential if you expect to get book performance from your multi-engine airplane, and you must know the appropriate airspeed for each condition of flight. Some of the airspeed designations will be familiar from your earlier training, while others will be unique to multi-engine flight. Your multi-engine examiner will ask you to recite the V-speeds and explain them. The following sections discuss the speeds you should know.

Piper Mojave

Minimum Controllable Airspeed

The red line on the airspeed indicator is V_{MC}—minimum-controllable airspeed, and it will be mentioned more than once in this book. The manufacturer, complying with conditions specified by the FAA (14 CFR Part 23), has determined that any attempt to take off and climb at a speed slower than V_{MC} with one engine inoperative and its propeller windmilling will result in loss of directional control. You should respect the red line as a minimum airspeed, and understand that as airspeed is reduced toward V_{MC}, your ability to control the aircraft is deteriorating. It's not an on-off, yes-no situation—if V_{MC} is 80 knots, you will still have a tiger by the tail at 82 knots with an engine out (meaning lots of rudder). As airspeed increases above the red line, controllability will improve, but you will still have a sick bird on your hands.

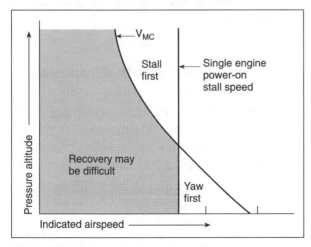

Figure 3-12. Stall speed, V_{MC} and altitude

I was careful to say that the manufacturer determined V_{MC} under certain conditions set forth in 14 CFR Part 23. Let's examine each of those conditions to see how it affects V_{MC}:

1. **Takeoff or maximum-available power on the engines.**

   The greatest yawing and rolling forces are created when one engine is developing maximum power and the other is suddenly made inoperative. An airplane engine and propeller combination develop maximum-rated horsepower at sea level; as density altitude is increased by higher pressure altitude or temperature, the power output decreases and the rolling and yawing forces are reduced. A greater angle of attack (lower airspeed) is then required for those forces to become great enough to endanger your ability to control the airplane. Figure 3-12 illustrates how V_{MC} decreases as density altitude increases. Note the indicated airspeed at which the airplane will stall stays constant as altitude changes, and that at some altitude, V_{MC} and stall speed will coincide. If an engine fails at a higher altitude, with an indicated airspeed near the power-on stall speed (a most unlikely situation), the airplane may enter a spin. It is safe to say that your airspeed needle should never be below the red line except during the landing flare. (Those few airplanes that require liftoff speeds at or near V_{MC} are discussed elsewhere.)

Although the manufacturer must establish V_{MC} with the operating engine at maximum horsepower, remember it is the good engine that is making your life miserable by trying to turn the airplane upside down. Don't hesitate to reduce the power on the operating engine if you can do so.

2. **The most unfavorable center of gravity.**

All three axes of control—pitch, roll, and yaw—act through the center of gravity (CG). If the CG is at or near the most rearward limit, the distance between the CG and the rudder is reduced, which reduces the amount of yawing leverage the rudder can exert. This means that your ability to control the airplane in an emergency is improved as the center of gravity is moved forward.

Part 23 does not address the question of lateral movement of the center of gravity, but a lateral imbalance might cause a lot of grief. You are already aware of the need to keep wing tank fuel in balance from your experience in single-engine airplanes, so nothing further needs to be said about fuel management. However, multi-engine airplanes that have wing lockers require special consideration in weight distribution. What happens if you put the tennis balls and racquets in the right wing locker, and load the golf clubs and the rest of the recreational equipment in the left wing locker, and the left engine fails? Supervise the loading of the wing lockers to be sure the weight is equally distributed.

3. **The maximum sea level takeoff weight (or any lesser weight necessary to show V_{MC}).**

Minimum controllable airspeed increases as weight is reduced, so during certification testing the manufacturer must gradually reduce the weight of the aircraft until the highest possible calibrated V_{MC} is obtained. That gives you a margin of safety because of the difference between calibrated and indicated airspeed. You and your instructor will never be able to duplicate the conditions under which the red V_{MC} marking was determined.

4. **Flaps in the takeoff position.**

The intent is to simulate, as closely as possible, the situation that would exist just after liftoff, at the beginning of the initial climb segment. Nor-

mally, you would have set the flaps to the manufacturer's recommended takeoff position.

5. **Landing gear retracted.**

This is the same scenario as for the flap setting. You may read in other texts that V_{MC} is lower if the landing gear is extended ... the FAA's Small Aircraft Directorate says that this statement does not apply to all airplanes and therefore is not accurate.

6. **The propeller of the inoperative engine windmilling.**

This is to create the most drag and the largest yawing moment for the V_{MC} certification tests. Feathering the offending propeller eliminates the drag and improves controllability.

7. **The airplane airborne and ground effect negligible.**

This requirement adds to the realism of the just-after-takeoff situation.

8. **A bank angle of not more than 5° toward the operating engine.**

Note that this is a requirement placed on a manufacturer seeking a type certificate; it is not a limitation on a pilot's reaction to an emergency. It might take more than 5° of bank to maintain control of the airplane, and it will certainly take less than 5° for best climb performance. Your goal is to establish zero sideslip angle.

The book V_{MC} figure, and the red line on the airspeed indicator, are based on a standard day at sea level. As density altitude increases, the red line becomes less reliable because V_{MC} decreases with altitude—which brings V_{MC} closer to stall speed.

Minimum Controllable Airspeed on the Ground

The airspeed we have been discussing is $V_{MC(A)}$; that is, the minimum controllable airspeed when you are airborne and can bank toward the good engine. Airplanes certificated under Part 25 must also observe $V_{MC(G)}$—minimum controllable airspeed on the ground where the airplane cannot be banked. This speed is almost always higher than $V_{MC(A)}$. It is entirely possible for the pilot of an airplane that has accelerated past $V_{MC(A)}$ and is feeling light on its wheels, or has begun to rotate, to lose directional control if an engine fails (or is failed intentionally, an important distinction). Although your Part 23 twin does not have a published $V_{MC(G)}$, be wary of anyone who wants to practice engine cuts at this critical juncture.

Minimum Safe Single-Engine Speed

The General Aviation Manufacturer's Association, following Beechcraft's lead, responded to a rash of multi-engine training accidents by suggesting that instructors observe a new V-speed, V_{SSE}. This is the minimum speed for intentional engine failures, and it is usually 5 or 6 knots above V_{MC}. Your instructor should know V_{SSE} for your airplane. V_{SSE} allows a comfortable margin above V_{MC}, yet it is slow enough to give you a workout. If your instructor insists on practicing low-altitude engine failures at red line airspeed, get another instructor.

Best Angle and Best Rate-of-Climb Speeds

The definitions of best angle-of-climb and best rate-of-climb speed do not change when you sit between two engines instead of behind one, and their designations (V_X and V_Y) do not change, either. These speeds are not marked on the airspeed indicator. Despite the emphasis that I must place on engine-out emergencies, in my opinion you should determine and use the two-engine performance speeds. The slight cushion they provide will prove invaluable during the critical first few seconds if something does go awry.

Landing Gear Extension and Operating Speeds

Most single-engine retractables have a single gear speed, which applies both to extension of the gear and operations with the gear down. Many twins have two gear speeds: V_{LO}, which governs the speed at which you can operate the gear, and V_{LE}, which limits the speed at which you can fly with it extended. If gear doors must open to let the wheels hang out

and then close again to cover the wheel well, V_{LO} will probably be slower to keep the gear doors from blowing away during the extension cycle. For those airplanes with nose gears that move forward during the retraction cycle, you may note a second V_{LO} speed: the maximum speed at which the gear should be retracted.

Engine-Out Climb Speeds

The Approved Flight Manual or Pilot's Operating Handbook (depending on the age of the airplane) will list the speeds to be maintained in the event of an engine failure. The single-engine best angle-of-climb speed (V_{XSE}) is of marginal importance, in my opinion. The operating manual says you should use the best angle speed until any obstacles have been cleared, and then accelerate to the best rate-of-climb speed. Believe me, if there is an obstacle in the take-off path high enough to worry you, considering the weight of the airplane and the density altitude, it would be wiser to choose another path than to plan on maintaining V_{XSE} until you clear the obstacle. Don't bet your life that you and your airplane can deliver book performance under actual conditions.

Manufacturers of light twins (less than 6,000 pounds) go to great lengths to ensure that the stall speed is less than 61 knots. This is because they need only *determine* the engine-out climb or descent rate — they do not have to prove that the airplane can climb on one engine. If the airplane weighs less than 6,000 pounds but stalls at a speed higher than 61 knots, the manufacturer must demonstrate a positive engine-out climb rate at a pressure altitude of 5,000 feet. Bottom line: Just because your airplane has two engines, a positive climb rate is not a sure thing if one of them has to be shut down and its propeller feathered. Airplanes weighing more than 6,000 pounds must demonstrate a positive climb rate with one propeller feathered.

The best single-engine rate-of-climb speed (V_{YSE}) is marked on the airspeed indicator by a blue radial line, and is usually called "blue line speed." According to the FAA's *Flight Training Handbook* (AC 61-21), this is your target speed if an engine fails just after takeoff. Figure 3-13, on the next page, illustrates that rate of climb will decrease at airspeeds higher or

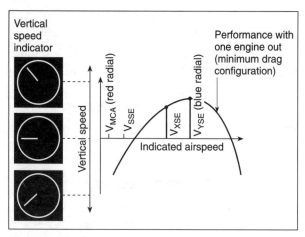

Figure 3-13. *Engine-out performance*

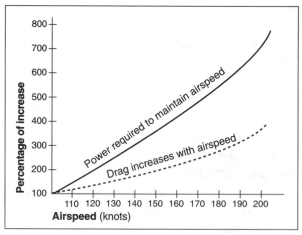

Figure 3-14. *Drag vs. airspeed*

lower than V_{YSE}. Many instructors (myself included) recommend you use the all-engine best rate-of-climb speed (V_Y) as a target, reasoning that you will lose a few knots while you are reacting to an engine failure. The FAA says to use the blue line speed, period. Work it out with your instructor.

There is nothing to be gained by accelerating beyond V_Y until you have attained a safe maneuvering altitude. In the early stages of a multi-engine takeoff, altitude is far more important than airspeed. Figure 3-14 illustrates why you shouldn't lower the nose and accelerate to cruise-climb airspeed too soon: drag increases as the square of the airspeed, and the power required to maintain that airspeed increases as the cube of the airspeed. You don't want to add drag by accelerating while the possibility exists that you might lose half of the thrust while close to the ground. The graph also explains why no dramatic performance increase is gained by retracting the gear early; if airspeed is held constant during the initial climb, the drag of the extended gear also remains constant. Retracting the rollers while there is still usable pavement ahead is foolhardy.

Maneuvering Speed, Normal Operating Speed and Never-Exceed Speed

The meanings of V_A, V_{NO}, and V_{NE} are the same in a twin as they are in a single-engine airplane. However, the fact that two engines make high speeds possible and weather penetration less formidable cause some multi-engine pilots to take chances they would not

take in a single. Don't do it. The aerodynamic forces that cause inflight structural failure are not dependent on the number of engines.

More Important V-Speeds

These are speeds you might hear mentioned around the airport or read about in aviation publications, but they have little or no relevance to light twin pilots. Pilots of turbine-powered airplanes calculate V_R and V_1 before takeoff, taking into account weight, density altitude, runway slope, and wind. V_1 is slower than V_R.

V_1 used to be called decision speed; that definition has been changed to "the maximum speed in the takeoff at which the pilot must take the first action to stop the airplane within the accelerate-stop distance."

V_R, or rotation speed, is defined as the speed at which a pilot makes a "control input with the intention of lifting the aircraft out of contact with the runway or water surface." You won't find it in your airplane's flight manual.

V_{EF} is now "the speed at which the critical engine is assumed to fail during takeoff," or, realistically, the speed at which the pilot must decide whether to stop or go.

V_{LOF} is liftoff speed; the speed at which a transport-category airplane's wheels will leave the ground—you won't find it in your airplane's flight manual.

Performance Airspeeds Versus Weight

When the aerodynamicists and engineers go over the data from test flights of new airplanes, they reduce all of the numbers to reflect what would happen to that airplane at maximum gross weight at sea level on a standard day. Those are the numbers that appear in the Pilot's Operating Handbook and are, in the case of V_{MC} and V_{YSE}, marked on the airspeed indicator. If you exercise some discretion and limit the load to less than gross, these performance airspeeds can be improved upon. Plan a reduction in V_X, V_{XSE}, V_Y, V_{YSE}, and V_A of about one-half the percentage reduction in weight. For example, the maximum takeoff weight of a Beech Duchess is 3,900 pounds and its blue line airspeed is 86 knots. If you load a Duchess to 3,500 pounds, a reduction of about 10%, the best single-engine rate-of-climb speed is reduced by 5% to 82 knots. Because the magnitude of the horizontal lift vector that offsets yaw is a function of weight (*see* Page 1-5), *adding* weight lowers V_{MC}, paradoxically making a twin at maximum gross weight easier to keep under control than one less heavily loaded at the moment of engine failure. When control has been established and the optimum performance bank angle attained, the effect of weight on V_{MC} is irrelevant. An engine-out emergency during takeoff is no time to be doing mental math, however; use the airspeed marked by a red line on the airspeed indicator.

Using Performance Charts
Takeoff Distance

From your very first takeoff in a multi-engine airplane, you should calculate the takeoff distance, the accelerate-stop and accelerate-go distances, and the single-engine climb rate. If the airplane is too heavy, the runway too short, or the obstacles too high, you should reconsider your decision to take off.

The takeoff distance chart, Figure 3-15, is another chase-around graph that takes into account pressure altitude, temperature, weight, wind component, and obstacle height (if any). The conditions in the sample problem are instructive: a fairly high density altitude, temperature warmer than standard, and an airplane loaded to gross takeoff weight.

Note that for normal takeoffs the brakes are held while the power is brought up to maximum. Under the stated conditions, you would lean the mixture for

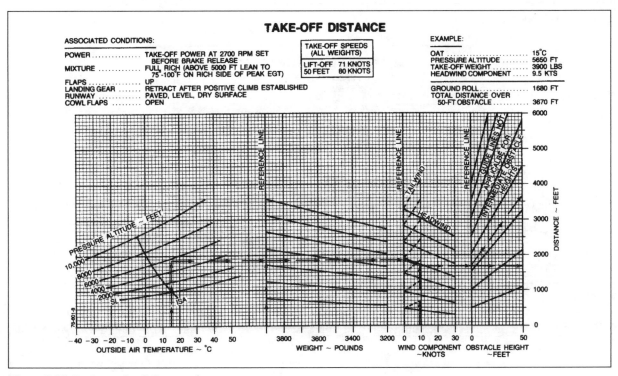

Figure 3-15. *Duchess takeoff distance chart*

best power after bringing the throttles up to takeoff power. Liftoff speed is given as 71 knots, which is V_{SSE}, and the initial climb speed through 50 feet is 80 knots. This is slower than V_{XSE}, which is given as 85 knots in the tabulation of emergency speeds for the Duchess. Moral: memorize the V-speeds in the front of the manual for the checkride, but fly the airplane at the speeds given in the performance section. It would appear that a runway at least 4,000 feet long would be about right for this takeoff, but we're not through yet.

Accelerate-Stop Distance

Accelerate-stop is a performance figure that allows you to determine whether the available runway is long enough for you to accelerate to decision speed, reject the takeoff, and bring the airplane to a stop without exploring the countryside. It is based on weight, pressure altitude, temperature, and wind. In many cases, the speed at which the engine is assumed to have failed varies with weight. This is not the case with all twins. For example, the Beech Duchess uses a speed of 71 knots at all weights. Figure 3-17 is a typical accelerate-stop chart, and it just happens to duplicate the normal takeoff chart sample conditions. According to the chart, you could begin your takeoff roll from the very end of a 4,000-foot-long runway, accelerate to 71 knots, lose an engine, and bring the airplane to a halt 750 feet from the departure end of the pavement—if you did everything right. My guess is that unless you enjoy the same perfect conditions as the factory test pilot did when the manual's figures were determined, you would need some as-

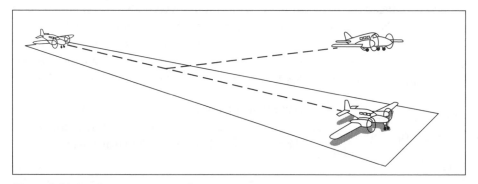

Figure 3-16. Accelerate-stop vs. accelerate-go

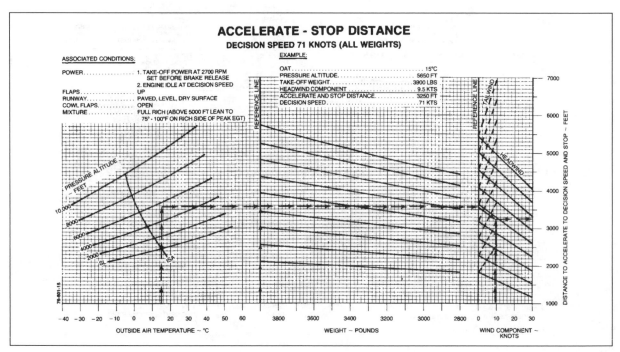

Figure 3-17. Accelerate-stop chart

sistance to get the airplane out of the dirt and back on the pavement. But could you have continued that takeoff? If the density altitude was higher than your airplane's single-engine service ceiling, continuing the takeoff would be impossible. Accelerate-go requires all of the conditions to be favorable—and that calculation comes next.

Accelerate-Go

Accelerate-go is a performance figure based on a multi-engine pilot's ability to accelerate to takeoff decision speed, lose an engine, continue the takeoff, and climb to clear a 50-foot obstacle. Figure 3-18 is used to determine it. As was the case with accelerate-stop, you need to know your aircraft's takeoff weight, the pressure altitude, temperature, and the wind component. Since Beechcraft didn't use the normal takeoff distance conditions for this graph, you will have to do it yourself.

Weight .... 3,900 lbs
Pressure altitude .... 5,650 feet
Temperature .... 15°C
Headwind component .... 9.5 kts

You don't have to get very far into the problem to learn that it isn't going to work. The intersection of 15 degrees and a 5,650-foot pressure altitude is up near the top of the graph, and a horizontal line over to the reference line runs right into the shaded area. This decision is a no-brainer: if you lose an engine at liftoff speed, you will have to get on the binders and screech to a stop. Also, did you notice that while decision speed is 71 knots, blue line airspeed (V_{YSE}) is 85 knots? Where do you plan to get the extra 14 knots so you can climb? Any attempt to fly on one engine under these conditions will result in an off-airport landing at a spot not of your choosing. When you have finished calculating the accelerate-stop and accelerate-go distances, add about 50% to those figures before you decide that you will be able to make it.

Note that the manufacturer does not always provide accelerate-stop and accelerate-go charts—this is a tacit admission that the airplane cannot do either.

Climb, One Engine Inoperative

Not willing to give up that easily? Go back and try the same conditions on Figure 3-9. It doesn't take a very sharp pencil to see that the climb rate would be less than 50 feet per minute, a rate that would be eroded by any turbulence or maneuvering. Of course,

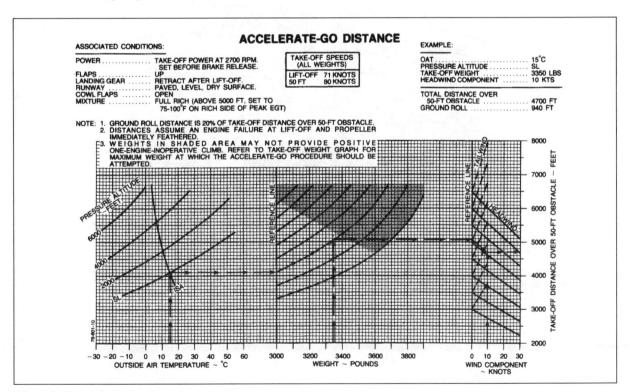

Figure 3-18. Accelerate-go chart

you could have avoided all of this calculation by using the Takeoff Weight chart in Figure 3-1, which indicates that you would have to offload 1,000 pounds of fuel and/or passengers to have a fighting chance. Unfortunately, a takeoff weight chart is not provided in all operating handbooks.

Note the steepness of the curves in the weight portion of the accelerate-go chart. Assuming a no-wind, standard day at sea level, a 10% increase in weight (from 3,300 pounds to 3,630 pounds) increases the accelerate-go distance by over 30% (from 4,900 feet to 6,500 feet). Consider that when your passengers show up with unexpected friends or extra baggage.

The manuals for some light twins do not include accelerate-go charts which should serve as a warning that their manufacturers do not consider those airplanes capable of climbing after losing an engine.

Time, Fuel and Distance to Climb

Assuming your takeoff distance calculations look good, the next planning step is to figure out how much fuel will be required to fly the trip and have legal reserves. Figure 3-19 looks complicated, but it isn't.

You can see in the sample problem the departure airport still has a pressure altitude of 5,650 feet, the temperature is 15°C and the airplane still weighs 3,900 pounds. The lesson that was learned from the accelerate-go chart has not been ignored, necessarily, but the odds are in favor of going.

The first step is to draw a vertical line from the outside air temperature at cruise altitude to the cruise altitude line, from that point horizontally to the weight, and then down to the baseline to read the time, fuel, and distance required if the departure airport was at sea level. The answers are 14 minutes, 6.1 gallons, and 24 miles.

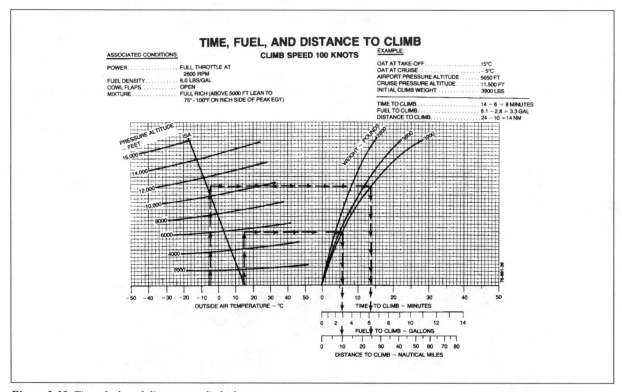

Figure 3-19. Time, fuel, and distance to climb chart

The next step is to start at the baseline with the surface temperature and draw a vertical line to the field elevation of the departure airport, then horizontally to the weight and down again to read time, fuel, and distance as if you hadn't climbed at all. That works out to be 6 minutes, 2.8 gallons, and 10 miles. Now subtract the second set of figures from the first set, and you have the time, fuel, and distance for a takeoff and climb from 5,650 feet to 11,500 feet: 8 minutes, 3.3 gallons, and 14 nautical miles. Your manual may also include an allowance for taxi fuel, which must be included in the total fuel burn.

These are important calculations, because your fuel burn calculations for the cruise segment will be in error if you don't account for the fact that you will have consumed some time, fuel, and distance by the time you reach cruise altitude. If the time to climb is more than 10 minutes for every hour at cruise altitude, rethink your choice of cruising altitude; fuel efficiency at that altitude will not overcome the increased fuel burned during the climb.

If you maintain a "howgozit" record (Figure 3-20) of fuel consumption, as you complete your cruise checklist after leveling off, you will record the fact that the fuel on board has diminished by the quantity you calculate using the Time, Fuel and Distance chart (be conservative) when you level off at cruise altitude.

Range and Endurance Profiles

Figures 3-21 and 3-22 enable you to predict either how far your airplane will fly or how long it will stay up in the air on full tanks. The range chart is based on zero wind at altitude and, accordingly, its predictions should be taken as advisory only. The endur-

Departure time	Time en route	gph	gals burned	gals remaining
0830				100
Top of climb	:24	26	10.5	89
Cruise	2:30	16	40	50
Descent	:18	12	4	55

Figure 3-20. A "Howgozit" chart

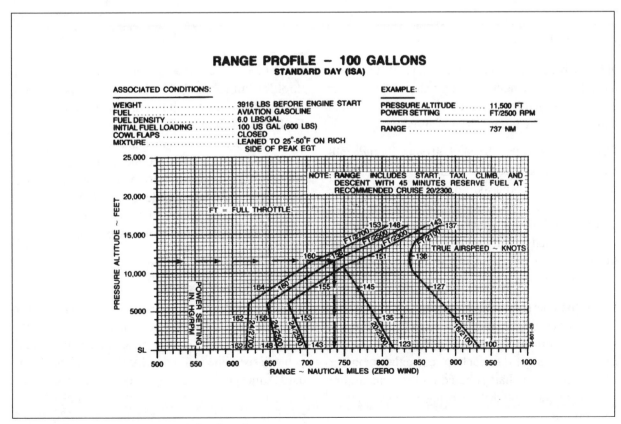

Figure 3-21. Determining range vs. fuel on board

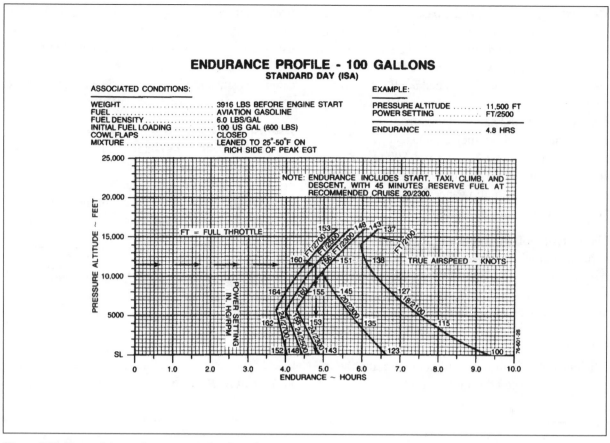

ENDURANCE PROFILE - 100 GALLONS
STANDARD DAY (ISA)

ASSOCIATED CONDITIONS:

WEIGHT .... 3916 LBS BEFORE ENGINE START
FUEL .... AVIATION GASOLINE
FUEL DENSITY .... 6.0 LBS/GAL
INITIAL FUEL LOADING .... 100 US GAL (600 LBS)
COWL FLAPS .... CLOSED
MIXTURE .... LEANED TO 25°-50°F ON
                              RICH SIDE OF PEAK EGT

EXAMPLE:

PRESSURE ALTITUDE .... 11,500 FT
POWER SETTING FT/2500

ENDURANCE .... 4.8 HRS

NOTE: ENDURANCE INCLUDES START, TAXI, CLIMB, AND DESCENT, WITH 45 MINUTES RESERVE FUEL AT RECOMMENDED CRUISE 20/2300.

FT = FULL THROTTLE

TRUE AIRSPEED ~ KNOTS

Figure 3-22. Determining endurance vs. fuel on board

ance chart is more objective in nature; if it predicts an endurance of 6 hours at a given altitude and power setting, you had better have a descent clearance in hand well before 6 hours have elapsed.

It is very unlikely that the winds at cruise altitude will be calm, and you should consider the forecast wind in the planning process. To be conservative, use 150% of a forecast headwind or only 50% of a forecast tailwind. If the wind is forecast to be quartering, rather than directly ahead or behind, use half of the value you got from applying the headwind/tailwind rule.

Using the charts is simple: draw a horizontal line from your cruise pressure altitude to the line representing the cruise power setting and drop a vertical line to the base of the graph to read either range or endurance. Each chart is based on the temperature at each pressure altitude level being the standard temperature for that level.

The charts themselves are instructive, however. Note how the lines for the higher power settings bend at

about 6,000 feet—that is where you will have the throttles full forward. The lines that slope upward from that altitude are all full throttle power settings. Each line has true airspeed (TAS) markings to enable you to predict the TAS at that altitude and power setting. Can you see why 20 inches and 2,300 RPM is a favorite cruise setting for many Duchess pilots? The flight might take a little longer at 20/2,300, but the increase in range and endurance at pressure altitudes below 10,000 feet is well worth it.

Cruise Power Tables

These tables allow you to fine-tune your planning for nonstandard conditions. Look back at the accelerate-stop, accelerate-go, or takeoff distance charts, and you will see a line marked "ISA" (International Standard Atmosphere) crossing through the pressure altitude lines. That line represents the standard temperature for each altitude, starting with 15°C at sea level. The Flight Service Station briefer will give you the forecast temperature at your selected cruising

RECOMMENDED CRUISE POWER - 24.0 IN. HG @ 2500 RPM (OR FULL THROTTLE)																						
	ISA −20°C (−36°F)							STANDARD DAY (ISA)							ISA +20°C (+36°F)							
PRESS ALT	IOAT		MAN. PRESS	FUEL FLOW/ ENGINE		IAS	TAS	IOAT		MAN. PRESS	FUEL FLOW/ ENGINE		IAS	TAS	IOAT		MAN. PRESS	FUEL FLOW/ ENGINE		IAS	TAS
FEET	°C	°F	IN.HG	PPH	GPH	KTS	KTS	°C	°F	IN.HG	PPH	GPH	KTS	KTS	°C	°F	IN.HG	PPH	GPH	KTS	KTS
SL	-3	27	24.0	61	10.2	152	147	17	63	24.0	59	9.8	148	148	37	99	24.0	57	9.5	144	149
1000	-5	23	24.0	62	10.3	152	149	15	59	24.0	60	10.0	148	151	35	95	24.0	58	9.7	144	151
2000	-7	19	24.0	63	10.5	153	152	13	55	24.0	61	10.2	148	153	33	91	24.0	58	9.7	144	154
3000	-9	16	24.0	64	10.7	153	154	11	52	24.0	61	10.2	149	155	31	88	24.0	59	9.8	144	156
4000	-11	12	24.0	64	10.7	153	156	9	48	24.0	62	10.3	149	158	29	84	24.0	60	10.0	144	159
5000	-13	9	24.0	65	10.8	153	159	7	45	24.0	63	10.5	149	160	28	82	24.0	61	10.2	144	161
6000	-15	5	23.6	66	11.0	153	161	5	43	23.6	63	10.5	148	162	26	79	23.6	61	10.2	144	163
7000	-17	1	22.7	63	10.5	150	160	4	39	22.7	61	10.2	145	161	24	75	22.7	59	9.8	141	162
8000	-19	-2	21.9	61	10.2	146	159	2	36	21.9	59	9.8	142	160	22	72	21.9	57	9.5	138	161
9000	-21	-6	21.0	59	9.8	143	158	0	32	21.0	57	9.5	139	159	20	68	21.0	55	9.2	135	160
10,000	-23	-9	20.2	57	9.5	140	157	-3	27	20.2	55	9.2	136	158	18	64	20.2	53	8.8	132	159
11,000	-25	-13	19.4	55	9.2	137	156	-5	23	19.4	53	8.8	133	157	16	61	19.4	51	8.5	129	158
12,000	-27	-17	18.7	53	8.8	134	155	-7	19	18.7	51	8.5	130	156	14	57	18.7	49	8.2	125	156
13,000	-29	-20	18.0	51	8.5	131	153	-9	16	18.0	49	8.2	126	154	11	52	18.0	47	7.8	122	155
14,000	-31	-24	17.3	49	8.2	127	152	-11	12	17.3	47	7.8	123	152	9	48	17.3	45	7.5	118	153
15,000	-33	-27	16.6	47	7.8	124	150	-13	9	16.6	45	7.5	120	151	7	45	16.6	44	7.3	115	151
16,000	-35	-31	16.0	45	7.5	121	148	-15	5	16.0	43	7.2	116	148	5	41	16.0	42	7.0	111	148

NOTES: 1. Full throttle manifold pressure settings are approximate.
2. Shaded area represents operation with full throttle.
3. Lean to 25° - 50°F on rich side of peak EGT.
4. Cruise speeds are presented at an average weight of 3600 lbs.

Figure 3-23. Cruise power chart

altitude, and you can determine whether it is warmer or colder than the standard temperature.

Figure 3-23 says that at 10,000 feet on a standard day (outside air temperature -3°C), full throttle and 2,500 RPM will give you an indicated airspeed (IAS) of 136 knots while burning 9.2 gallons per hour per engine. The Winds and Temperatures Aloft Forecast, however, says that the temperature is expected to be 2°C, five degrees warmer than standard. Now what can you expect for airspeed and fuel burn?

The columns on the right side of the chart are for a temperature 20 degrees warmer than standard, and the indicated airspeed at that temperature is 132 knots, a difference of 4 knots. For every degree of temperature increase above standard, the IAS decreases 4/20, or .2 knot. If the forecast temperature is five degrees warmer than standard, the IAS will decrease by 5 x .2, or 1 knot. Too much trouble? Just eyeball it. The temperature increase is about a quarter of 20 degrees, so figure that the airspeed will fall one-quarter between 136 and 132 and the fuel burn will fall one-quarter between 8.8 and 9.2 gph per engine. Use the degree of accuracy you feel comfortable with, but be conservative. Round the fuel burn up to the next highest whole gallon-per-hour and you'll have some fuel in the bank.

Descent Planning

The manufacturer provides a chart of time, fuel, and distance to descend (Figure 3-24 on the next page). It is similar to the Time, Fuel, and Distance chart for the climb to altitude in that you look up two sets of numbers and subtract one from the other to get the information for your flight. First, draw a horizontal line from your cruise altitude to the reference line and from that point, drop vertically to the baseline to read the time, fuel, and distance for a descent from cruise altitude all the way to sea level.

Repeat the process, using the field elevation of the destination airport, to determine how much time, fuel, and distance would be required to descend from field elevation to sea level, and subtract those figures from the first set to get the information you want. You now know that the distance you will fly at cruise altitude is the point-to-point measurement from your navigational chart minus the calculated distances for climb and descent. Therefore you can figure the total time en route using that distance at cruise speed, plus the times you got from the climb and descent charts. You also have a handle on the total fuel required and can enter your fuel order. Finally, you have two conflicting desires: to have more than enough fuel on board, and to try to stay well below maximum gross weight. Good luck.

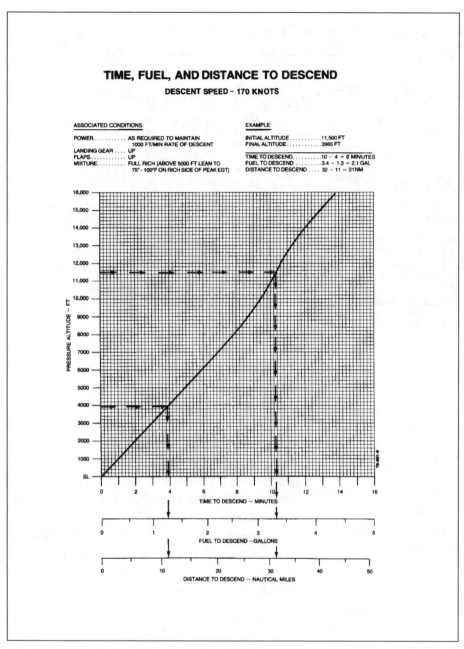

TIME, FUEL, AND DISTANCE TO DESCEND

DESCENT SPEED - 170 KNOTS

ASSOCIATED CONDITIONS:

POWER . . . . AS REQUIRED TO MAINTAIN
　　　　　　　　　　 1000 FT/MIN RATE OF DESCENT
LANDING GEAR . . . . UP
FLAPS . . . . UP
MIXTURE . . . . FULL RICH (ABOVE 5000 FT LEAN TO
　　　　　　　　　　 75° - 100°F ON RICH SIDE OF PEAK EGT)

EXAMPLE:

INITIAL ALTITUDE . . . . 11,500 FT
FINAL ALTITUDE . . . . 3965 FT

TIME TO DESCEND . . . . 10 – 4 = 6 MINUTES
FUEL TO DESCEND . . . . 3.4 – 1.3 = 2.1 GAL
DISTANCE TO DESCEND . . . . 32 – 11 = 21NM

Figure 3-24. *Time, fuel, and distance to descend chart*

Chapter 3
Review Questions

There is no FAA Knowledge examination for the multi-engine rating. There is a more difficult test, however—real life. Be conservative when making performance calculations; your airplane and its engines are probably not new, you are not a factory engineering test pilot, and conditions are probably not standard (you can count on the temperature at the runway surface being hotter than the reported temperature for the airport). *Always* give yourself a cushion; *never* expect to achieve book figures.

1. The distance required to accelerate to decision speed, lose an engine, and continue the takeoff to a height of 50 feet is called

   A—accelerate-stop distance.
   B—accelerate-go distance.
   C—ground roll.

2. An increase in aircraft weight will have what effect on accelerate-go distance?

   A—Increase
   B—Decrease
   C—No effect

3. What is the relationship between V_{MC} and indicated V_{SO} as density altitude increases?

   A—V_{MC} stays constant; indicated V_{SO} decreases.
   B—V_{MC} decreases, indicated V_{SO} stays constant.
   C—Both V_{MC} and indicated V_{SO} decrease as density altitude increases.

4. Referring to Figure 3-1 (Page 3-2), if the pressure altitude is 3,000 feet and the temperature is 20°C, is it safe to take off in a Duchess that weighs 3,700 pounds?

   _____

5. Using Figures 3-2 and 3-3 (Page 3-3), determine if this Seneca is safe to fly:

   Weight .... 3,136 lbs
   Pilot and front passenger .... 280 lbs
   Passengers, center seats (fwd facing)... 270 lbs
   Baggage forward .... 200 lbs
   Baggage aft .... 50 lbs
   Fuel .... 500 lbs

   _____

6. When an engine fails, a multi-engine airplane

   A—rolls, then yaws, so stopping the roll is most important.
   B—yaws, then rolls, so stopping the yaw is most important.
   C—rolls and yaws simultaneously.

7. Use Figure 3-9 (Page 3-7) to determine engine-out climb performance.

   Pressure altitude .... 1,000 feet
   Temperature .... 10°C
   Weight .... 3,500 lbs

   _____

Continued

8. Calculate the takeoff distance, using Figure 3-15 (Page 3-13).

    Pressure altitude .... 2,000 feet
    Temperature .... 20°C
    Weight .... 3,600 lbs
    Headwind .... 10 knots
    Obstacle .... none

_____

9. Calculate the accelerate-stop, using Figure 3-17 (Page 3-14) and the same parameters.

_____

10. What does it mean if the manufacturer provides only an accelerate-stop chart?

_____

Preflight Preparation

4

The Preflight Inspection

From the walkaround inspection to the runway hold line, operating a twin is more demanding than a single-engine airplane. A multi-engine airplane has more things to check on the preflight inspection than a single, and the consequences of missing an item can be more serious.

Expect to find more fuel drains, because the twin you are preflighting may have several tanks plus a crossfeed drain. Also, if the airplane has only one fueling point on each wing, a visual inspection at that point might not give a true indication of the amount of fuel on board unless the tanks have been topped off. Follow the recommendations in the airplane's flight manual.

Look for static system drains as well—many twins provide them as a precaution against water freezing in the static lines and disabling the pitot-static instruments.

Ensuring that all baggage compartment doors are locked is critical, especially if the airplane has a nose baggage compartment. Chapter 3 warned about lateral weight-and-balance considerations for airplanes with wing lockers. The walkaround checklist will require a check of the heater safety switch—finding that the heater is inoperative after you are airborne is embarrassing at best.

Taxiing

A multi-engine airplane is heavier than a single-engine airplane, and more power is required to get one moving. Similarly, more distance is required to bring the airplane to a stop and you must plan accordingly. If your airplane is parked in a row of tiedowns and space is tight, moving it out of the parking space manually may be safer than using power—a twin can make tight turns using differential power, but the economic consequences of an error can be considerable. Anyway, blasting the airplanes behind yours is not good form.

Staying in the center of the taxiway will require additional attention; your eye position will be more off-center than it is in a single, and the greater wingspan of a typical twin requires more concern for obstacles near the runway.

Even at sea level, taxiing with the mixture in its full-rich position can lead to fouling of the many, many, expensive spark plugs you are flying with, and as density altitude increases the problem gets worse. At the very least, stand the mixture controls straight up when taxiing—you're not going to hurt anything. Lean more aggressively at high altitude airports or on hot days. The pre-takeoff checklist will remind you to richen the mixture for takeoff.

A multi-engine airplane will pick up speed while taxiing, even without the tailwind component to be expected when taxiing toward the runup area. Do not ride the brakes, because they will heat up and might fail when you need them. With consideration for your passengers (no sudden stops), apply brake pressure to bring the airplane almost to a halt, then let it move forward again.

Student and Instructor Relationship

Before the throttles are pushed forward for takeoff, both the student and the instructor should know what to expect if an engine failure, real or simulated, occurs during the takeoff roll. "You are going to lose an engine before rotation" takes nothing away from training effectiveness. Most multi-engine accidents happen during training, and the reason is usually either both pilots were trying to fly the airplane, or each thought the other had control.

FAA operations inspectors and civilian designated examiners are required to simulate engine failure below 3,000 feet AGL by reducing power, not by use of the mixture control or fuel selector. Many multi-engine flight instructors kill engines with the mixture or fuel selector—you should discuss this with your instructor. Keep in mind that sudden, complete engine stoppages, such as those experienced in training, are exceedingly rare (except for fuel exhaustion/starvation incidents).

Passenger Briefing

Brief your passengers before beginning the runup, so the noise will not disconcert them. Tell them where the emergency exit is located ("In case I am busy with an unexpected situation"), and how to use the oxygen masks if flight at oxygen altitudes is a possibility. Communicating with concerned passengers in flight is never easy, and demonstrating things is nearly impossible unless there are two pilots up front. (Note: Many passengers are unfamiliar with the bayonet fittings used on most oxygen systems and must be shown how to use them.)

If a door is going to pop open, it will probably be just after rotation. Make sure your passengers understand it will be noisy but not dangerous, and that you will return to the airport to close it.

Preflight Runup

Because it has many redundant systems, the pre-takeoff checklist for a multi-engine airplane is longer than that for a single, and you might be inclined to rush through it. Do not fall into this trap; you need to assure yourself before takeoff that each system is capable of operating independently. Multi-engine airplanes frequently have systems that were either optional equipment or were added after manufacture, and the checklists for these systems will be found in the appendices to the flight manual—they are no less important because they are in the back of the book. This is especially true of autopilot systems; you do not want to be fighting the autopilot for control of the airplane if it malfunctions, and the time to find existing malfunctions is before takeoff.

Check the magnetos and propeller governor on one engine at a time. It is tempting to push both throttles up and do the checks in a flurry of switch throwing and knob pulling, but it is important you listen to each engine for clues to possible problems, and the sound of both engines at mag check RPM does not permit this. Exercise the prop control three times: Once to get fresh oil into the prop governor, once to check that the manifold pressure increases as RPMs decrease, and once into the feather detent to be sure the propeller will go into feather. Do not let RPM decrease more than 500 RPM (or the manufacturer's recommendation) during this check. You will be able to hear the blades changing pitch toward the feathered position.

Last Thoughts...

Do you know what terrain and obstacles lie in the departure path? Will you be able to clear them at a severely restricted rate of climb? If not, which way will you turn, and will the loss of lift in the turn make the situation worse? Is there a reasonable place beneath the climb path to put the airplane down if that becomes necessary? How far from the airport will you be by the time you have climbed high enough to return for landing? Are you carrying so much weight that single-engine performance will be inhibited at the existing density altitude? What if you have to accelerate-stop—is there an overrun or is there a fast-food restaurant at the end of the runway?

Chapter 4
Review Questions

1. To expedite the pretakeoff check, you should do the magneto check for both engines at once. (true, false)

2. Because a twin is more maneuverable than a single-engine airplane, it can be taxied out of its tiedown space. (true, false)

3. The sample you have drawn from a sump drain is straw colored, and feels greasy between your fingers. What is it?

   A—80/87 octane avgas
   B—Jet fuel/kerosene
   C—Soapy water

4. The pretakeoff check procedure for the autopilot and oxygen system will be found

   A—on the manufacturer's printed checklist.
   B—in the POH, under "Normal Procedures."
   C—in the back of the POH, with the Supplements.

5. After checking the density altitude and calculating weight and balance, what should you calculate next?

   A—Takeoff distance
   B—Engine-out rate of climb
   C—Accelerate-stop distance

Takeoff and Departure

5

Your planning is complete, the airplane is loaded, and it's time to taxi out for takeoff. The takeoff phase of flight is generally perceived to be the most hazardous, no matter how many engines your airplane has. It's time for constructive paranoia.

Paranoia is defined in part as a tendency toward excessive suspiciousness or distrustfulness, and if your Aviation Medical Examiner thinks that you are paranoid you won't be issued a medical certificate. No matter. When you are the pilot of a multi-engine airplane, a little paranoia can save you.

Engine Failure on Takeoff

Most pilots will go through an entire flying career without having an engine failure, but that is no reason for complacency. The Golden Rule of multi-engine flying is this: convince yourself that you will have an engine failure at some point during every takeoff and be ready for it. You won't know which engine will fail or at what point in the takeoff the failure will occur, but always expect a failure.

This is my reasoning: Medical experts who try to figure out why pilots do the things they do have identified four stages in an engine-out emergency. The first stage, *confusion*, lasts about 3 seconds; during this period the pilot experiences either an unexpected reaction to a control input or gets no reaction at all. This, quite understandably, is confusing.

It takes two more seconds for the pilot to realize the cause of the problem is that an engine has failed. This is the *recognition* phase. For one more second the pilot's reaction is, "No, this can't be happening to me!" This is called the *denial* phase. After 7 seconds have elapsed, the pilot begins to take the appropriate *action*, if the airplane has not already hit the ground or become uncontrollable.

The most effective way to avoid having these four stages end in disaster is to expect a failure on every takeoff. For example, there will be no confusion phase if you convince yourself that every unusual noise, vibration, or steering difficulty is caused by engine failure and make mental preparations to react appropriately. What you should do depends on where you are in the takeoff and climb procedure, and we will discuss that in detail. Recognition be-

Piper Seneca III

comes acceptance: you expected it to happen, and it did. No lost time. The same is true of denial. You can't deny something is happening when you expected it all the time. That brings you to the action phase without losing 7 seconds.

During the takeoff roll, and when you are airborne with the gear down and runway available, the appropriate action is to stop the airplane straight ahead. If that means running off the departure end of the runway and banging up the airplane, so be it. It is better to hit something while at 30 knots and decelerating than to fall 100 feet out of control.

You are most vulnerable when the airspeed needle is between the red line (V_{MC}) and the blue line (V_{YSE}); because below V_{MC} the airplane is uncontrollable on one engine, and above V_{YSE} performance on one engine is marginal. If an engine fails when the airspeed needle is between the red and blue lines, once again, your best bet might be to land straight ahead. If your airplane will allow you to do so without wheelbar-rowing on the nose wheel, keep the airplane on the ground until blue-line airspeed is achieved. Some airplanes (the Seneca series is an example) are ready to fly before the airspeed needle reaches the red line, and if you apply forward pressure to stay on the ground until V_{SSE}, you will end up wheelbarrowing along with the nose strut compressed and little or no weight on the mains. In those airplanes, you have to let the airplane fly when it is ready, and accept the fact that you are momentarily vulnerable.

Once airborne, you should accelerate through that area as the gear is retracted or in transit (this should not happen until there is no longer any usable runway), and you should consider yourself committed to continue with the climbout.

There is no set procedure if you lose an engine while in the area of vulnerability between the red and blue lines. That is why pretakeoff planning is important. Do you put it back down *in an area you know is available beneath the departure path*? Do you know where the towers and apartment buildings are? Do you climb straight ahead for ten miles while struggling up to pattern altitude? There are no pat answers, because every situation will be different. You must have a plan and stick to that plan.

If you will be taking off into instrument meteorological conditions, consider the climb rate required for the departure procedure. Could you make it on one engine? Would you have to make any climb-killing turns before reaching a safe altitude? Is the weather at the departure airport good enough for you to make a "no sweat" single-engine approach? Where is the nearest airport with VFR conditions? Can you handle an engine-out emergency under IFR? Be hard on yourself.

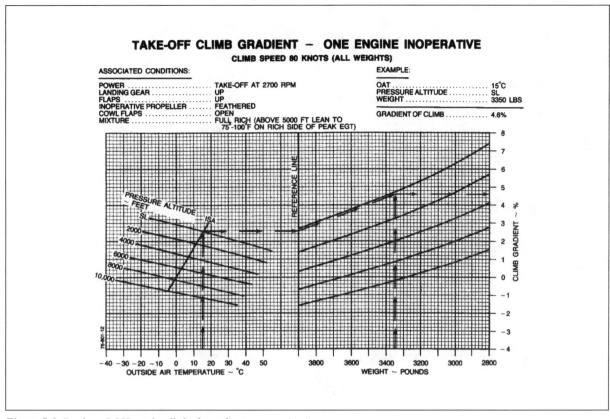

TAKE-OFF CLIMB GRADIENT — ONE ENGINE INOPERATIVE
CLIMB SPEED 80 KNOTS (ALL WEIGHTS)

ASSOCIATED CONDITIONS:

POWER .... TAKE-OFF AT 2700 RPM
LANDING GEAR .... UP
FLAPS .... UP
INOPERATIVE PROPELLER .... FEATHERED
COWL FLAPS .... OPEN
MIXTURE .... FULL RICH (ABOVE 5000 FT LEAN TO
                              75°-100°F ON RICH SIDE OF PEAK EGT)

EXAMPLE:

OAT .... 15°C
PRESSURE ALTITUDE .... SL
WEIGHT .... 3350 LBS

GRADIENT OF CLIMB 4.6%

Figure 5-1. Duchess POH—takeoff climb gradient, one engine inop

Calculating Climb Rates Before Takeoff

Will obstruction clearance be a problem for this take-off? Every manufacturer lists airspeeds for best all-engine angle-of-climb and for best single-engine rate-of-climb, using the FAA standard 50-foot obstacle as the hurdle you are going to try to jump. Figure 5-1 allows you to calculate just how many feet of altitude you will gain per 1,000 feet of horizontal distance if you follow the procedure recommended by the POH. This is the climb gradient, or slope, not the rate-of climb.

As you can see from the sample problem in Figure 5-1, a Duchess takes off from a sea level airport on a standard day at a gross weight of 3,350 pounds (550 pounds below maximum gross weight), can lose an engine at rotation, the pilot can clean up the airplane, climb at 80 knots (which is slower than V_{XSE}), and gain 46 feet of altitude per 1,000 feet of forward progress in no-wind conditions. That's about 276 feet per mile, or 368 feet per minute, during the initial climb. Not much, especially when you consider it is based on everything being done perfectly.

Unless the runway you are departing from is really short, with that 50-foot tree or apartment house right at the departure end, the smartest action you could take following a failure immediately after liftoff is to put the airplane back down again, accepting the possibility of damage and injuries. Too many pilots expose themselves and their passengers to the possibility of a fatal accident in attempts to get the airplane back on the ground without a scratch. If you have done your accelerate-stop and accelerate-go calculations (*see* Chapter 3), you will have a good idea of what you can accomplish safely. The climb gradient chart gives you an idea of how much clearance you will have over those apartment houses 2 miles from the end of the runway.

Figure 5-2 on the next page assumes that you have cleared all of the close-in obstacles and want to climb to a safe altitude with the gear and flaps up and the dead engine's propeller feathered. Note that the airspeed is now 85 knots, the single-engine best rate-of-climb speed. Using the same conditions that were used to determine the engine-out climb gradient (3,350 pounds on a standard day at sea level),

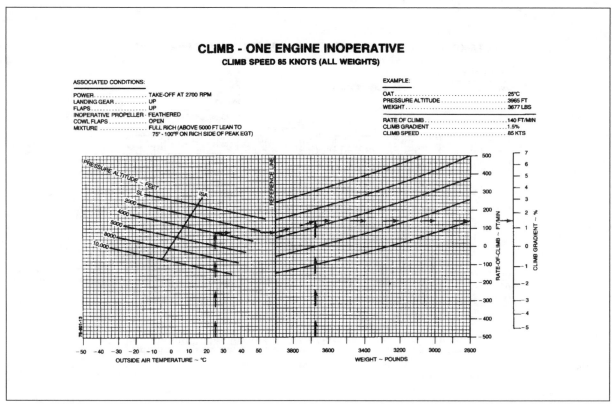

Figure 5-2. *Duchess POH—climb performance*

the rate of climb improves to about 420 feet-per-minute. Considering that any turning will erode this minimal climb performance, how far from the airport will you be when you have gained enough altitude to maneuver?

The Takeoff Roll

Do not accept an intersection takeoff, and when you are cleared for takeoff from the hold line, don't sacrifice runway distance by making a rolling takeoff. Use every foot of the available runway by taxiing toward the end of the paved surface and then turning to align the airplane with the runway. *(This is a good time to note that a little extra throttle on the upwind side will help with directional control in a crosswind situation.)* All takeoff performance charts are based on the brakes being locked as the power is brought up to the takeoff setting—very few pilots do this, which makes book takeoff distances impossible to achieve—but you will do it, won't you?

As the airplane accelerates, check the fuel flow and exhaust gas temperature gauges—they will be better indicators of impending problems than any other instruments. The power instruments may mislead you, for the following reasons: During the takeoff roll, manifold pressure will be at or near ambient outside pressure (non-turbocharged airplanes, of course), and prop speed will be near the red line. When an engine fails, its manifold pressure gauge will read ambient outside pressure, which will be very close to the full-throttle manifold pressure—looking at the MAP gauge will not tell you which engine has failed. Similarly, unless the engine has experienced massive internal damage, the propeller will not spin down immediately, so looking to the tachometer for clues is not a good idea.

As the airplane nears rotation speed, the pressure differential between the inside and outside of the fuselage will reach the point at which poorly latched access or baggage compartment doors will open, or at which the end of a seat belt hanging outside a door will set up an earsplitting racket. Be ready to pull the throttles back to the stops in either case. Maybe you will hear an unintelligible transmission on the radio; was it *"Have a nice flight!"* or was it *"Your left engine has black smoke coming out of it!"*? If you don't know, stop the airplane and find out what was said.

When the airspeed needle reaches V_{MC} plus 5 knots (for most twins), rotate to a positive climb attitude—and be ready for an engine to fail before the airspeed reaches the blue line. With the VSI needle indicating a climb rate of at least 300 feet-per-minute, lower the nose slightly and accelerate to V_Y, the best all-engine rate-of-climb speed. The rationale for using V_Y is that there will be an unavoidable loss of airspeed as you react to a failure, and a deceleration from V_Y to V_{YSE} won't cause the problems that slowing from V_{YSE} toward V_{MC} might cause.

Engine Fails!

Imagine that despite your best plans and lucky rabbit's foot, the left engine burps twice and quits just as the altimeter indicates you are 100 feet above the ground. The airplane swerves hard to the left and begins to roll in that direction. Reacting instinctively, you rotate the yoke all the way to the right—and lose directional control. Why?

The purpose of flight training is to substitute trained reactions for instinctive reactions, isn't it? Let's go back to the instant of failure and start over, using trained reactions. As the airplane swerves and rolls to the left, you push the right rudder pedal all the way to the floorboard, stopping the turn. Simultaneously,

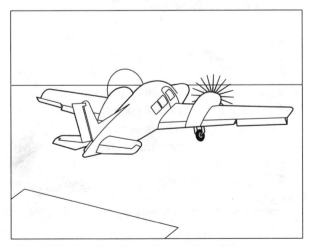

Figure 5-3. *Lots of rudder and just enough aileron*

you apply enough right aileron to establish a bank into the good engine, and regain directional control by developing a horizontal lift component to offset the turning moment. This time, you don't lose control.

Tests by the FAA have shown that it takes a bank of *at least* 5 degrees toward the good engine to overcome the initial roll and maintain control of the airplane (the "*not more than* 5 degrees" you may have heard is a certification limitation placed on the manufacturer when the published minimum control speed is determined). This establishes a slight sideslip into the good engine, and because the airplane is slipping toward the fully deflected rudder, the increased airflow makes the rudder more effective. You can bank more than 5 degrees and make the rudder so effective that you can almost give your foot a rest.

Unfortunately, this good medicine has bad side effects. Increasing the bank eats into climb performance at a time when you have none to spare, with a 10°-bank completely eliminating any climb capability. With the airplane under control, however, climb performance will be improved if you relax the aileron pressure and reduce the bank to about 3 degrees—or less, depending on a lot of variables. Just don't level the wings completely.

Because the conditions that create zero sideslip can vary from one airplane to another, you can determine the best combination of bank angle and ball deflection by taping a piece of string to the nose of the airplane. (Glider pilots call it a yaw string—*see* Figure 1-6.) Zero sideslip has been attained when the loose end of the string streams straight back, parallel to the longitudinal axis. Without a yaw string, the slip/skid indicator is a better guide to being "just right" than is the attitude indicator at small bank angles such as these. The ball should be about halfway out of its cage on the good engine side, and the turn coordinator should be showing zero rate of turn.

The best performance indicator is the vertical speed indicator, because the goal of all of this drag reduction is to enable the crippled airplane to climb out of danger. Don't forget that the horizontal component of lift isn't a gift—it comes from a reduction in vertical lift.

While your right foot has been exerting 150 pounds of pressure on its rudder pedal and your left hand has been busy rolling the airplane into the good engine—remember, it was the left engine that failed—your right hand has not been idle. Its duty, whenever you suspect an engine failure, is to move across the throttle quadrant from right to left (pilots of older Beech aircraft please bear with me for a while), pushing the mixture and prop controls full forward and adding sufficient power to avoid loss of altitude. Figure 5-4 shows the sequence.

Many instructors (and the FAA's *Flight Training Handbook*) advocate pushing both throttles full forward in every situation. I suggest a more reasoned approach—as reasoned as you can get when you are in a crisis situation. Full power is great when you are in a takeoff or climb situation close to the ground. It is not necessary if an engine fails in cruising flight, and full power on one side will drive the airplane off of the localizer and glideslope if used during an ILS approach. Add just enough power to avoid losing altitude or slowing below V_{YSE} and yet enough to develop sufficient differential rudder pressure for you to identify the failed engine. I like author Richard L. Taylor's advice: go to the next higher power setting. If you have set climb power, go to takeoff power; if you have set cruise power, go to climb power; if you

Figure 5-4. Right-to-left at the instant of failure

are on an approach, go to cruise power. When in doubt, more power is better than less. It's easy to be fooled if you haven't added enough power on the good engine to identify the failed engine through rudder pressure alone.

It's a tough decision to make, but because it is the good engine and not the failed engine that is giving you control problems, it might be better to reduce power on the good engine and accept an under-control landing on something soft and inexpensive. Attempting a single-engine climb could possibly be more dangerous than putting it back down. Airplanes are easier to replace than people.

Cleaning Up the Airplane

You have done all you can on the thrust side of the equation, so drag reduction comes next. Form the habit of always checking the gear and flap position. You are most vulnerable during takeoff and initial climb, when the gear is extended and the flaps, if they are used at all, are in the takeoff position. The gear-flap sequence varies between different airplane models, but more often than not, the manufacturer calls for gear retraction first, since the flap setting for take-off creates more lift than drag. If the gear retraction sequence involves doors that must open to accept the wheels, as is the case with the Cessna Skymaster, the drag caused by the sudden appearance of cavernous holes in the bottom of the fuselage is the reason the landing gear is not retracted immediately. Accept the fact that you will lose altitude while getting rid of the gear and flaps.

The sequence for securing a failed engine is **identify**, **verify**, **feather**. You identify the dead engine by rudder pressure; one foot is pressing the rudder pedal on the good engine side nearly to the firewall (and your leg muscles are beginning to ache), while the other foot is idle. The memory aid is: dead foot = dead engine. In our example, the left engine has given up the ghost and your left foot is doing absolutely nothing. You verify by retarding the throttle while listening for a change in engine sound and checking for a change in rudder pressure. If you can pull the throttle back without any apparent change, you have verified that the left engine has failed.

Figure 5-5. Left-to-right to secure the failed engine

Figure 5-6. Baron power levers

The last step is to feather the propeller on the engine that you have identified and verified. Figure 5-5 shows the sequence for securing the dead engine. With those items taken care of and the airplane under control, everything else is housekeeping. You will want to pull the failed engine's mixture control to idle cutoff. If the airplane is equipped with cowl flaps, open them on the good engine side. Get out the manufacturer's checklist and follow its recommendations for securing the electrical system. The emergency is over. All you have to do now is get the airplane to a suitable location for landing.

The control sequence for securing the failed engine in the last paragraph (throttle, propeller, mixture) agrees with the recommended procedure in almost all piston twins. You may find an owner's manual or text that counsels the sequence should be throttle, mixture, propeller. Your instructor and examiner might say that you should follow the manual in every case, or they might opt for standardization. Piper says either method is acceptable. Cessna, for reasons that I assume have to do with product liability, makes no such concession. *All Beechcraft twins use the throttle, prop, mixture sequence.* In my opinion, standardization of procedures reduces the possibility of error as you transition from one type of twin to another.

There is at least one good reason to delay pulling the mixture until the propeller has been feathered: pilots aren't perfect. If you inadvertently retard the wrong throttle or propeller control, the change in engine noise will alert you to the error and you can correct it quickly. However, if you inadvertently lean the mixture on the operating engine to idle cutoff, and, upon hearing it begin to spin down, push the mixture back to full rich, the odds are that you are going to hear a dandy backfire. Why blow the exhaust system off a perfectly good engine? You have enough trouble already. If you save the mixture for the securing phase, after aircraft control has been regained, you can take the time to look for the correct mixture control. The Duchess manual, which we have been using as a reference throughout this book, lumps pulling the mixture to idle cutoff in with such housekeeping measures as closing the cowl flaps and turning off the magnetos and alternator.

Those of you who fly older Beechcraft twins deserve an explanation. The quadrant layout on older Beeches is, from left to right, propeller, throttle, mixture (Figure 5-6 above). You can see why my left-to-right instructions wouldn't work. Newer Beechcraft twins, such as the Duchess, follow the now-conventional quadrant layout.

The securing procedure just described did not mention taking any action with regard to the fuel selectors, because unless the engine is on fire, there is no immediate requirement to shut off the fuel. Crossfeeding the operating engine from tanks on the dead engine side is not usually required until lateral imbalance demands it or until that fuel is needed to get the airplane to a safe landing spot. It is really a cruise consideration, not something you must think of at takeoff time. Most, but not all, crossfeed procedures call for the fuel selector on the dead engine side to be placed in the OFF position, and the fuel selector on the operating engine side to be placed in CROSSFEED. There are enough differences between different airplanes, however (the Twin Comanche and Beech Travel Air come to mind), that you should check the crossfeed procedure for your airplane before you need it.

With the airplane airborne, gear and flaps up and the offending propeller feathered, you are either on your way back to the airport, or, if weather conditions will not permit you to return and land, you are en route to your takeoff alternate. You did have a takeoff alternate in mind, didn't you?

"Abnormal" Takeoffs

In a crosswind situation you can offset any weathervaning tendency during the takeoff roll by using a tad more power on the upwind engine—this eliminates the necessity for rudder pressure.

For short fields, manufacturer's recommendations differ—are flaps required, or not? This is a situation that definitely calls for holding the brakes until takeoff power has been set.

Chapter 5
Review Questions

1. What is the climb gradient?

   Weight .... 3,800 lbs
   Pressure altitude .... 2,000 feet
   Temperature .... 20°C

2. During the takeoff roll, which instruments give the best indication of engine health?

   A—Manifold pressure and tachometer
   B—Airspeed and manifold pressure
   C—Exhaust gas temperature and fuel flow

3. The bank angle for best performance with a propeller feathered is approximately

   A—five degrees toward the good engine.
   B—five degrees toward the dead engine.
   C—two degrees toward the good engine.

4. The best climb speed to maintain with both engines operating is

   A—V_{YSE}.
   B—V_Y.
   C—V_{XSE}.

5. When engine failure is suspected, the correct sequence of actions is

   A—verify, identify, feather.
   B—identify, verify, feather.
   C—feather….

6. Without an unfeathering accumulator, what are your options for getting an air-start?

   _____

7. You are most vulnerable to engine failure between _____ and _____. (V speeds)

   _____

8. Book takeoff distance performance charts are based on the brakes being locked as power is increased to the takeoff setting. (true, false)

   _____

9. The manifold pressure gauge on a normally-aspirated engine reads approximately 30 inches when the engine is shut down. What will the MAP gauge read if the engine fails during the takeoff roll?

   _____

10. At the moment of engine failure, you should bank _____ degrees toward the operating engine to maintain control.

    A—not more than five
    B—not less than five
    C—whatever it takes

Cruising Flight

6

The Cruise Checklist

Cruising flight is where having two operating engines pays off, because the excess power that got you to altitude at a brisk rate of climb can now be converted into forward speed. Your job is now to monitor the systems so the cruise portion of the flight will be accomplished with maximum efficiency.

If your airplane's Pilot's Operating Handbook does not have a cruise checklist, you should make up your own. Some of the items on such a checklist would be switching to the auxiliary or tip tanks, closing the cowl flaps, and setting the power and mixture. Be sure to check the procedure for the fuel pump switches — some models suggest the fuel pumps be left in the "low" position when cruising above 12,000 feet. Never turn both fuel pump switches off simultaneously. If an engine-driven pump has failed while the electric pumps were performing their backup function and you kill them both at once, there will be a moment of confusion when that pump's engine begins to wind down. Far better to turn one pump off, wait ten seconds or so, and then turn the other pump off. You would be surprised at how long it takes for an engine to consume the fuel in the plumbing.

Before you reach for the fuel selectors, however, be sure you understand how to manage your airplane's fuel system. In many airplanes with fuel-injected engines (the Cessna 310 comes to mind), fuel vapor and excess fuel from the engines returns to the main tanks, and if you haven't been on the mains long enough to make room for the return fuel, it will be vented overboard. That's not good for fuel planning. In these situations the Pilot's Operating Handbook will require that you continue to burn fuel out of the main tanks for a specified period of time before switching to auxiliary or tip tanks.

Most operating handbooks are noncommittal about cowl flaps, simply telling you to use them as required to maintain cylinder head temperatures within limits. Don't make closing the cowl flaps an automatic action without checking the cylinder head temperatures. Unless air pressure on the open cowl flaps at cruise speed will cause vibration or possible damage, leave them open for a few moments after leveling off at cruise altitude. The engines have been working hard and deserve an extra shot of cooling air before you close the cowl flaps completely. You might even want to close them in increments to moderate the temperature change.

When it comes time to set cruise power, you have many options. Don't be put off by the myth that says the manifold pressure in inches should never be a larger number than the RPM in hundreds. This hoary old story, based on experience with radial engines, has no relevance to modern aircraft. Figure 6-1 shows an acceptable operating area with manifold pressures greater than RPM by four: 28 inches and 2,400 RPM fall into this area. The manufacturer's recommended cruise power settings are more conservative, with 24

The tradeoff you must consider is high manifold pressure and low RPM versus low manifold pressure and high RPM.

A pilot shouldn't assume that using low manifold pressure and high RPM will extend engine life. Without sufficient pressure in the cylinder, the pistons will rattle up and down and the rings will scrape and scar the cylinder walls. That may be a slight exaggeration, but you get the picture. Piston ring flutter is a result of low manifold pressure in combination with high RPM.

Take a few moments to analyze Figure 6-2 (cruise power chart). Note that for a given manifold pressure, reducing propeller speed cuts both true airspeed and fuel flow. However, the percentage reduction in fuel flow is twice the airspeed penalty. For example, if, while pulling 28 inches of manifold pressure, you reduce horsepower from 75% to 64% through use of a lower prop speed (2,500 down to 2,200), you will burn 15% less fuel while only losing 8% true airspeed.

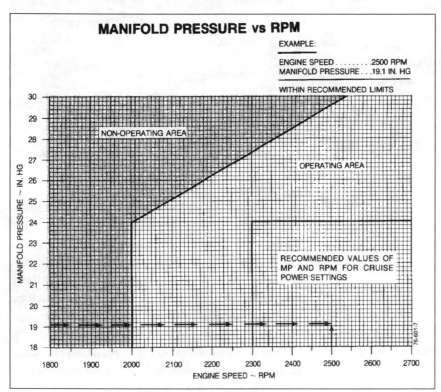

Figure 6-1. *Engine power envelope*

inches over 2,300 RPM the largest gap. The 180-horsepower Lycomings of the Beechcraft Duchess do not differ greatly from other normally aspirated engines in their cruise power settings.

During World War II, Colonel Charles Lindbergh passed on to military pilots some power management techniques he refined from his history-making transatlantic flight, and the methods he taught allowed fighter and bomber pilots to stretch the range of their aircraft. Simply put, the rule was low propeller speed and high manifold pressure. In the days of radial engines, 1,600 to 1,700 RPM was considered low. The manufacturers of today's flat opposed engines consider 2,100 RPM as being low for cruise power.

The most efficient enroute altitude for normally-aspirated airplanes is between 6,000 and 8,000 feet at 75% power. Within that range you will find the highest altitude at which 75% power can be maintained and also the highest true airspeed for a given rate of fuel consumption. I'm not recommending that you operate at 75%, however; if you use lower power settings, in addition to the reduction in fuel burn mentioned above, the optimum altitude will increase. You will find that 55% power gives the best tradeoff between speed and fuel economy. Slow and easy wins the race, as the tortoise said to the hare; a fuel stop will add 30 to 45 minutes to your trip.

		Standard Temperature 3°C		
RPM	MP	% BHP	KTAS	GPH
2500	30	81	132	17.8
	28	75	127	16.4
	26	69	122	15.1
	24	63	116	13.8
	22	56	109	12.4
2400	30	76	128	16.6
	28	71	123	15.4
	26	65	118	14.2
	24	59	112	13.0
	22	53	105	11.8
2300	30	73	125	15.9
	28	68	121	14.8
	26	62	115	13.7
	24	56	109	12.5
	22	50	102	11.3
2200	30	69	122	15.1
	28	64	117	14.0
	26	58	111	12.9
	24	53	111	11.8
	22	47	98	10.7

Figure 6-2. Cruise power chart

Depending on the make and model of twin you are flying, you may not be able to determine the exact percentage horsepower that a given combination of manifold pressure and propeller speed will deliver. Some operating handbooks are silent on the subject, and you will have to refer to the engine manufacturer's manual for that information.

Throughout this book, I have suggested that you go by the numbers in the Pilot's Operating Handbook. When it comes to setting cruise power, however, there are several combinations of numbers to choose from. An excellent rule to follow is this: use the lowest prop speed at which the engines run smoothly, without noise or vibration. Based on my own experience, I suggest that you standardize on 2,300 RPM. With normally-aspirated engines at cruise altitudes above 5,000 feet, you will be able to open the throttles fully without exceeding 75% power if you leave the props at 2,300 RPM.

There is another plus to operating at low RPM: if the pistons are traveling up and down at a leisurely pace, the fuel-air mixture will spend more time in the cylinder, cooling it down before the compression stroke begins.

Lean to the book fuel flow for the power setting you are using. If an EGT gauge or other source of analytical information is available, of course, use that information to the fullest extent. You will seldom go wrong by leaning to 50 degrees on the rich side of peak exhaust gas temperature, and Lycoming says you can operate their engines at peak if the cylinder head temperatures stay within limits.

If you leave the throttle at the initial cruise setting as fuel is consumed and weight is reduced, you will notice an increase in true airspeed. Why not tweak the throttle back to maintain the planned airspeed and conserve some fuel? At this point, fuel conservation (which translates into more time in the air) takes precedence over having the throttle fully open.

You may be working on your multi-engine rating in an airplane with auxiliary or tip tanks, and this will help you to prepare for the fuel systems in more sophisticated aircraft. If this is the case, you may be tempted to use all of the fuel in the auxiliary tanks during cruise. Don't do it. When you allow the fuel lines to fill with air, you deprive the fuel pumps of their ability to work for you. They are not designed to move air. It can take an uncomfortably long time to restart a fuel-injected engine that has been deprived of fuel, but that's not the only drawback. You lose the advantage of dual systems while the dry engine is sucking frantically for some liquid refreshment, and if you are drawing a heavy load from both alternators or running the de-icing boots with the vacuum pumps, purposely failing an engine may create more problems than you can easily handle.

Service and Absolute Ceilings

Every multi-engine airplane has an all-engines "service ceiling," which is the highest density altitude at which the airplane can maintain a climb rate of 100 feet per minute; the single-engine service ceiling is the highest density altitude at which the airplane can maintain a climb rate of 50 feet per minute with one propeller feathered. The absolute ceiling, with both engines or with one prop feathered, is the highest density altitude the airplane can maintain using maximum available power. These numbers are not found in all approved flight manuals; they are provided at the manufacturer's discretion. As a multi-engine pilot you should not consider operating at an altitude close to your airplane's service ceiling—always have power in reserve if a climb is necessary to get out of icing conditions.

Service ceilings are determined with new airplanes that have new engines, so the chances are your airplane cannot reach the published altitudes anyway.

"Minimum Airspeed in Icing Conditions" is not a ceiling, but it is a cruise consideration. When your airplane is accreting structural ice and you attempt to maintain altitude by increasing angle of attack, ice can begin to form on the unprotected underside of the leading edge, behind the deicing boots (if installed). To forestall this, some manufacturers include a "minimum speed in icing conditions" in their manuals—when the airspeed decreases to this value, you must give up altitude in order to maintain the minimum airspeed. Even without such a manufacturer's edict, attempting to maintain altitude while picking up ice is not a good idea. If you are unable to get a lower altitude from ATC, declare an emergency.

Engine Failure During Cruise Flight

The sudden cessation of sound from one side of the fuselage is never welcome, but if it has to happen, let it be in cruise. With a comfortable quantity of air between the airplane and the ground, an engine failure should be more of an inconvenience than an emergency. Unfortunately, National Transportation Safety Board (NTSB) statistics indicate that most accidents involving multi-engine aircraft begin during the cruising phase. This does not imply that the airplanes fell from the sky like dead ducks, but that the loss (or partial loss) of an engine at altitude began a series of pilot errors or misjudgments that culminated in a mishap. Of course, there are no NTSB statistics on how many twins experienced some sort of problem during cruise and landed without incident.

The reason that, despite statistics, you would rather have a power loss at altitude than during takeoff or approach is that altitude gives you the luxury of time. At 10,000 feet above the terrain, with the airplane under control and trimmed for hands-off flight, you

can reach into the back seat for the Pilot's Operating Handbook and read the emergency procedure section in detail.

Unless you have had a catastrophic failure, such as losing part of a propeller blade or blowing a cylinder through the nacelle, you will have time to experiment with sources of fuel and ignition in an attempt to regain full or partial power. Most total power losses are fuel-related, either fuel starvation, caused by mismanagement of the fuel on board, or fuel exhaustion, caused by poor planning on the part of the hapless pilot.

No matter what the cause of the failure, however, after the airplane is under control you will have to deal with the loss of one alternator, one vacuum pump, one source of pressure for the deicing system, and one source of bleed air for the pressurization system. Loss of power is the most important element of engine failure, but not the *only* element that must be considered.

There is no question that any unusual noise or vibration during what should be the most relaxed portion of the flight can be unsettling, and that in the event of an actual power loss, there will be some delay in reaction caused by the "This can't be happening to me!" syndrome.

At the instant of failure, the airplane will lurch toward the ailing engine, the propellers will go out of synchronization, and the passengers will start peppering you with questions. However, the airplane will not immediately roll over on its back and dive for the ground as television viewing might lead you to expect. You will be able to establish lateral control easily, because aileron control will be very effective at cruise speeds. Heading control is another matter. The plane will want to yaw toward the sick engine, and full rudder-pedal deflection may be required until you can get the rudder trim to help out. The airplane will not lose altitude solely because of the engine problem; in fact, you may be able to convert excess airspeed into a shallow (and momentary) climb.

Trim for hands-off flight and start looking for reasons the engine quit (I am assuming a non-catastrophic failure). Fuel flow OK? Is the answer as simple as throwing a fuel pump switch or moving a fuel selector? If that's the answer, hold on a minute— pull the throttle back near idle before you force-feed the engine with a big gulp of fuel and cause a power surge. If fuel is available to the engine, could the problem be ignition? Try operating on each magneto individually. If one mag has jumped out of time, the engine may run perfectly well on the other one. Again, to avoid backfiring, reduce the throttle setting before you experiment with the magnetos. If there is fuel and ignition, is the engine having trouble breathing? Could the air intake be blocked by ice, wet snow, or some failure in the plumbing? Try the alternate air source, which bypasses the normal air intake. Will the engine run at a lower power setting? Try adjusting the mixture. If the engine is getting too much air because of a leak in the intake manifold, you may be able to re-establish a viable fuel-air ratio. When in doubt, though, kill the engine and feather the prop. An engine that is surging or cutting in and out might decide to deliver a burst of power at the worst possible moment. Deal with a known situation, not a mystery.

If an engine fails on a pressurized airplane during cruising flight and cabin altitude begins to rise toward flight altitude, initiate an emergency descent to 10,000 feet MSL or below. Pull the throttles back, push the propeller controls forward, and roll into a 45° bank to put a positive load on the wings. Extend the landing gear when the airspeed falls below V_{LO}.

Drift Down

What is the single-engine service ceiling for your airplane? It is the altitude at which the airplane has essentially lost all climb capability. The official definition is a climb rate of 50 fpm, but that minuscule rate will be erased by control movement in reaction to even light turbulence. It's a good number to keep in mind, though, especially if you are flying in mountainous terrain. Let's assume the worst: you have tried all of the suggested methods above and nothing has worked. Both magnetos are out to lunch, or there is a blockage that keeps fuel from the engine. You have, reluctantly but calmly, feathered the propeller of the offending engine and completed the shutdown checklist. What now? If the failure occurred above the single-engine service ceiling, not much. If you trim to maintain blue line airspeed, the airplane will lose altitude very slowly as it drifts down toward the service ceiling, and it will cover a lot of ground while doing so. When the single-engine service ceiling is reached, of course, the airplane will stop losing altitude. Don't consider this as a means of making it to your destination on one engine. Use the drift down capability as a means of getting to a suitable airport.

Chapter 6
Review Questions

1. When setting power, you want to avoid

   A—high manifold pressure, low rpm.
   B—low manifold pressure, high rpm.
   C—high manifold pressure, high rpm.

2. Service ceiling has been reached with a multi-engine airplane when it can climb at no more than _____ feet per minute on one engine.

   A—50
   B—100
   C—0

3. If an engine fails in cruise and its propeller is feathered, maintaining V_{YSE} (blue line) airspeed will result in the airplane gradually losing altitude down to

   A—its service ceiling.
   B—its absolute ceiling.
   C—the density altitude equivalent of its single-engine service ceiling.

4. The single-engine service ceiling of a twin _____ as weight is added.

   A—increases
   B—decreases
   C—is not affected

5. The quickest way to lose altitude in an emergency, such as fire or depressurization, is to

   A—roll into a 45-degree bank to keep a positive load on the wings.
   B—roll into a standard rate turn to avoid over-banking.
   C—lower the nose, reduce the power to idle, and dive.

6. Your twin is picking up ice at the assigned altitude, and you ask for a lower altitude. ATC says "Unable." You should

   A—maintain altitude despite loss of airspeed.
   B—declare an emergency and descend.
   C—ask to speak to the supervisor.

7. The best way to adjust the mixture in cruise is to use

   A—the fuel flow gauges.
   B—the exhaust gas temperature gauges.
   C—the cylinder head temperature gauges.

Descent, Approach and Landing

Descent Planning

Although you ran through the time, fuel and distance-to-descend calculations as a part of preflight planning, as you near the destination, conditions will probably be different than anticipated.

Under instrument flight rules, some descent decisions are forced on you by air traffic control, and you must make the best of them. However, a little judicious bugging of the air traffic controller might get you "expect lower in ten miles" or something similar, giving you time to make preparations. Your goal is to establish a comfortable descent rate at cruise speed without extreme power changes. You should know how many minutes you are from the destination by reference to the DME, the GPS, the LORAN, or through exercising your pilotage navigation skills; allow 3 minutes per 1,000 feet of altitude loss. Your passengers will appreciate a 300 fpm descent.

Beginning the Descent

Earlier, I recommended a "one size fits all" propeller setting of 2,300 RPM during cruising flight, with manifold pressure set by the book to provide 65 to 70% power, and the mixture set 50° on the rich side of peak EGT. The first step in preparing to descend is a reduction in prop speed to the bottom of the governing range; this should be about 2,000 to 2,100 RPM. Note that this is my recommendation; the engine manufacturers suggest an initial throttle reduction. I use this method and it works. If you are cruising at 14,000 feet and the manifold pressure has

fallen to 20 inches at full throttle, pulling the props back from 2,300 to 2,000 RPM will bring the pressures up no more than three inches; pull the throttles back to their cruise setting. You should now be showing 20 inches and 2,000 RPM, and descending at a comfortable rate.

The situation you want to avoid is high prop speed and low manifold pressure. This is what Lycoming says on the subject in the Lycoming Flyer: "Unless the pilot takes certain precautions, fast descents carrying high cruise RPM and low manifold pressure cause broken piston rings from ring flutter, and also cause cracked cylinders at the spark plug and valve ports, and warped exhaust valves due to sudden cooling…we recommend that the pilot maintain at least 15 inches MP or higher with pressurized aircraft and set the RPM at the lowest cruise setting…"

Reducing prop RPM will increase the load on the propeller and keep the engine working so it will stay toasty warm on the way down. As manifold pressure increases in the descent, reduce the setting to keep manifold pressure at the cruise setting. Leave the mixtures alone. I know, I know, most handbooks tell you to go to full rich when descending, but think of the effect on the engines of suddenly increasing the percentage of fuel in the mixture.

Remember that the fuel in the tanks has been subjected to some fairly cold temperatures for a long period of time, and that little warming will occur as it makes its way through the fuel selector and pumps. RAM Aircraft Corporation, a major overhauler and modifier, says, "The rich mixture manifests itself as a lot of cold fuel entering a hot cylinder intake air port at the fuel injection nozzle outlet. The conditions for 'shock' cooling have been met…" Your goal should be to keep the engines warm, so don't go for the mixture knobs until the engines tell you they are beginning to run lean. Try to keep the exhaust gas temperature 50° cooler than the peak temperature you used for cruise. Believe me, if the engines don't like what you are doing, they will let you know by running rough, and your reaction should be to richen only enough to make them run smoothly again. RAM says that you should not go to full rich until you are on the runway with engines at idle. A check of the exhaust gas and cylinder head temperatures should show that leaving the mixture untouched has kept the cylinder head temperature in the middle of the green and the exhaust gas temperature about two-thirds of the way to peak.

Leveling Off

Within the gradual-power-reduction guidelines mentioned earlier, keep the manifold pressure close to what it was in cruise (because MAP increases 1 inch per 1,000 feet of descent, this will require a reduction of about 1 inch every 2 minutes). When you have descended to pattern altitude or initial approach altitude, put the props back at 2,300 RPM and leave them there until the wheels are on the runway; 17 inches MAP should result in approach speed. This raises another point: prop pitch changes make noise, and pitch changes at low altitude cause people on the ground to reach for their binoculars with one hand and their telephone with the other hand. If you push the prop controls full forward because of a possible go-around, make sure that the final RPM change is made after the governors have driven the propeller blades to their flattest pitch.

Remember when zero thrust was discussed? The zero-thrust power setting is used in training to simulate an engine-out situation while keeping the engine available for use. When the manifold pressure is higher than the zero-thrust setting, the propeller is pulling the airplane forward through the air, and the bearings and seals in the drive train are experiencing the loads they were designed to handle. At power

settings below zero thrust, however, the airplane is moving through the air faster than the propeller can turn, causing the propeller to drive the engine. This reverses the loads on the seals and bearings, which is not good, and also creates a tremendous amount of drag. This is called flat-plate drag, because the effect is the same as if a 72-inch or 84-inch (depending on propeller blade length) flat plate is attached to the crankshaft. Retarding the throttles past the zero-thrust setting places the propellers in the flat-plate drag range; accordingly, you should avoid power settings below those that deliver zero thrust.

Flat-plate drag can be a useful tool if used wisely. If you have allowed the engines to cool gradually and find that you need to lose some altitude, pulling the throttles back to the stops will cause the airplane to sink dramatically. Leaving them there, however, can result in a hard landing. Two (imaginary) flat plates attached to the nacelles mean disturbed airflow over the horizontal stabilizer, and reduced elevator authority. You might attempt to flare and find out too late that back pressure on the yoke has no effect. Never be in the flat-plate drag manifold pressure range on short final.

On Final

When you make your first landing in a twin, it will be apparent that you will see things differently than you did in a single-engine airplane; there won't be an engine cowling to obscure a portion of the approach path. Instead of eyeballing the descent path, you will use a combination of airplane configuration and attitude control (as reflected by airspeed). Flying by the numbers is the only way to land a multi-engine airplane.

The manufacturer provides a landing configuration and airspeed in the Pilot's Operating Handbook; the recommended airspeed may vary with your airplane's landing weight. When you extend landing flaps and maintain the suggested airspeed, the resulting pitch attitude ensures that you will land on the main wheels. Watch an air carrier jet land and transfer that mental picture into your twin. The jet pilot configures the airplane for landing several miles from the touchdown point and maintains a reference speed all the way to touchdown. "Ref," as it is called, is based on landing weight and stall speed, and the captain flies a profile based on the reference speed. It might call for ref plus 20 knots until intercepting the final approach course, ref plus 10 to the final approach fix, and ref plus no more than 5 knots on final. Because flight at reference speed in the landing configuration results in a slightly nose-high attitude, little or no flare is used— they just fly it onto the runway.

Your propeller twin will deliver the best results if you fly it just as an airline captain flies a jet, making speed control paramount—use power as required to control rate of descent. Because the reference speed typically allows only a 20% cushion over the stall, you may add a correction factor for gusting crosswinds, such as one-half of the gusts. This is intended to keep a sudden lull in the wind from dropping the airplane onto the runway. Remember to use more power on the upwind engine to offset the effect of a crosswind.

Landing Distance

In the case of the Duchess, Figure 7-1 indicates a recommended approach speed of 76 knots and 600 fpm with full flaps. Note that the charted landing distances are achieved with maximum braking, a method you will probably not use. Also, if there is a 50-foot obstacle right at the threshold, you will land at least 633 feet down the runway after barely clearing it. Under the conditions in the sample problem in the figure, much warmer than standard temperature at a pressure altitude of almost 4,000 feet, the ground roll begins 920 feet beyond the obstacle.

All of these elements are involved in multi-engine descent planning, and a thorough, conservative pilot will go through all of the planning steps before each trip.

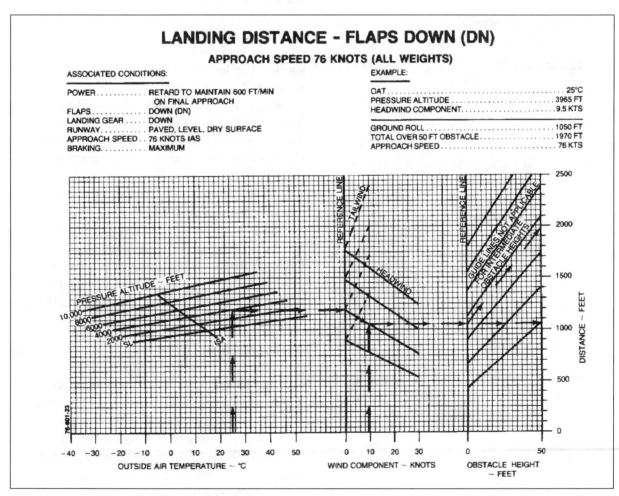

Figure 7-1. Landing distance

Getting It Stopped

As the pilot of a multi-engine airplane, you must remember that getting it stopped on the ground is a question of energy management, and you must reduce the total energy to virtually zero before you will be able to turn off at an intersection. The amount of energy under your control is a combination of weight and airspeed.

When you are loading and fueling the airplane before departure, landing distance at the destination may not seem a very high priority; when you are on short final, however, you may wish you didn't have quite so many pounds to bring to a halt. You already know the importance of a low touchdown speed; the energy present when the rubber meets the runway must be dissipated by friction, either the rolling friction of the tires on the runway or the use of brakes. Unless you are landing at Cape Canaveral, rolling to a stop is impractical. Aerodynamic drag is a function of the square of the airspeed, and once the airplane has slowed to 60 or 70% of touchdown speed, that source of drag is pretty useless. The flaps played their role when you established the landing configuration, by permitting a lower approach speed, and once you are on the runway they are out of the picture.

The smartest action you can take is to get on the brakes just as soon as the full weight of the airplane is on the tires. It takes just as much braking energy to slow from 85 knots to 65 knots, early in the landing roll, as it does to decelerate from 55 knots to 7 knots as you approach the end of the runway—you are not saving the brakes by waiting. The brakes are most effective if you retract the flaps, transferring any weight still being carried by the wings to the landing gear. I know all of the arguments against going for the flap handle before turning off the runway for fear of retracting the gear by mistake, but you must balance that risk against the importance of a short landing roll. Don't shrug off a slight tailwind; when the tailwind component is 5% of touchdown speed, the ground roll will be 50% longer than it would be if you were landing into the same wind.

Multi-engine flying and instrument weather go together, and you must consider the effect that a wet or slippery runway will have on the rollout. Remember: the maximum speed to avoid hydroplaning is 9 times the square root of the tire pressure. Beechcraft recommends that Duchess tires be inflated to 38 pounds, which suggests the danger of hydroplaning at speeds higher than 57 knots. That's the kind of calculation you can make well before takeoff.

Single-Engine Approach and Landing

According to the National Transportation Safety Board, most fatal twin accidents occur during the approach and landing after losing an engine during cruise or descent, yet during your multi-engine training you will land time after time with one engine operating properly and the other one operating at or close to zero thrust.

This would suggest either that pilots landing with an engine feathered are making poor decisions at critical times, or the apparent ease of single-engine approaches during training has not prepared them for the real thing. One possibility is the pilots are getting low and slow and forgetting that punching up the power on the operating engine causes both roll and yaw problems. You should prepare for that eventuality by deciding you will never let the airspeed deteriorate below the blue line, and you will always be a little high on final. A dot above the glide slope or pink over white on the visual approach slope indicator (VASI) is sufficiently high. This may result in a longer landing than you would like, but as I mentioned when discussing engine loss immediately after takeoff, it is better to slide off the end of the runway at 40 knots than to fall out of the sky.

Another possible reason pilots lose control on final approach is cascading problems; because of the engine failure, some aircraft systems do not work and the pilot becomes overloaded. A typical scenario might find a pilot flying on one engine and unable to extend the landing gear. You don't want to leave the airport area in order to extend the gear by emergency means, because the airplane probably won't maintain altitude on one engine with the gear down. In other words, the pilot gets the gear down but can't make it back to the airport. Remember that an aircraft in distress has priority; if you have to, don't hesitate to tie up the whole airport area while you get your problem solved.

When should the wheels be lowered for landing if one prop has been feathered? At the point where you normally begin the descent to land. If the extension system is not going to work, you need to know this while you have plenty of altitude. Don't let the drag of the gear take you below the glide slope or, in level flight, cause the airspeed to fall below the blue line. *Never let the speed get below V_{YSE} until you have the runway made.* If you can't maintain altitude without slowing below blue line airspeed, put the wheels back in the wells until you need to extend them for landing. It's better to land with the gear up than to lose control because of limited engine-out performance.

Do not extend full flaps when landing with an engine out; the additional drag might cause you to land short. When you are sure your touchdown will be well down the runway, you can add partial flaps.

A go-around on one engine in a light-to-medium twin is something that is taught, practiced, and written about, but is seldom successful under actual conditions. Remember that a light twin does not have to demonstrate a positive climb capability on one engine, and that the FAA does not even require an applicant for the multi-engine rating to demonstrate the ability to wave off on one engine. Do not consider a single-engine go-around as a viable option unless you make the decision with airspeed and altitude to spare. When you have descended to less than 500 feet above the ground, you should consider yourself committed to land, even if it is on the grass or on a taxiway. Les Berven, the FAA's guru for multi-engine flight, says that he would not attempt a single-engine go-around in anything smaller than a King Air.

Landing with a Propeller Feathered

Landing with a propeller feathered is one thing you will probably never practice, so your first such landing will be cold turkey—mine was. When you reduce power to flare, the airplane will want to turn toward the good engine (in no-wind conditions), because of the drag of the windmilling propeller and the fact that there is absolutely no drag on the failed engine side. Expect to float farther than normal because of the reduced drag. Once the airplane has touched down, the wing on the side with the feathered propeller will tend to lift, again because it is relatively clean aerodynamically in comparison to the good engine side (*see* Figure 7-2). For that reason, the tire on that side will have less weight on it. If you treat the situation normally and apply even braking, the airplane will swerve toward the good engine side and possibly blow a tire. Use intermittent light braking on the failed engine side until the weight rests solidly on both wheels. Wind from the good engine side will make things worse, while a wind from the failed engine side will help. And you will be in no position to shop around for runways with favorable winds.

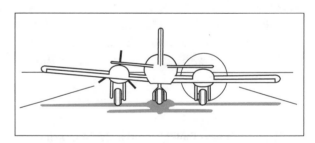

Figure 7-2. Landing with a propeller feathered

Taxiing with an engine feathered is another challenge, because the airplane will refuse to turn toward the good engine. Expect a series of 270°-turns toward the dead engine as you make your way to the ramp. If taxiing is difficult, don't abuse the remaining engine by pulling lots of power with little cooling. Get the airplane off the runway and call for help.

Chapter 7
Review Questions

1. Label the items below with their effect upon landing distance:

    A—increased weight _____
    B—increased altitude _____
    C—increased temperature _____
    D—headwind _____
    E—landing over an obstacle _____

2. When should maximum braking be applied?

    A—At touchdown.
    B—When the full weight of the airplane is on the wheels.
    C—At midfield.

3. Using Figure 7-1 (Page 7-3), determine the landing distance.

    Pressure altitude .... 3,000 feet
    Temperature .... 30°C
    Weight .... 3,700 lbs
    Tailwind .... 5 knots
    Obstacle height .... 20 feet

4. The ATIS says that the wind is 2718G30 and you are landing on runway 24. How much airspeed should you add to the normal approach speed?

    A—18 knots
    B—15 knots
    C—33 knots

5. When landing with a crosswind, a little extra power on the (upwind, downwind) engine will reduce the amount of rudder required.

6. Reducing the power to idle on short final will have what effect?

    A—Turbulent airflow over the horizontal stabilizer.
    B—Reduced elevator authority.
    C—Inability to flare as much as you would like to.

7. When should the propeller control be placed in low pitch/high rpm during a landing approach?

    A—When the descent from pattern altitude is begun.
    B—On short final.
    C—Before the final power reduction.

Preparing for the Checkride

8

Assuming you are adding the multi-engine rating to your private pilot certificate, your examiner will be using the Practical Test Standards for that rating during your checkride. Because a few pilots do get their original Private tickets in twins (the late comedian Danny Kaye, for one), the test standards include several tasks which you completed for your single-engine rating. Don't worry—your MEL checkride will not duplicate any of those tasks. Prepare for the oral portion of the test by reading the *Multi-Engine Oral Exam Guide*, an ASA publication.

If you are reading *The Complete Multi-Engine Pilot* as a certificated Commercial pilot who is adding the multi-engine rating, you will find that the Commercial checkride duplicates the Private ride almost exactly, except for the stalls. The major difference is that each task includes the following as an Objective: "Exhibits commercial pilot knowledge by explaining…," whereas the Private pilot must only "exhibit knowledge." After reading this book and the *Oral Exam Guide*, a Commercial certificate applicant will be able to satisfy an examiner as to his or her "Commercial pilot knowledge," and a Private pilot applying for a Multi-engine certificate will have no trouble with the oral.

Certificates and Documents

Be prepared to show the examiner not only the airframe log but two engine logs. In addition to showing the examiner that the airplane is not out of a 100-hour inspection or an annual, check the time on the propellers. They, too, must be inspected at regular intervals that do not always coincide with airframe inspection times.

Become familiar with the weight-and-balance records and find the most recent Form 337. When you are asked to perform a weight-and-balance calculation, you must use the most current information. If you intend to fly the airplane on instruments after you pass the checkride, this would also be a good time to determine how recently the pitot-static and transponder inspections were performed.

Airplane Systems

The examiner will ask you to explain how the flight controls are actuated, the power source of each flight instrument, and how the landing gear is extended, both normally and in an emergency. You will be asked how the propeller blade angle is changed and the effect of problems with the governor. You should be able to explain the fuel system and tell the examiner how you would ensure continued fuel flow to an engine if a particular pump or valve failed.

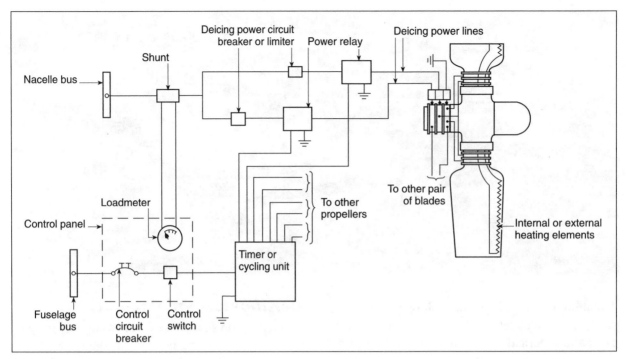

Figure 8-1. *Typical engine deicing system*

The same types of questions will be asked about the electrical system: If you lose part of your electrical supply, how will you cope with the loss? If your airplane is equipped with deice and/or anti-ice, be prepared to tell the examiner how the system works. Know how the environmental system works. Where is the heater safety switch? Can you warm up the passengers without toasting the cockpit crew? Can you operate the windshield defroster without frosting the passengers?

Normal Procedures

Be able to name every V-speed applicable to the test airplane and tell the examiner when each speed is appropriate. Know the various limiting weights. If you take off at maximum gross takeoff weight and lose an engine, will the airplane be at or below its maximum gross landing weight if you try a turn back to the runway? Are there any other limitations (zero fuel weight, prop RPM caution arcs, etc.) that apply? If there are any placards or limiting markings, be ready to tell the examiner why they are there and what might happen if you ignored them. Do you know how to start an engine using external power, without frying the electrical system?

Determining Performance and Flight Planning

You should be able to use every chart and graph in the performance section of the Pilot's Operating Handbook. Prepare for the checkride by planning imaginary trips and calculating takeoff distances, fuel burn to altitude, landing distance, and other relevant factors.

Do some weight and balance problems that involve shifting passengers between seats (or removing weight) to place the center of gravity within limits. Your twin gives you more loading flexibility as well as more opportunities to load the airplane improperly.

Minimum Equipment List

Your light twin is subject to 14 CFR §91.213 ("Inoperable instruments and equipment") and its requirement that all installed equipment must be operative or the airplane is considered unairworthy. There may be a Master Minimum Equipment List (MMEL) for your airplane that designates some pieces of equipment as not required for flight; if that is the case, have a copy of the MMEL and any supporting documents available to show to the examiner.

Piper Cheyenne 1A

It may be that some pieces of installed equipment can be placarded as inoperative and the airplane determined to be airworthy without that equipment. Know which items, if any, can be so designated. The key is to show the examiner that you are aware of the requirement for Minimum Equipment Lists, how your operation is affected, and that you know how to work around the restrictions if allowed to do so by 14 CFR §91.213.

Flight Principles: Engine Inoperative

The examiner will ask you to explain the effect on single-engine flight of density altitude and airplane loading, and how single-engine service ceiling might affect your plans at a higher density altitude. You will be asked to explain the term "critical engine" and tell the examiner which engine is critical (if any) on your airplane. Be prepared to explain V_{MC}, how it is determined, and its relationship to indicated stall speed and altitude. You should be ready to discuss takeoff planning from determining safe runway length to single-engine climb gradient after takeoff.

Ground Operations

Carry a checklist in your hand while doing the preflight walkaround. Know exactly how many fuel drains there are and which sump or filter each one serves. Be able to explain each and every knob and switch in the cockpit. Although your instructor may not let you use the autopilot during training, the examiner expects you to know how to use it and, most importantly, how to disengage it in case of a malfunction. The same is true of oxygen systems.

Don't forget to check that the door is closed properly and the examiner has both seat belt and shoulder harness fastened. Brief the examiner on how to open the seat belt and door if you are disabled—remember, the examiner is playing the role of a passenger. Examiners have a nasty habit of popping a door open to check your reaction.

Use a checklist during engine start and the preflight runup. The FAA encourages checklist use and the examiner will look for it. Be ready to explain why you perform runup actions, such as the alternator check, exercising the propeller, and the feather check. Do the magneto and prop checks one engine at a time. If you try to check the magnetos on both engines simultaneously you won't be able to hear subtle changes in engine sound.

Normal and Crosswind Takeoffs and Climbs

Refer to the Normal Takeoff Distance chart in the performance section and follow the procedure and airspeed listed there. It will probably recommend standing on the brakes and running the throttles up to takeoff power. If no liftoff speed is listed, rotate at V_{MC} plus 5 knots. Climb at V_Y (not V_{YSE}), plus or minus 5 knots, to a safe maneuvering altitude before the first power reduction.

The examiner may fail an engine before you reach liftoff speed—be ready to chop the throttles and get on the brakes. Know your crosswind takeoff procedure, and remember that a little additional throttle on the upwind engine can help offset a crosswind.

Maximum Performance Takeoffs and Climbs

Again, check the charts in the performance section and fly the airplane using the procedure shown. You should definitely stand on the brakes and apply full power for an obstacle clearance takeoff, and rotate at the recommended speed. The only difference between a normal takeoff and a maximum performance takeoff is the initial climb speed of V_X until the obstacle is cleared.

Instrument Flight

If you hold an Instrument rating on your single-engine certificate, you will be required to demonstrate your ability to handle engine-out emergencies under simulated instrument conditions (wearing a view-limiting device) and to perform instrument approach procedures with one engine inoperative.

A proficient instrument pilot should have no trouble meeting these requirements. You will be amply warned when the examiner simulates engine failure, because the props will go out of sync and the airplane will lurch toward the failed engine. The ball will deflect toward the good engine. You must fix your eyes on the flight instruments and maintain heading with rudder pressure. That pressure will help you identify the failed engine, and you can then go through the verification and feathering procedure by feel, keeping your eyes fixed on the flight instruments.

Note that the Practical Test Standards call for securing the engine before attempting to determine the reason for the failure. And if the examiner fails an engine while you are in a turn, you will find it easier to identify the failed engine if you roll out of the bank.

Remember that a bank toward the good engine is required to maintain a heading. If you level the wings during an instrument approach, the good engine will drive you off of the final approach course. This is the most difficult aspect of a single-engine ILS; if you relax the bank, you will lose the localizer. Having said that, remember the discussion of zero sideslip in Chapter 1: The optimum bank angle for best performance will be only a couple of degrees and certainly not as much as five degrees. On approach, the power output of the operating engine and the yaw that it causes will be considerably reduced.

Slow Flight and Stalls

You will be expected to confidently and competently maneuver the airplane through climbs, descents, and turns at speeds as low as 1.2 V_{S1} or V_{MC}, whichever is greater, plus 10 or minus 5 knots. Slow flight is an excellent confidence builder—it helps avoid the "10 extra knots for the family" mindset that leads to long landings and heavy braking. At least one training session should be devoted exclusively to exploring the low-speed end of the airplane's operating envelope. Unlike a single-engine airplane, much of a twin's lift comes from propeller discharge air, and a power reduction will have a greater effect on your ability to hold altitude than it would in a single.

You will also be expected to demonstrate your ability to recognize the onset of a stall, both power-on (departure) and power-off (approach and landing) and to recover smoothly to level flight through the coordinated use of the flight controls and throttle. Because you have more power at your command, the pitch attitude for recovery will be much closer to level flight than that required for stall recovery in a single. Single-engine stalls are specifically prohibited by the Practical Test Standards. The examiner will expect you to announce the first aerodynamic indication of the oncoming stall, but you should not recover until the stall breaks.

Power-on full stalls are hard on airplanes, because the rotating propellers are excellent gyroscopes. A rapid pitching moment, such as you might use in an over-zealous stall recovery, will exert lateral bending forces on the crankshaft extensions to which the propeller is attached.

The commercial checkride differs from the private checkride only in that it has tighter tolerances.

Spins

Part 23 does not require a manufacturer to investigate the spin characteristics of a multi-engine airplane, and any recommended spin recovery technique in the Approved Flight Manual has not been tested by the manufacturer. Conventional spin recovery technique is:

1. Both throttles to idle.
2. Full rudder opposite the spin (no aileron input).
3. Brisk forward movement of the control yoke.
4. Hold until rotation stops, then positive control pressure to recover from the ensuing dive.

If this doesn't work, try to help the rudder with power on the inside engine. Whatever you do, you are a test pilot in this situation.

Steep Turns

You will be asked to perform a 40-50° banked 360°-turn while maintaining altitude, and rolling out within 10° of the entry heading. With this degree of bank, both load factor and induced drag increase, and extra power may be required to maintain altitude. Be sure you know what the maneuvering speed is for your twin, and don't begin the steep turn at a speed higher than V_A. Expect the overbanking tendency to be more noticeable than it was in single-engine airplanes. If you pick a point on the windscreen directly in front of your eyes and keep that point on the horizon, as you would in a single-engine airplane, you will find this maneuver to be no more difficult in a twin.

Instructors (and examiners) like to fail engines while the airplane is turning, because the aerodynamic clues can be confusing—failing the inside engine while the airplane is banked will cause overbanking, and failing the outside engine will cause the airplane to try to roll out of the turn. If you suspect engine failure (sound is the obvious clue), roll toward level flight and properly identify the failed engine before taking corrective action.

Drag Demonstration

The examiner may ask you for a drag demonstration, giving you an opportunity to show that you are aware of the effect on performance of different configurations and the part that this knowledge plays in reacting to an engine-out situation. Begin with plenty of altitude.

With the propeller of one engine at zero thrust, and with the airplane established in level flight at blue line airspeed, extend the landing gear. Lower the nose to maintain airspeed; after waiting for the airspeed to stabilize, note the vertical speed. Retract the landing gear and re-establish level flight at V_{YSE}. Extend full flaps, lower the nose to maintain blue line airspeed, and note the vertical speed. Lower the landing gear, maintain blue line, and note the effect on vertical speed of the landing configuration. Retract the gear and flaps and re-establish V_{YSE}.

Now push the propeller control for the "failed" engine full forward, and pull its throttle full back. Maintain V_{YSE} and note the effect on vertical speed of the windmilling propeller. Restore level flight with both engines operating (give the "failed" engine time to warm up).

You should see that the landing gear creates the least drag, that full flaps create more drag than the gear, and that the landing configuration creates the most drag. Accordingly, with an engine out you should not fully configure the airplane for landing until a landing on the runway is assured.

The windmilling prop will create about the same amount of drag as full flaps, but retracting the flaps is a one-control function. That's why you hit the gear and flap switches before starting the feathering process.

Note: The manuals for some airplanes recommend against retracting the landing gear after an engine fails. Follow the recommendations of your airplane's manual.

V_{MC} Demonstration

The examiner will ask you to demonstrate your knowledge of the engine-out loss of directional control caused by flight at V_{MC}. Establish level flight at V_{YSE} with wing flaps and cowl flaps in the takeoff position and the landing gear retracted. Put the trim control at the takeoff setting. Push both propeller controls to their full-forward position, where they would be immediately after liftoff.

Reduce the power on the critical engine to idle and increase the power on the operating engine to takeoff power or maximum available power—you will have to bank toward the operating engine (the Practical Test Standard does not mention a specific bank angle). Increase the pitch attitude to reduce airspeed approximately one knot per second while feeding in rudder to maintain heading. Be alert as the airspeed indicator nears the red line.

Tell the examiner when you cannot maintain heading with full rudder applied *or* at the first indication of a stall, either mechanical or aerodynamic. Recover by reducing power on the operating engine and re-

ducing the angle of attack to regain airspeed and directional control. Do not expect loss of directional control to occur exactly at red line airspeed—you cannot exactly match the conditions under which the manufacturer determined V_{MC}.

Because indicated stall speed remains constant with increasing altitude, while V_{MC} decreases with altitude due to the loss of engine power with altitude, V_{MC} will equal stall speed at some altitude. A stall with one engine idle and the other at takeoff power could lead to a spin; so when density altitudes are high, a V_{MC} demonstration can be hazardous. If your checkride will be out of a high-altitude airport on a hot day, express your concern to the examiner. This will have the salutary effect of demonstrating your knowledge of this hazard and should also serve as a reminder when you have your rating and are contemplating a takeoff with a load of passengers.

System and Equipment Malfunctions

This is an inflight extension of your explanation of the airplane systems in that the examiner will simulate failure of a system to observe how you respond. Fortunately for you, there is no way that the examiner can set an engine on fire, cause a loss of oil pressure, or dump the hydraulic fluid. However, examiners can do just about everything else. Expect one landing without operative pitch trim and another without flaps, and don't be surprised if a door pops open during a takeoff. The examiner needs to evaluate not only your knowledge of the airplane's systems, but how you react to unfamiliar situations. An imaginative instructor can do a lot to prepare you for this part of the checkride, but you can do a lot for yourself by sitting down with the manual and playing "what if?"

Maneuvering with One Engine Inoperative

This should be easy, because your instructor will be pulling engines throughout your training. The examiner will want to see how you react to an in-flight failure, and if you can perform normal flight maneuvers with an engine out. You will be expected to maintain heading and altitude in straight-and-level flight, climb and descend to assigned altitudes, and perform turns both toward and away from the dead engine. Your mind will be on the failed engine and the control problems it will cause, and it will be easy to let the heading or altitude slip a little. Don't let it happen.

There is no airspeed standard other than "Attains the best engine-inoperative airspeed" listed under Objectives. In level flight, a high airspeed suggests that the good engine is being overworked, while a speed below V_{YSE} is unacceptable. You won't find a recommended engine-out cruise speed in the performance charts. I suggest V_{YSE} plus 10 knots. You should be able to attain that speed without beating up on the good engine, affording an airspeed cushion for turbulence and maneuvering. If your instructor knows that your type of twin operates best at a certain speed, by all means go with his or her experience.

When the examiner fails an engine, by whatever means, identify the failed engine and then go through your troubleshooting routine before feathering the propeller on the offending engine. Because an in-flight restart may be part of this task, don't be surprised if the examiner lets you go all the way to feather. Don't look over at the examiner and say "Do you want me to feather it?" If going to full feather is not on the examiner's agenda, he will keep the prop control out of the feather detent with a strategically placed thumb on the quadrant or by quickly moving the prop control back to high pitch.

It won't take much effort to turn toward the dead engine, because the good engine has been waiting for you to give it an opportunity to take charge of directional control. Watch out for overbanking. On the other hand, banking toward the good engine will require more aileron deflection than usual. I am assuming you already have the rudder trim set toward the good engine side to give your leg a rest.

If the examiner allows you to feather the propeller and then demonstrate an air start, be sure to use the restart checklist, and expect the engine to be hard to start. Remember that cooling air has been passing through the nacelle at 100 knots or so for the past few minutes and that the fuel-air mixture will be reluctant to vaporize in that chilly environment.

Engine Failure En Route

The examiner may combine this task with "Maneuvering with One Engine Inoperative." There is no difference in your required actions, except that you will be expected to establish a minimum sink rate (drift down). Use V_{YSE} if the airplane manual does not specify an airspeed.

Engine Failure on Takeoff Before V_{MC}

This is easy, because you should be spring-loaded to reduce the throttles to idle and get on the brakes if *anything* unusual happens before the airspeed needle reaches the red line.

Engine Failure After Liftoff

The examiner will expect you to ensure that all of the engine controls are set at full power and that drag items have been cleaned up before you identify, verify, and feather. With the airplane under control, use the checklist to secure the failed engine. Don't go through your troubleshooting routine until the airplane has reached a safe altitude.

Approach and Landing with an Inoperative Engine

If the examiner fails an engine after you have reduced power to initiate the descent for landing, you may have to add power to get enough differential rudder pressure to identify the dead engine. Don't let the confusion of the moment make you forget the Prelanding Checklist. Airspeed should be within plus 5 knots of the blue line. Don't let the airspeed get below the blue line. Use power on the good engine to maintain a stabilized descent rate, and be alert on the rudders as you reduce power to land. Keep the airplane aligned with the runway.

Landing with "zero thrust" on one engine does not prepare you for landing with an engine feathered, because the manufacturer's zero thrust settings are based on flight at V_{YSE}. Those settings will result in some drag as speed is reduced in the flare for landing. In contrast, a feathered propeller would create no drag.

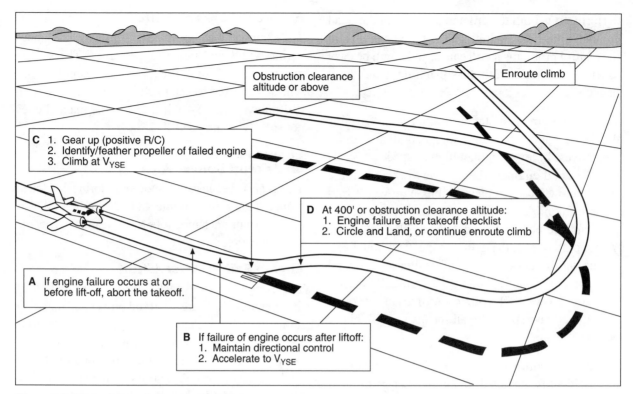

Figure 8-2. *Engine failure during takeoff procedures*

Within the figure:

> Obstruction clearance altitude or above

> Enroute climb

> **C** 1. Gear up (positive R/C)
> 2. Identify/feather propeller of failed engine
> 3. Climb at V_{YSE}

> **D** At 400' or obstruction clearance altitude:
> 1. Engine failure after takeoff checklist
> 2. Circle and Land, or continue enroute climb

> **A** If engine failure occurs at or before lift-off, abort the takeoff.

> **B** If failure of engine occurs after liftoff:
> 1. Maintain directional control
> 2. Accelerate to V_{YSE}

You can add a little realism to your engine-out landing practice (without shaking up the tower controllers by landing with one prop standing still) by calculating a touchdown-zero-thrust setting. First determine the ratio between V_{YSE} and touchdown speed. If blue line is 87 and you normally touch down at 70, the ratio is 70/87 or 0.8. Then fly at V_{YSE} using 12 inches (or the manufacturer's recommended manifold pressure for zero thrust), push the prop control full forward, and note the resulting RPM; let's say that it is 2,300 RPM. Multiply 2,300 by .8 to get 1,840. The next time you flare for touchdown with a simulated engine out, adjust the RPM to 1,840 with the throttle (the propeller pitch will be as flat as it can get, the governor will have lost control, and you will be able to control RPM with the throttle).

Balked Landing

The FAA does not require that you demonstrate the ability to execute a missed approach on one engine. However, you are expected to demonstrate to the examiner that you can recognize a bad landing approach and go around for another try. The examiner will be watching to see how you handle the gear, the flaps, and the cowl flaps (if installed) and to see if you use a checklist to ensure that you didn't miss anything. Climb out at V_Y plus or minus 5 knots.

Figure 8-3. *Feathered propeller reduces drag*

Normal and Crosswind Approaches and Landings

Know the demonstrated maximum crosswind for your airplane and, if there is no crosswind, be ready to explain crosswind landing procedure to the examiner. The examiner will be looking for a constant approach speed and a constant descent path. Whether or not that means a constant rate of descent depends on the wind. Expect to make small pitch and power adjustments all the way down the descent path. Maintain the indicated airspeed within plus or minus 5 knots of the recommended approach speed. Check the landing distance graphs in the performance section of the operating handbook for the speed. Make sure you don't reduce the throttle below about 12 inches to avoid getting into the flat-plate drag range.

Maximum Performance Approach and Landing

Refer to the charts in the performance section of the operating handbook for the airspeed and flap setting to use for a short field landing. You will learn more from the performance charts than you will from reading the normal procedures section. Don't let your desire to land short fool you into pulling the throttles back to idle at the low airspeeds recommended for maximum performance landings.

With reduced airflow over the horizontal stabilizer due to the low speed, the disturbed airflow that results from idling propellers may degrade elevator effectiveness to the extent that you will be unable to flare. That's hard on nosewheels.

Congratulations! You made it through the checkride; now enjoy your multi-engine rating.

Appendix A

Multi-Engine Rating Syllabus

Enrollment Prerequisites

The student must be able to read, speak, write, and understand the English language and must possess a valid Private, Commercial, or ATP certificate with instrument, single-engine, land ratings, and a third-class medical certificate (or higher) prior to enrollment.

Training Course Objectives

The student will obtain the aeronautical skill and knowledge necessary to meet the requirements of a Private, Commercial, or ATP certificate (depending upon the certificate held at time of enrollment), with an airplane category, instrument rating, and multi-engine land class rating.

Course Completion Standards

The student will demonstrate, by way of a flight and written test, the aeronautical skill and knowledge necessary to obtain a Private, Commercial, or ATP certificate (depending upon the certificate held at time of enrollment), with an airplane category, instrument rating, and a multi-engine land class rating. Each task in each area of operation in the Practical Test Standards will have been accomplished by the student. The instructor will not proceed to the next lesson until the student is able to explain and/or demonstrate the elements of the procedure or maneuver as required by the Practical Test Standards.

Recommended Materials for the Multi-Engine Rating

- *The Complete Multi-Engine Pilot*, by Bob Gardner (ASA-MPT)

- FAA Practical Test Standards (referred to as PTS) (Private ASA-8081-14.1S, Commercial ASA-8081-12A, ATP ASA-8081-5D, Instrument ASA-8081-4C)

- *FAR/AIM* (ASA-FR-AM-BK, published annually)

- *Multi-Engine Oral Exam Guide*, by Michael Hayes (ASA-OEG-ME)

Training Syllabus

The FAA does not require a specified amount of experience to obtain a multi-engine rating. Hours shown for each lesson for flight training, preflight briefing, and post-flight critique are offered as a guide to the instructor. Time used for an individual lesson may be adjusted to the student's needs. The instructor is responsible for ensuring all requirements are met. Points at which normal student progress should meet the requirements of the Practical Test Standards for a *task* in an *area of operation* will include a note indicating this, listed under the Completion Standards. Instructors should then reference the Practical Test Standards appropriate to the certificate currently held by the student.

Multi-Engine Rating Course Hours

The FAA does not specify how much time should be spent training for a multi-engine rating. Instructors may choose to have the student practice solo (or with a safety pilot), in addition to the following Dual Flight lessons. Ground instruction includes preflight briefings, post-flight critiques, and classroom or personal study.

Instructors and students are encouraged to integrate Personal Computer-based Aviation Training Devices (PCATDs) technology with existing methods of aviation instruction and training. Instructors are encouraged to challenge students by altering the virtual environment within which the lessons take place. This can be done by changing the weather (adding turbulence, altering the winds, or assigning the ceiling and visibility to the approach minimum conditions), and/or simulating a system or engine failure. These changes can be set to occur randomly or within a specified time frame, allowing the students to learn flight and decision-making skills simultaneously. In conjunction with training to the Practical Test Standards at all times, this method will encourage a willing suspension of disbelief and maximize the value of PCATDs in a curriculum. The practice of flying the lesson in a PCATD before heading out to the airplane will result in a more efficient training program.

Lesson	Dual Flight	Dual X/C	Dual Night	Instrument Instruction	Ground Instruction
1	1.0				2.0
2	1.0			0.3	2.0
3	1.5			0.5	2.0
4	1.5			0.5	2.0
5	1.0		1.0	0.3	2.0
6	2.0	2.0		1.0	2.0
7	1.0			0.3	2.0
8	1.0			0.3	2.0
Totals	10.0 hours	2.0 hours	1.0 hour	3.2 hours	16.0 hours

Lesson 1   Dual

1.0 hour flight
2.0 hours ground instruction

Ground Training

Objective:

For the student to be introduced to the Multi-Engine Rating program, and learn the flight school requirements, procedures, regulations, and grading criteria. Student will also be introduced to multi-engine aerodynamics, regulations associated with multi-engine training, and the training airplane Pilot's Operating Handbook (POH).

Content

____ Review of course and objectives
____ School requirements, procedures, regulations
____ Grading criteria, student's expectations
____ Federal Aviation Regulations, Parts 61, 91, 23
____ Multi-engine aerodynamics
____ Service ceiling
____ Absolute service ceiling
____ Single-engine service ceiling
____ Single-engine absolute service ceiling
____ Centerline thrust
____ Critical engines
____ P-factor
____ Counter-rotating propellers
____ Review POH associated with training airplane

Completion Standards

Student must complete all review questions following the assigned reading.

Assignment

The Complete Multi-Engine Pilot, Introduction and Chapter 1; Pilot's Operating Handbook

Flight Training

Objective:

For the student to be introduced and become familiar with the multi-engine preflight inspection, checklist operations, starting and taxi procedures, and the airplane controls and systems.

Content

____ Preflight inspection and aircraft documents (certificates and documents, aircraft logbooks, airplane servicing)
____ Discuss cockpit management
____ Starting Procedures
____ Taxi
____ Run-up procedures
____ Checklist introduction and use
____ Normal takeoff
____ Four Basics: straight and level, climbs, descents, turns
____ Steep turns
____ Demo slow flight
____ Demo power-on stall
____ Demo power-off stall
____ Collision avoidance procedures
____ Normal approach and landing
____ Postflight procedures

Completion Standards

Student must conduct the preflight with minimum assistance, properly use all checklists, start and taxi the airplane, and operate the airplane system and controls.

Lesson 2 Dual

1.0 hour flight
0.3 hour instrument work
2.0 hours ground instruction

Ground Training

Objective:

For the student to have an understanding of the systems and engines associated with a multi-engine airplane.

Content

___✓__ Multi-engine cockpit instrumentation
___✓__ Propeller systems
___✓__ Engine failures and effect on other systems
___✓__ Air starts
___✓__ Fuel system
___✓__ Electrical system
___✓__ Hydraulic system
___✓__ Turbocharging
___✓__ Pressurization
___✓__ Landing gear system
___✓__ Trim
___✓__ Flaps
___✓__ Environmental system
___✓__ Vacuum system
___✓__ Ice protection system
___✓__ Emergency exit system
___✓__ Avionics, autopilot, FMS
_____ Oxygen systems
_____ Glass-cockpit systems

Completion Standards

Student must complete all review questions following the assigned reading.

Assignment

The Complete Multi-Engine Pilot, Chapter 2

Flight Training

Objective:

For the student to become proficient with the four basics of flight, demonstrate sound collision avoidance procedures, and gain experience with steep turns, slow flight, and stalls.

Content

___✓__ Preflight
___✓__ Aircraft systems
___✓__ Discuss emergency procedures
_____ Discuss principles of flight with engine
___✓__ inoperative
___✓__ Normal takeoff and climbout
___✓__ Climbs
___✓__ Straight and level

Turns

___✓__ 90 degrees
___✓__ 180 degrees
___✓__ 360 degrees
___✓__ Turns to headings
___✓__ Cruise configuration
___✓__ Steep turns
___✓__ Slow flight
___✓__ Power-on stall
___✓__ Power-off stall

Descents

_____ With flaps
___✓__ Without flaps
___✓__ Scanning procedures
___✓__ Normal approach and landing
___✓__ Postflight procedures

Completion Standards

Student must maintain altitude within 200 feet, airspeed within 20 knots, and heading within 20 degrees, while performing the maneuvers listed in the content of this lesson.

Lesson 3 Dual

1.5 hours flight
0.5 hour instrument work
2.0 hours ground instruction

Ground Training

Objective:

For the student to have a working understanding of the factors affecting multi-engine airplane performance.

Content

____ Weight and balance
____ Empty weight
____ B.O.W.
____ Zero fuel weight
____ Effects of CG on performance
____ Performance planning
____ Minimum controllable airspeed
____ Multi-engine V-speeds: V_S, V_{S0}, V_{SSE}, V_X, V_Y, V_{XSE}, V_{YSE}, V_A, V_{FE}, V_{LE}, V_{MC}, V_{NO}, V_R, climb-out speed, approach speed
____ Conditions that affect V_{MC}
____ Takeoff and landing distance
____ Accelerate-stop distance
____ Accelerate-go distance
____ One-engine performance
____ Time, fuel, and distance to climb
____ Range and endurance profiles
____ Cruise power tables
____ Descent planning

Completion Standards

Student must complete all review questions following the assigned reading.

Assignment

The Complete Multi-Engine Pilot, Chapter 3

Flight Training

Objective:

For the student to demonstrate a working knowledge of the airplane weight and balance and performance characteristics, and gain proficiency in slow flight and stalls.

Content

____ Preflight
____ Aircraft V-speeds
____ Performance data
____ Weight and Balance
____ Normal takeoff
____ V_X and V_Y climbs
____ Cruise configuration
____ Steep turns
____ Slow flight
____ Power-on stall
____ Power-off stall
____ Spin awareness
____ Demo one-engine shutdown
____ Demo emergency gear extension
____ Normal approach and landing
____ Go-around procedures
____ Postflight procedures

Completion Standards

Student must maintain altitude within 200 feet, airspeed within 20 knots, and heading within 20 degrees, while performing the maneuvers listed in the content of this lesson.

Lesson 4 Dual

1.5 hours flight
0.5 hour instrument work
2.0 hours ground instruction

Ground Training

Objective:

For the student to have a working knowledge of the preflight preparation necessary for a multi-engine flight.

Content

- ✓ Taxiing a twin
- ✓ Differential taxiing
- ___ Preflight inspection
- ✓ Passenger briefings
- ✓ Abnormal situations
- ✓ Run-up and takeoff checks
- ✓ Minimum equipment lists
- ___ Multi-engine cockpit instrumentation

Completion Standards

Student must complete all review questions following the assigned reading.

Assignment

The Complete Multi-Engine Pilot, Chapter 4

Flight Training

Objective:

For the student to demonstrate proficiency in slow flight, stalls, and emergency procedures.

Content

- ✓ Preflight
- ✓ Discuss minimum equipment lists
- ✓ Differential taxiing
- ✓ Short-field takeoff and climbout
- ✓ Cruise configuration
- ✓ Steep turns
- ✓ Slow flight
- ✓ Stalls
- ✓ One engine shutdown
- ✓ Emergency gear extension
- ✓ V_{MC} demonstration
- ✓ Drag demonstration
- ✓ Identify, verify, feather dead engine
- ✓ 4 basic maneuvers with feathered engine
- ✓ Re-start engine
- ✓ Short-field approach and landing
- ✓ No-flap landing
- ✓ Postflight procedures

Completion Standards

Student must maintain altitude within 150 feet, airspeed within 15 knots, and heading within 15 degrees, while performing the maneuvers listed in the content of this lesson.

Lesson 5 Dual

1.0 hour flight
1.0 hour night
0.3 hour instrument work
2.0 hours ground instruction

Ground Training

Objective:

For the student to have a working understanding of the factors that affect multi-engine takeoff and departure.

Content

____ ✓ Climb rates
____ ✓ The takeoff roll
____ ✓ Engine failure
____ ✓ Multi-engine takeoff procedures
____ ✓ Departure procedures

Completion Standards

Student must complete all review questions following the assigned reading.

Assignment

The Complete Multi-Engine Pilot, Chapter 5

Flight Training

Objective:

For the student to gain proficiency in specialty take-offs and landings, engine-out procedures, and night operations.

Content

____ Preflight
____ Discuss supplemental oxygen
____ Differential taxiing
____ Short-field takeoff and climbout
____ Cruise configuration
____ 4-basic maneuvers, instrument, both engines
____ 4-basic maneuvers, instrument, single engine
____ Steep turns
____ Slow flight
____ Stalls
____ One-engine shutdown
____ Emergency gear extension
____ V_{MC} demonstration
____ Drag demonstration
____ Identify, verify, feather dead engine
____ 4 basic maneuvers with feathered engine
____ Re-start engine
____ Short-field approach and landing
____ Postflight procedures

Completion Standards

Student must maintain altitude within 150 feet, airspeed within 15 knots, and heading within 15 degrees, while performing the maneuvers listed in the content of this lesson.

Lesson 6 Dual

2.0 hours flight
2.0 hours cross-country
1.0 hour instrument work
2.0 hours ground instruction

Ground Training

Objective:

For the student to have a working understanding of the factors affecting multi-engine cruise flight.

Content

____ Cruise checklist
____ Engine failure during cruise flight
____ Drift down

Completion Standards

Student must complete all review questions following the assigned reading.

Assignment

The Complete Multi-Engine Pilot, Chapter 6

Flight Training

Objective:

For the student to gain proficiency in engine-out procedures, cross-country procedures, and instrument approaches (for instrument-rated students only).

Content

____ Preflight
____ Discuss performance ceilings and density altitude
____ Differential taxiing
____ Short-field takeoff and climbout
____ Round-robin cross-country flight
____ Simulated system failures (electrical, hydraulic, mechanical)
____ Holding pattern (both engines, single engine)
____ Precision approach (both engines, single engine)
____ Nonprecision approach (both engines, single engine)
____ Missed approach procedure (both engines, single engine)
____ Circle-to-land approach (single engine)
____ Postflight procedures

Completion Standards

Student must maintain altitude within 150 feet, airspeed within 15 knots, and heading within 15 degrees, while performing the maneuvers listed in the content of this lesson, and maintain approach minimums.

Lesson 7 Dual

1.0 hour flight
0.3 hour instrument work
2.0 hours ground instruction

Ground Training

Objective:

For the student to have a working knowledge of the factors affecting multi-engine descent, approach and landing.

Content

____ Descent planning
____ Descent
____ Leveling off
____ Final approach
____ Landing distance
____ Stopping
____ Single-engine approach and landing
____ Landing with a propeller feathered

Completion Standards

Student must complete all review questions following the assigned reading.

Assignment

The Complete Multi-Engine Pilot, Chapter 7

Flight Training

Objective:

For the student to gain proficiency in single-engine operations.

Content

____ Preflight
____ Simulated engine failure on takeoff roll
____ Short-field takeoff
____ Engine failure at V_Y climb
____ Engine failure at V_X climb
____ Engine failure in steep turns
____ Engine failure in slow flight
____ Engine shut down and re-start
____ Engine failure in simulated go-around
____ Engine failure in landing configuration
____ Engine failure on approach
____ Engine failure on simulated go-around
____ Simulated feathered landing
____ Simulated single-engine landing
____ Simulated single-engine landing from an approach (instrument students only)
____ Postflight procedures

Completion Standards

Student must maintain control of the airplane throughout all emergency procedures and adhere to standards outlined in the Practical Test Standards.

Lesson 8 Dual

1.0 hour flight
0.3 hour instrument work
2.0 hours ground instruction

Ground Training

Objective:
For the student to gain proficiency in all areas included in the Practical Test Standards.

Content
____ Certificates and documents
____ Airplane systems
____ Normal procedures
____ Determining performance and flight planning
____ Minimum equipment list
____ Flight principles: engine inoperative
____ Ground operations
____ Normal and crosswind takeoff and climb
____ Maximum performance takeoff and climb
____ Instrument flight
____ Slow flight and stalls
____ Steep turns
____ Maneuvering with one engine inoperative
____ Drag demonstration
____ V_{MC} demonstration
____ Engine failure en route
____ Engine failure on takeoff before V_{MC}
____ Engine failure after liftoff
____ Approach and landing with an inoperative engine
____ Balked landing
____ Normal and crosswind approach and landing
____ Maximum performance approach and landing

Completion Standards
Student must complete all review questions following the assigned reading.

Assignment
The Complete Multi-Engine Pilot, Chapter 8; Practical Test Standards; *Multi-Engine Oral Exam Guide*

Flight Training

Objective:
For the student to demonstrate competency in passing the multi-engine checkride.

Content
____ Preflight
____ Differential taxiing
____ Starting and runup checks
____ Simulated engine failure on takeoff roll
____ Short-field takeoff
____ Normal and crosswind takeoff
____ Engine failure at V_Y climb
____ Engine failure at V_X climb
____ V_{MC} demonstration
____ Drag demonstration
____ Steep turns
____ Slow flight
____ Stalls
____ Spin awareness
____ 4 basic maneuvers on instruments
____ Engine shut down and re-start
____ Engine failure in simulated go-around
____ Engine failure in landing configuration
____ Engine failure on approach
____ Simulated feathered landing
____ Simulated single-engine landing
____ 2-engine instrument approach (precision or nonprecision), instrument students only
____ Single-engine approach (precision or nonprecision), instrument students only
____ Go-around procedures
____ Normal and/or crosswind landing
____ Short-field approach and landing
____ Postflight procedures

Completion Standards
All maneuvers must be completed according to Practical Test Standards, and the Multi-Engine Written Exam must be passed with a minimum 80% score (*See* Appendix B).

Appendix B

Written Exam for Multi-Engine Checkout

There is no knowledge test for the multi-engine rating, as you know. However, many FBOs have a written exam pilots must take and pass before renting or checking out in the twin. For further guidance, use ASA's *Multi-Engine Oral Exam Guide*.

1. After a normal liftoff with no obstacles ahead, climb at

   A—V_{XSE}.
   B—V_{YSE}.
   C—V_Y.

2. The alternator on each engine is capable of supplying 100 percent of the airplane's electrical requirements. (true, false)

3. Takeoff performance charts are based on

   A— a rolling start.
   B— the brakes being locked until the takeoff power setting is reached.
   C— smooth power application as the airplane accelerates.

4. Takeoff performance charts are based on

   A—temperature, wind, and pressure altitude.
   B—weight, temperature, and field elevation.
   C—temperature, weight, wind, and pressure altitude.

5. What speed should be maintained on final approach to a short field?

   A—V_{MC}
   B—V_Y
   C—Manufacturer's recommended approach speed

6. With one propeller feathered, which bank angle will result in the greatest rate of climb?

   A— 4°
   B—5°
   C—2°

7. The single engine service ceiling is

   A—the maximum altitude at which the airplane can climb 100 fpm.
   B—the maximum altitude at which the airplane can climb 50 fpm.
   C—the maximum altitude at which the airplane can sustain a climb.

8. What is the result of pulling the throttles to idle on short final with the propeller control full forward?

   A—Disturbed airflow over the horizontal stabilizer, degrading elevator effectiveness.
   B—Reduced stopping distance.
   C—Increased braking effectiveness.

9. When the manufacturer establishes V_{MC},

   A— landing gear is down, flaps are at takeoff setting.
   B— landing gear is retracted, flaps are at takeoff setting.
   C— landing gear down, flaps retracted.

10. What is V_{SSE}?

   A—Rotation speed on takeoff.
   B—V_{MC} plus 5 knots.
   C—minimum safe speed for an intentional engine cut.

11. Your multi-engine airplane has a maximum gross weight of less than 6,000 pounds and a V_{SO} of less than 61 knots. What single-engine climb performance does the FAA require at sea level, under standard atmospheric conditions?

   A—No climb performance is required; the airplane must be controllable.
   B—A rate of .0127 x V_{SO}.
   C—A minimum climb rate of 50 feet per minute with one propeller feathered.

12. When an engine fails on a multi-engine airplane, the loss of performance is

   A—50 percent.
   B—80 percent.
   C—a function of weight.

13. If you calculate that the accelerate-stop distance is greater than the available runway length, and the density altitude is above the single-engine service ceiling, what action should you take?

   A—Accelerate to $V_{Y(SE)}$ before rotating for liftoff.
   B—Offload passengers or cargo, or wait for cooler conditions.
   C—Plan to lift off as soon as possible.

14. In a multi-engine airplane with normally-aspirated engines, V_{MC} (increases, decreases) with increasing altitude.

   _____

15. Assume that you are landing with the right engine's propeller feathered; the wind is calm. As you reduce the left engine's throttle to idle after touchdown, (right, left) rudder pressure will be required.

   _____

16. The most common cause of engine failure in cruising flight is

   A—ignition problem.
   B—mechanical failure.
   C—fuel exhaustion/starvation.

17. Which engine instrument presents the best indication of engine failure during the takeoff roll?

   A—Manifold pressure gauge
   B—Exhaust gas temperature gauge
   C—Tachometer

It will be necessary for you to become intimately familiar with the aircraft's operating characteristics and systems. Answers to the following questions can be found by researching the Pilot Operating Handbook for the aircraft.

18. Define the following speeds and their values for your aircraft:

   V_{FE} _____

   _____

   V_{LE} _____

   _____

   V_{LO} _____

   _____

   V_{LOF} _____

   _____

   V_{NE} _____

   _____

V_{MC} _____

_____

V_{NO} _____

_____

V_R _____

_____

V_{SO} _____

_____

V_S _____

_____

V_{S1} _____

_____

V_X _____

_____

V_{XSE} _____

_____

V_Y _____

_____

V_{YSE} _____

_____

V_{SSE} _____

_____

V_A _____

_____

19. Does this aircraft require a positive single-engine climb rate?

_____

_____

20. What is the service ceiling for this aircraft? Single-engine service ceiling? Absolute ceiling?

_____

_____

_____

_____

21. What is the accelerate-stop distance required for this airplane?

_____

_____

22. Calculate the total takeoff distance required to clear a 50-foot obstacle.

_____

_____

23. What is the accelerate-stop distance if an engine failure occurs at takeoff decision speed?

_____

24. What is the accelerate-go distance if an engine failure occurs at takeoff decision speed?

_____

25. Calculate the total time, distance traveled, and fuel burned in a standard cruise climb to 10,000 feet.

_____

_____

26. Determine the fuel consumption, range, and endurance of this airplane.

_____

_____

27. What is the time and point of descent from cruise altitude to pattern altitude for this airplane?

_____

_____

28. Define the following terms and their values for your aircraft:

maximum takeoff weight _____

_____

maximum landing weight _____

_____

basic empty weight _____

_____

maximum allowable zero fuel weight _____

_____

29. Calculate a weight and balance computation for your aircraft using the following data: pilot and copilot, passengers, fuel and oil, baggage. Also, calculate a weight and balance computation for after 2 hours of flight.

_____

_____

_____

_____

_____

_____

30. Which is the critical engine in this airplane?

_____

31. Describe the procedures for recovering from an inadvertent spin.

_____

_____

32. Describe the procedures for an engine failure on takeoff, immediately before takeoff, and below V_{MC}.

_____

_____

_____

_____

_____

_____

33. Where are the emergency exits for this airplane?

_____

_____

34. How are the various flight controls operated?

ailerons _____

_____

elevator _____

_____

rudder _____

_____

35. What type of trim system is installed in this airplane?

_____

_____

36. What procedure should be followed if loss of elevator control occurs?

_____

_____

37. What type of wing flaps are used on this aircraft and how do they operate?

_____

_____

38. What is the maximum degree of flap extension available? What is the maximum flap extension for takeoff?

_____

_____

39. What kind of ice protection does this aircraft have?

_____

_____

40. What source of power is utilized for the landing gear system for extension and retraction operations? How does the manual system work?

_____

_____

_____

_____

41. How is inadvertent gear retraction on the ground prevented?

_____

_____

42. What are normal climb and cruise power settings?

_____

_____

43. How are the propellers synchronized in flight?

_____

_____

44. Describe the procedure for feathering a propeller on an inoperative engine (for both the inoperative and operative engine sides).

_____

_____

_____

45. Describe the in-flight engine restart procedures.

_____

_____

_____

46. What are the capacities of the fuel tanks (usable and total)?

_____

_____

47. Is it possible to crossfeed fuel from one engine to the other?

_____

_____

48. What equipment is considered hydraulic on this aircraft?

_____

_____

49. During the before-takeoff static runup, what is the normal drop expected when checking the magnetos?

_____

_____

50. What type of cabin heating system is this aircraft equipped with?

_____

_____

51. What are the minimum and maximum safe oil capacities? oil temperatures and pressures? What type of oil is used in this system?

_____

_____

_____

_____

_____

_____

_____

52. What aircraft system failures will cause the autopilot to operate erratically?

_____

_____

53. Is it possible to manually overpower the autopilot?

_____

_____

Appendix C

Answers to Review Questions

Chapter 1

1. Answer C is correct. The 12,500-pound figure found in the regulations separates "small" airplanes from "large" airplanes—number of engines is not a factor.

2. Answer C is correct. The drag of the windmilling prop and the loss of discharge air over the wing cause the airplane to yaw and roll toward the failed engine.

3. Answer C is correct. An airplane weighing more than 6,000 pounds or which has a stall speed greater than 60 knots must demonstrate a positive climb rate under standard conditions—no specific rate is required—but a "light" twin must simply be controllable.

4. Answer B is correct. This is the reason why the "drag items," (gear, flaps, windmilling prop) must be cleaned up.

5. Answer B is correct. Drag caused by skin friction, cooling drag, etc., is close to zero during the takeoff run and increases with airspeed.

6. Answer B is correct. The descending blade has a greater angle of attack than the ascending blade. You know that a greater angle of attack means greater lift—on a propeller the force of lift is exerted along the longitudinal axis, and it is referred to as thrust because it forces air to the rear.

7. Answer A is correct. A windmilling propeller is, in effect, a solid disc; a stopped propeller creates less drag than a windmilling prop, but more drag than a feathered prop.

8. Answer C is correct. With the descending blades of both propellers equally distant from the airplane's centerline, neither engine is critical.

9. True. The pilot would have to take a checkride in an airplane with wing-mounted engines and have the "Centerline Thrust Only" restriction removed.

10. Answer A is correct. You lose 50 percent of the power, but 80 percent of the climb performance.

Chapter 2

1. Answer B is correct. Poor fuel planning or mismanagement of the fuel system leading to fuel exhaustion (all tanks empty) or starvation (running on an empty tank while other tanks still have fuel) is the leading cause of bent metal on twins.

2. False. Each alternator is rated to carry 80 percent of the total electrical load.

3. True. Although fuel-injected engines cannot develop carburetor ice, their intakes can ice over due to wet snow or ice. Alternate air must be selected, manually or automatically.

4. Answer C is correct. If some mishap dumped all of the oil overboard, wouldn't you want to prop to move toward the feathered position?

5. Answer B is correct. Something to think about when deciding whether or not to let a tank run dry.

6. Answer A is correct. You still have to move the prop control into the feather position just in case there is a temporary hiccup in the oil supply.

7. It releases oil, stored under pressure, into the prop hub. It is a one-shot deal; if the prop does not unfeather, try the starter and look for a place to land.

8. Answer C is correct. Answers A and B are the opposite of the remedies available.

9. Answer A is correct. You can't be sure, and you should never leave the ground in an airplane with a questionable system. Air or gas pressure starts the feathering action, helped by counterweights—but the counterweights can't do the job by themselves. Take the time to do a thorough pretakeoff check.

10. Answer B is correct. Under 14 CFR Part 23, a fuel gauge must read empty when it contains only unusable fuel; there are no other accuracy requirements.

Chapter 3

1. Answer B is correct. Think long and hard before taking off from a runway that is not much longer than the book accelerate-go figure. Better to slide off the end of the runway than to find out too late that the airplane won't climb on one engine.

2. Answer A is correct. Weight will make it longer, as will uphill slope and high density altitude. Less weight, cooler temperature, and increasing headwind are all favorable factors.

3. Answer B is correct. V_{MC} decreases with increasing altitude, while indicated stall speed remains constant. That means there will be an altitude at which the airplane will stall and do a V_{MC} roll at the same time, and you will be too busy to figure out which is which.

4. No. Under those conditions, takeoff weight should be 3,180 pounds or less. Offload fuel or passengers (passengers are easier to offload).

5. Yes. My CG position is 90.6 inches; yours may vary. If something goes wrong, you will have to fly around for awhile before landing because the takeoff weight is greater than the maximum landing weight; but you would have to weigh (no pun intended) that decision against the seriousness of the problem.

6. Answer B is correct. It is the drag of the windmilling prop and the thrust of the operating engine that cause the yaw. Loss of lift due to discharge air from the failed engine's prop does not occur instantaneously, but yaw does. Your corrective actions should be full rudder against the yaw and whatever aileron it takes to maintain control.

7. My answer is 300 feet per minute, which isn't bad until you compare it with Figure 3-10 and learn that under the same conditions, the airplane would climb about 1,400 feet per minute. Always calculate the engine-out climb rate to determine if a takeoff is safe—if the airplane can get out of the departure airport with a failed engine, it can certainly do the job if both are running.

8. I get about 800 feet. I would want 2,000 feet of pavement, even before figuring out the accelerate-stop.

9. I get 2,500 feet; my estimate was wrong. Now I want 3,000 feet of pavement. Calculating an accelerate-go is a waste of time—you can't rely on any light twin to climb after losing an engine on the runway.

10. The manufacturer provides information that has been tested. If the airplane will not accelerate-go at any weight or density altitude, no chart will be provided.

Chapter 4

1. False. Take your time, check one engine at a time so that you can hear any unusual noises.

2. False again. It is good manners, and potentially less harmful to your pocketbook, to pull a twin out of its tiedown space manually. The smallest ding can be very expensive.

3. Answer B is correct. Gasoline of any octane rating will evaporate quickly, while jet fuel will feel greasy. Another way to test is to place a couple of drops of the suspect fuel on a piece of paper—gas will evaporate, leaving a dye stain, while kerosene will make an expanding greasy spot.

4. Answer C is correct. Unless a piece of equipment is installed as standard on each airplane of a given model, its operating instructions will be added to the POH as a supplement. A wise pilot makes a checklist that includes *everything* that should be checked before takeoff.

5. My answer would be B. If the airplane will not climb on one engine under the existing conditions, what difference does it make how long the runway is or whether I can keep going if an engine fails?

Chapter 5

1. I get two percent, or 20 feet per 1,000 feet of forward progress (120 feet per nautical mile). The Fahrenheit temperature is 67, which isn't really hot, and 2,000 feet is not a high pressure altitude, but the airplane is going to be almost nine miles from the airport before it has gained 1,000 feet. If this imaginary airport was in an urban area or surrounded by mountains, the pilot would be in trouble. Offload fuel or passengers. Note that gradient is in percent, not degrees. Two degrees would be 200 feet per nautical mile.

2. Answer C is correct. The manifold pressure gauge and tachometer will continue to show takeoff values even if an engine is failing; the exhaust gas temperature will drop as soon as power begins to decrease.

3. Answer C is correct. The best answer is "whatever gives the best climb performance," but it will be closer to two degrees than it will be to five degrees.

4. Answer B is correct. You will invariably lose speed during the cleanup process, so climbing at V_Y lets the speed bleed off to V_{YSE} while you are handling the situation.

5. Answer B is correct. "Dead foot, dead engine" is as good a rule as any. Just don't pull the prop control into feather until you are sure you are reaching for the correct knob.

6. Using the starter is your first choice, of course, because little or no loss of altitude is involved. The second option is diving until the propeller windmills, then turning on the magnetos and richening the mixture, in that order. Keep the power setting low until the engine has had a chance to warm up.

7. V_{MC} and V_{YSE}. Remember, V_{SSE} is an airspeed that only applies to a training situation—intentional engine shutdown by an instructor. The closer you are to V_{YSE} when you rotate, the better off you will be if an engine fails.

8. Absolutely true. If you perform a rolling takeoff, without setting the brakes, the book performance numbers are meaningless.

9. About the same, which is why looking at the manifold pressure gauge to determine which engine has failed is a waste of time. When the engine is started, the MAP gauge drops to 10 inches or so, and it increases toward the local barometric pressure as the throttle is opened to develop takeoff power. When the engine quits, the throttle is still open, and the manifold pressure does not change.

10. Answer C is correct. The factory test pilot was limited to answer A, when determining V_{MC}; answer B is a good answer, but you should not have any specific bank angle in mind—just maintain control and accept some loss of altitude.

Chapter 6

1. Answer B is correct. This is to avoid ring flutter. Insofar as high rpm and high manifold pressure is concerned, refer to the manufacturer's recommendation. There is a lot of bad word-of-mouth information about power settings (*see* Figure 6-1, Page 6-2).

2. Answer A is correct, according to the *Airplane Flying Handbook*. 14 CFR 61.31 refers to "maximum operating altitude or service ceiling, whichever is lower," but there is no definition of service ceiling in the regs.

3. Answer C is correct. When the airplane has descended to a density altitude equal to its single-engine absolute ceiling it *should* stop descending—but don't count on it. Any maneuvering will cost altitude that is very difficult to regain.

4. Answer B is correct. With more weight to lift, the airplane can't gain as much altitude—a good reason to stay below gross weight.

5. Answer A is correct. You know that load factor increases with bank angle, and in a steep descent you don't want objects flying around the cabin or fuel intakes unporting because of negative G-forces.

6. Answer B is correct. Never let regulatory concerns outweigh your responsibility for the safe conduct of your flight. Unless ATC gives you priority over other aircraft, no paperwork will ensue.

7. Answer B is correct. The CHT reacts far too slowly to use as a guide, and the fuel flow gauges actually measure pressure, not flow rate. The EGT reacts quickly (although not instantly) when the mixture is changed.

Chapter 7

1. A—increase; B—increase; C—increase; D—decrease; E—increase

2. Answer B is correct. Apply the brakes too early and you will scrub rubber off the tires; wait too long and maximum braking might not be enough. Get rid of the kinetic energy as soon as possible.

3. My answer is 2,500 feet—yours may vary (note that the obstacle height lines are not applicable for intermediate heights—*all* obstacles are at least 50 feet high). Under these conditions, a hard-surfaced runway a minimum of 4,000 feet long is called for by a prudent pilot; add a minimum of 50 percent to the calculated distance.

4. Answer B is correct. With the wind only 30 degrees off runway heading, almost all of the wind is headwind; add one-half the gust (15) to your normal approach speed.

5. Upwind. The airplane wants to weathercock into the wind, so you oppose the tendency by adding power on the upwind side.

6. All three. Never pull the power back to less than 11-12" of manifold pressure to avoid flat-plate drag.

7. The best answer is B, because by the time you are on short final, the power setting should be below prop governing range and airport neighbors will not hear a br-a-a-a-p as you move the prop control forward. Unless there is some reason to anticipate a go-around (cow on the runway, airplane at the hold line, variable visibility), why move the prop control at all?

Appendix D

Further Study in FAA Source Material

AC 61-9B — Pilot Transition Courses for Complex Single Engine and Light Twin Engine Airplanes

Date: **1974**

Preface

This publication is intended for use by certificated airplane pilots who wish to transition to more complex single engine or light twin engine airplanes.

An extremely wide range is available today in the single engine class and in the light twin engine class of airplanes. Change from the simple to the sophisticated has occurred rapidly in recent years. Pilots who have been inactive or who have not been introduced to the more modern airplanes are encouraged to follow the syllabus of training offered in this advisory circular. Greater knowledge and skills are needed for the efficient and safe operation of today's more powerful aircraft.

This publication is offered as a guide to the procedures and standards to be followed for a thorough and comprehensive checkout in these airplanes. The conscientious application and adherence to the scope of coverage recommended in the syllabus should result in a more competent, effective, and efficient pilot.

The transition courses have been prepared by the Flight Standards Service of the Federal Aviation Administration and issued as Advisory Circular 61-9B.

Comments regarding this publication should be directed to Department of Transportation, Federal Aviation Administration, Flight Standards Technical Division, P.O. Box 25082, Oklahoma City, Oklahoma 73125.

Training for Checkouts

Pilots preparing to check out in additional types of airplanes may find it helpful to follow a prescribed set of procedures and standards in training. This guide outlines a course of training for each of the two classes of airplanes: the complex single engine and the light twin engine.

This training should be conducted by a competent flight instructor who is certificated in the class of airplane and who is thoroughly familiar with the make and model. Characteristics of classes of airplanes as well as makes and models vary considerably, one from another.

While this guide is complete in its outline of the material to be covered, the recommended syllabus for transition training is to be considered flexible. The arrangement of the subject matter may be changed and the emphasis may be shifted to fit the qualifications of the trainee, the airplane involved, and the circumstances of the training situation, provided the prescribed proficiency standards are achieved.

The training times indicated in the syllabuses are based on the capabilities of a pilot who is currently active and fully meets the present requirements for the issuance of at least a private pilot certificate. The time periods may be reduced for pilots with higher qualifications, or increased for pilots who do not meet the current certification requirements or who have had little recent flight experience.

Complex Single Engine Airplanes

The syllabus in figure 1 is designed to prepare a certificated single engine pilot, without previous experience in "complex" airplanes, to operate one such airplane type competently.

For purposes of this syllabus, a "complex" single engine airplane is one equipped with flaps, a controllable propeller, and a retractable landing gear.

Figure 1. Complex Single Engine Airplane Transition Training Syllabus.

Ground Instruction, 1 hour
1. Operations sections of flight manual.
2. Line inspection.
3. Cockpit familiarization.

Flight Instruction, 1 hour
1. Flight training maneuvers.
2. Takeoffs, Landings and Go-Arounds.

Directed Practice*, {none}

Ground Instruction, 1 hour
1. Aircraft loading, limitations, and servicing.
2. Instruments, radio, and special equipment.
3. Aircraft systems.

Flight Instruction, 1 hour
1. Emergency operations.
2. Control by reference to instruments.
3. Use of radio and autopilot.

Directed Practice*, 1 hour
As assigned by flight instructor.

Ground Instruction, 1 hour
1. Performance section of flight manual.
2. Cruise control.
3. Review.

Flight Instruction, 1 hour
1. Short & Soft Field Takeoffs & Landings.
2. Maximum Performance operations.

Directed Practice*, 1 hour
As assigned by flight instructor.

1 hour
Checkout

*The directed practice indicated may be conducted solo or with a safety pilot, at the discretion of the instructor.

Light Twin Engine Airplanes

The syllabus in figure 2 may be used for either of two purposes; (1) to check out a private or commercial pilot who holds a multiengine rating on a new type of light twin engine airplane; or (2) to prepare a private or commercial pilot without previous multi-engine experience to take the required multiengine class rating flight test from a qualified pilot examiner or FAA inspector. The training program assumes that the student is currently qualified in at least one complex airplane type.

To be fully effective, this syllabus should be followed and the training conducted by a flight instructor familiar with the performance and characteristics of light "twins" in general and with the significance and use of critical performance speeds. The instructor should be fully qualified in the airplane type concerned.

Figure 2. Light Twin Engine Airplane Transition Training Syllabus.

Ground Instruction, 2 hours
1. Operations sections of flight manual.
2. Minimum engine out control speed.
3. Climb Speeds.
4. Line Inspection.
5. Cockpit familiarization.

Flight Instruction, 2 hours
1. Flight training maneuvers.
2. Takeoffs, Landings and Go-arounds.

Directed Practice*, {none}

Ground Instruction, 1 hour
1. Aircraft systems, radio, instruments, autopilot, and emergency gear.

Flight Instruction, 1 hour
1. Engine feathering or shut-down.
2. Enroute engine operations.
3. Control by instruments.
4. Use of radio and autopilot.

Directed Practice*, 1 hour
As assigned by flight instructor.

Continued

Ground Instruction, 1 hour
1. Performance section of flight manual.
2. Aircraft servicing, loading, and limitations.

Flight Instruction, 1 hour
1. Emergencies, including engine failure on take-off
2. Short and soft field takeoffs and landings.

Directed Practice*, 1 hour
As assigned by flight instructor.

Ground Instruction, 1 hour
Review.

Flight Instruction, 1 hour
Checkout for flight test recommendation.

2 hours
Multiengine Rating Test
*The directed practice indicated may be flown solo or with a safety pilot, at the discretion of the instructor.

Checkout Procedures and Standards
Preflight Examination

Before taking off on his checkout flight, a pilot should pass a test on the airplane to be used, its systems, limitations, performance, emergency procedures, and approved operating procedures. This test may consist in part of a written quiz, or may be wholly an oral examination by the check pilot.

The preflight examination should cover at least:

a. The approved Airplane Flight Manual, Owner's Handbook, and official placards which prescribe operating procedures and limitations.

b. A working knowledge of cruising speeds at various altitudes, power settings, fuel consumption, endurance, takeoff and landing distances, and rates of climb and descent.

c. Normal and emergency operation of aircraft systems and special equipment.

d. Practical computation of various combinations of the permissible loadings using available loading diagrams or graphs.

e. A thorough line check of the airplane to be used, using a checklist provided by the manufacturer or operator. If no official checklist is available, the check must be made in accordance with an orderly procedure that covers all critical items. The presence of all required certificates, documents, and placards, and the fuel and oil supply should be checked. The inspection must cover all airworthiness items that can be investigated by an external examination. The pilot must know the significance of all unsatisfactory items noted, and the appropriate corrective action to be initiated by the pilot for each.

Flight Maneuvers and Procedures
Coordination and Planning Maneuvers

Standard coordination and planning maneuvers should be performed to demonstrate that the pilot is familiar with the airplane's performance and flight control responses. These may be very simple maneuvers or relatively complex, ranging from medium banked turns (20 deg to 30 deg) and 720 degree power turns to chandelles and lazy eights. Coordination and planning maneuvers should be demonstrated in both directions, at various speeds within the normal airspeed range of the airplane, and with various flap and landing gear configurations.

The pilot should perform all standard coordination maneuvers without completely deflecting the ball outside the center reference lines of a standard slip-skid indicator. Prolonged turns should be stopped within 10 degrees of the assigned heading, and altitude should be maintained within 100 ft of the assigned altitude during level flight maneuvers.

Ground Pattern Maneuvers

Any of several standard training maneuvers may be used to demonstrate that the pilot is able to accurately control this path over the ground, and anticipate turns to new courses. Among these are S-turns across a road, rectangular courses, turns about a point, or eights around pylons. The demonstration of rectangular courses may be accomplished in the airport traffic pattern if other traffic permits.

The pilot should be able to maintain the desired track over the ground by crabbing into any existing wind, anticipating the crab on recovery from turns, and maintaining proper coordination of the rudder and aileron controls. During pattern maneuvers, he should hold his altitude within 100 ft of the altitude assigned. He should be able to operate by ground references without prolonged diversion of attention from his engine instruments and his vigilance for other traffic.

Flight at Minimum Controllable and Landing Approach Airspeeds

Climbs, descents, and level flight on straight courses and in medium banked turns should be demonstrated at minimum controllable and landing approach airspeeds with appropriate power settings. The minimum controllable speed used should be such that any further reduction in airspeed or increase in load factor would result in immediate indications of a stall. The landing approach speed should be 1.3 to 1.4 times the power-off stalling speed in cruise configuration.

The pilot should also demonstrate the smooth, prompt transition from cruising to landing approach airspeed, and the use of flaps and gear to effect descents from level flight at approach speed without changing the power setting.

The pilot should be able to control his airplane positively and smoothly at the appropriate speed, and maintain an airspeed within 5 kts. of the desired speed. He should make the transition from cruising speed to landing approach speed without varying more than 10 deg from the desired heading nor more than 100 ft from the desired altitude.

Stalls from All Normally Anticipated Flight Attitudes

The recovery from stalls entered with and without power should be demonstrated. Emphasis should be placed on the recovery from the three critical stall situations: takeoff and departure, approach to landing, and accelerated stalls.

Recovery should be initiated as soon as the first physical indication of a stall is recognized, except that in single engine airplanes at least one stall should be allowed to develop until the nose pitches through level flight attitude before recovery is initiated. Stall warners should be deactivated for stall demonstrations, except in airplanes for which they are required equipment. Stall recoveries should be demonstrated with and without power, and with various configurations of gear and flaps.

Stall recovery performance will be evaluated on the basis of prompt stall recognition and smooth positive recovery action. The pilot's ability to establish a precise stall entry situation is not a requirement, so he may be coached or assisted in setting up the required stall situations. Recovery should be effected smoothly with coordinated use of the flight controls and the least loss of altitude consistent with prompt recovery of positive flight control.

Maximum Performance Operations

Short field and soft field takeoffs and landings should be required in accordance with procedures specified in the Airplane Flight Manual or Owner's Handbook and the FAA Flight Test Guides. Special attention should be paid to flap and trim settings, power usage, and the use of correct airspeeds. The use of the best angle of climb and rate of climb airspeeds becomes more critical as speeds increase and the cleanness and efficiency of airplanes improve.

In multiengine airplanes, it is important for the pilot to know and observe two sets of performance speeds: one for normal use and one applicable to operation with one engine inoperative. To demonstrate maximum performance short field and soft field takeoffs, liftoff should be initiated just below the all engine best angle of climb speed, unless it is slower than the engine out minimum control speed, in which case the engine out minimum control speed should be used. The best all-engine angle of climb speed should be attained, and maintained to the height of an assumed obstruction, such as a fence or row of trees, after which normal climb speed should be smoothly attained.

Optimum power, loading, and flap settings for various density altitudes may be found in the Airplane Flight Manual or Owner's Handbook. In efficient high performance airplanes the proper application of these factors will produce a significantly better performance which can be readily demonstrated.

Control by Reference to Flight Instruments

During his checkout in a new airplane type, the pilot should demonstrate his ability to control the airplane manually in flight by reference to instruments. No IFR flight procedures, as such, need be performed, but the pilot should be able to perform the following maneuvers smoothly and with confidence, using all instrumentation installed in the airplane.

1. Level flight, climbs, turns, and descents. Climbs and descents should be performed at constant airspeeds, using standard rates of climb and descent, usually 400 to 500 ft per minute depending on the performance of the airplane used. Turns should be performed at the standard rate, and be stopped within 10 deg of an assigned heading.

2. Recovery from unusual attitudes. The pilot should be able to recover positively and smoothly from both nose-high and nose-low unusual attitudes established by the check pilot. The attitudes used should be moderate displacements from normal flight, characteristic of errors due to diversion of attention from the instruments during instrument flight. They should include climbing turns, incipient power spirals, increasing or decreasing angles of bank, and significant variations in airspeed. Recovery should be smoothly effected to a straight and level flight by reference to instruments without imposing arty excessive load factors or involving airspeeds which are dangerously close to the placarded maximum speed or to stalling speed.

Use of Radio, Autopilot, and Special Equipment

Radio

The pilot should demonstrate the use of all radio equipment in the airplane for communications and VFR navigation. The pilot should be able to operate each transmitter and receiver and use radio navigation equipment to establish bearings and tracks by radio signals received. He should be able to operate DME (distance measuring equipment) and transponder if installed, and have a general knowledge of their principles of operation and limitations.

Operation of radio equipment should include a knowledge of the location of associated fuses and circuit breakers, and how to replace or reset them. It should also include a general knowledge of the capabilities and limitations of each radio installation.

Autopilot

If an autopilot is installed, the pilot should demonstrate its use, including indexing, engaging, disengaging, and resetting course and altitude while it is engaged, if permissible.

He should also demonstrate a working knowledge of its limitations, possible malfunctions, overpowering by the pilot, and emergency disengagement.

Special Equipment

The pilot should be familiar with and demonstrate the use of any special equipment installed, such as flight director, oxygen systems, pressurization systems, and automatic feathering devices. The demonstration should include a working knowledge of the limitations and the common failures of the equipment. and of the special precautions to be taken in equipment operation.

Emergencies

Emergency Operation of Aircraft Systems

The emergency operation of all airplane systems should be performed when practicable. Such operations should include the emergency extension of gear and flaps, the use of boost pumps, fuel transfer, replacement or resetting of fuses or circuit breakers, and the isolation of specified electrical circuits. The operation of pressure fire extinguisher systems, and such operations as the emergency extension of the landing gear by CO_2 should be explained and simulated. The emergency operation of the pressurization and oxygen system should be covered on airplanes so equipped.

Forced Landings
(Single Engine Airplanes Only)

The examiner should close the throttle smoothly at unannounced times during the checkout, and request the applicant to proceed as he would in the event of an actual power failure. No simulated forced landing will be given where an actual safe landing would be impossible. At least once, during the checkout, the pilot should demonstrate a landing from a glide with the engine throttled at traffic pattern altitude. Performance will be evaluated on the basis of the pilot's judgment, planning, technique, and safety.

Engine Out Emergencies
(Multiengine Airplanes)

A pilot checking out for the first time in a multiengine airplane should practice and become thoroughly familiar with the control and performance problems which result from the failure of power in one engine during any normal flight condition. He should practice the control operations and precautions necessary in such cases, and be prepared to demonstrate these on his multiengine rating flight test.

1. Propeller feathering or engine shutdown. The feathering of one propeller should be performed in all airplanes equipped with propellers which can be safely feathered and unfeathered in flight. If the airplane used is not equipped with featherable propellers, or, is equipped with propellers which cannot be safely feathered and unfeathered in flight, one engine should be shut down in accordance with the procedures in the Airplane Flight Manual or Owner's Handbook. The prescribed propeller setting should be used, and the emergency setting of all ignition, electrical, hydraulic, and fire extinguisher systems should be demonstrated.

   Proficiency will be evaluated on the basis of the control of heading, airspeed, and altitude; the prompt identification of a simulated power failure; and the accuracy of shutdown and restart procedures as prescribed in the Airplane Flight Manual or Owner's Handbook.

   Feathering for training and checkout purposes should be performed only under such conditions and at such altitudes and positions that a safe landing on an established airport could be readily accomplished in the event of difficulty in unfeathering.

2. Engine out minimum control speed (V_{MC}) demonstration (small multiengine airplanes only). Every small multiengine airplane checkout (except airplanes with centerline thrust) should include a demonstration of the airplane's engine out minimum control speed. The engine out minimum control speed given in the Airplane Flight Manual, Owner's Handbook, or other manufacturer's published limitations is determined during original airplane certification under conditions specified in the Federal Aviation Regulations. These conditions are normally not duplicated during training or on flight tests. It is also recognized that in all airplanes there is a density altitude above which the stalling speed is higher than the engine out minimum control speed.

A thorough discussion, prior to flight, of the factors affecting engine out minimum control speed will be required. This discussion and the following demonstration will satisfy the operational objective in regard to identifying the controllability problems which can result from flight at too slow an airspeed when an engine failure occurs. The demonstration should be performed at a safe altitude. This maneuver will demonstrate the engine out minimum control speed for the existing conditions and makes no effort to duplicate V_{MC} as determined for airplane certification.

With the gear and flaps tip, the airplane will be placed in a climb attitude representative of that following a normal takeoff. With both engines developing as near rated takeoff power as possible, power on the critical engine (usually the left) will be reduced to idle (windmilling, not shutdown). The airspeed will then be reduced slowly with the elevators until directional control can no longer be maintained. At this point, recovery will be initiated by simultaneously reducing power on the operating engine and reducing the angle of attack by lowering the nose. Should indications of a stall occur prior to reaching this point, recovery will be initiated by reducing the angle of attack. In this case, a minimum engine out control speed demonstration is not possible under existing conditions.

If it is found that the minimum engine out control speed is reached before indications of a stall are encountered, the pilot should demonstrate his ability to control the airplane and initiate a safe climb in the event of a power failure at the published engine out minimum control speed.

For this demonstration, with the gear and flaps set for takeoff, the airspeed should be slowed at reduced power to the minimum speed determined above. Rated takeoff power should be applied smoothly, and a climb initiated at the minimum engine out minimum control speed specified in the approved Airplane Flight Manual or Owner's Handbook. The check pilot should throttle one engine to simulate a loss of power, and request the pilot to maintain heading and continue a climb (or minimum sink) at the engine out best rate of climb airspeed.

The gear and flaps should be retracted in accordance with the emergency procedures prescribed in the Airplane Flight Manual, or Owner's Handbook, and the throttle on the windmilling engine may be advanced sufficiently to simulate a feathered propeller (on airplanes with feathering propellers only).

Performance will be evaluated on the basis of the pilot's being able to maintain his heading within 15 deg and his bank within 10 deg, and the accuracy of his operation and trim procedures. Any attempt to continue level or climbing flight at less than the published minimum engine out control speed after a simulated or actual power failure will result in immediate disqualification on a flight test in a multiengine airplane.

3. Engine out best rate of climb demonstration. The pilot should practice and demonstrate the use of the best engine out rate of climb speed shown in the Airplane Flight Manual or Owner's Handbook.

This speed should be demonstrated with one engine set to simulate the drag of a feathered propeller or a propeller actually feathered, except that in airplanes without feathering propellers one engine should be cut off or idling. The

prescribed speed should be carefully maintained for at least 1 minute after the airspeed has stabilized, and the resulting gain or loss of altitude should be carefully noted. For comparison, climbs may be attempted at other airspeeds within the normal operating range of the airplane used.

4. Effects of configuration on engine out performance. The pilot should also practice and demonstrate the effects (on engine out performance) of various configurations of gear, flaps, and both; the use of carburetor heat; and the failure to feather the propeller on an inoperative engine. Each configuration should be maintained, at best engine out rate of climb speed long enough to determine its effect on the climb (or sink) achieved. Prolonged use of carburetor heat at high power settings should be avoided.

5. Maneuvering with an engine out. Engine out maneuvering is usually practiced in conjunction with the feathering demonstration described in para. 1, above. It is acceptable, however, to conduct this demonstration with one engine set to simulate the drag of a feathered propeller if the airplane is equipped with feathering propellers. In airplanes which are not so equipped, maneuvering should be demonstrated with an engine cut off completely, or idling.

Straight and level flight and medium (20 deg to 30 deg) banked turns toward and away from the inoperative engine should be practiced. The pilot should be able to maintain altitude within 100 ft of the initial altitude if the airplane is capable of level flight with an engine out, or the airspeed within 5 kts. of the best rate of climb speed in an airplane that is not capable of level flight under the existing conditions.

6. Approach and landing with an engine out. At least once during his checkout, the pilot should perform an approach and landing with an engine throttled to simulate the drag of a feathered propeller, or, if featherable propellers are not installed, an engine throttled to idling.

Continued

Evaluation will be based on the correct operation of the airplane systems, the appropriate handling of trim, observance of the proper traffic pattern or approach path, airspeed and altitude control, accuracy of touchdown, and control during rollout.

Emergency Descents
(Pressurized Airplanes Only)

During checkout in a pressurized airplane, the pilot should practice and demonstrate emergency descents, such as may be necessitated by explosive decompression, in accordance with procedures prescribed in the Airplane Flight Manual or Owner's Handbook.

Descents should be initiated and stabilized, but prolonged descents should be avoided because of possible hazard to air traffic. The airspeed or Mach number used for the demonstration should be approximately 10 percent less than the airplane's structural limitation (V_{MO}, M_{MO}) to provide a margin for error. When a Mach limitation is controlling at operational altitudes for the airplane used, the descents should be arranged to require the transition from the observance of a Mach limitation to an airspeed limitation. No emergency descents should be practiced near or through clouds.

Flight Instructor's Endorsements and Recommendations
Logbook Endorsements

A flight instructor who has checked out a certificated pilot in a new type of airplane, single engine or multiengine, should enter and certify the checkout in the pilot's logbook. Such certification should include the date, precise designation of the airplane type involved, and the extent of the checkout conducted. Figure 3 is an example of such a certification.

Checkout in Piper Comanche Model PA-24-260 in accordance with FAA Advisory Circular 61-9B Satisfactory, 3/14/74.

David Livingston, CFI 386423

Signed, CFI No.

Figure 3. Flight Instructor's Certification

Multiengine Rating Recommendation

A certificated flight instructor who has checked out a certificated pilot in a multiengine airplane should execute the certification in the pilot's logbook illustrated in figure 3.

If the pilot does not already hold a multiengine rating, the flight instructor should also provide him with an official recommendation for the multiengine rating practical test, using FAA Form 8420-3, as depicted in figure 4.

Instructor's Recommendation
I have personally instructed the applicant and consider him ready to take the test for which he is applying.

Date

Instructor's Signature

Certificate No.   Certificate Expires

Figure 4. Instructor's Recommendation

Graduation Certificate

An agency or operation that conducts transition courses for pilots, at pilot training clinics or in the course of its regular pilot training operations may wish to award formal graduation certificates in addition to the regular endorsements and recommendations. A sample for such a graduation certificate is illustrated in figure 5.

Graduation Certificate
This is to certify that

Pilot Name and Number
has satisfactorily completed each required stage of the approved course of training including the tests for those stages, and has received___ hours of multi-engine training.

_____ has graduated from the Federal Aviation Administration approved Multi-Engine Rating Course conducted by

School and Certificate Number

Chief Instructor   Date of Graduation

Figure 5. Graduation Certificate

AC 61-107 — Operations of Aircraft at Altitudes Above 25,000 Feet MSL and/or Mach Numbers (M_{MO}) Greater Than 0.75

Date: **01/23/91**   Initiated by: **AFS-840**

Foreword

1. **PURPOSE.** This advisory circular (AC) is issued to alert pilots transitioning to complex, high-performance aircraft which are capable of operating at high altitudes and high airspeeds of the need to be knowledgeable of the special physiological and aerodynamic considerations involved within this realm of operation.

2. **CANCELLATION.** AC 91-8B, Use of Oxygen by Aviation Pilots/Passengers, dated April 7, 1982, is cancelled.

3. **RELATED READING MATERIAL.** Additional information can be found in the latest edition of AC 67-2, Medical Handbook for Pilots.

4. **BACKGROUND.** On September 17, 1982, the National Transportation Safety Board (NTSB) issued a series of safety recommendations which included, among other things, that a minimum training curriculum be established for use at pilot schools covering pilots' initial transition into general aviation turbojet airplanes. Aerodynamics and physiological aspects of high-performance aircraft operating at high altitudes were among the subjects recommended for inclusion in this training curriculum. These recommendations were the result of an NTSB review of a series of fatal accidents which were believed to involve a lack of flightcrew knowledge and proficiency in general aviation turbojet airplanes capable of operating in a high-altitude environment. Although the near total destruction of physical evidence and the absence of installed flight recorders have inhibited investigators' abilities to pinpoint the circumstances which led to these accidents, the NTSB is concerned that a lack of flightcrew knowledge and proficiency in the subject matter of this AC were involved in either the initial loss of control or the inability to regain control, or both, of the aircraft. A requirement has been added to the Federal Aviation Regulations (FAR) Part 61 for high-altitude training of pilots who transition to any pressurized airplane that has a service ceiling or maximum operating altitude, whichever is lower, above 25,000 feet mean sea level (MSL). Recommended training in high-altitude operations that would meet the requirements of this regulation can be found in Chapter 1 of this AC.

5. **DEFINITIONS.**

   a. Aspect Ratio is the relationship between the wing chord and the wingspan. A short wingspan and wide wing chord equal a low aspect ratio.

   b. Drag Divergence is a phenomenon that occurs when an airfoil's drag increases sharply and requires substantial increases in power (thrust) to produce further increases in speed. This is not to be confused with MACH crit. The drag increase is due to the unstable formation of shock waves that transform a large amount of energy into heat and into pressure pulses that act to consume a major portion of the available propulsive energy (thrust). Turbulent air may produce a resultant increase in the coefficient of drag.

   c. Force is generally defined as the cause for motion or of change or stoppage of motion. The ocean of air through which an aircraft must fly has both mass and inertia and, thus, is capable of exerting tremendous forces on an aircraft moving through the atmosphere. When all of the above forces are equal, the aircraft is said to be in a state of equilibrium. For instance, when an aircraft is in level, unaccelerated 1 G flight, thrust and drag are equal, and lift and gravity (or weight plus aerodynamic downloads on the aircraft) are equal. Forces that act on any aircraft as the result of air resistance, friction, and other factors are:

Continued

(1) *Thrust.* The force required to counter-act the forces of drag in order to move an aircraft in forward flight.

(2) *Drag.* The force which acts in opposition to thrust.

(3) *Lift.* The force which sustains the aircraft during flight.

(4) *Gravity.* The force which acts in opposition to lift.

d. MACH, named after Ernst Mach, a 19th century Austrian physicist is the ratio of an aircraft's true speed as compared to the local speed of sound at a given time or place.

e. MACH Buffet is the airflow separation behind a shock-wave pressure barrier caused by airflow over flight surfaces exceeding the speed of sound.

f. MACH (or Aileron) Buzz is a term used to describe a shock induced flow separation of the boundary layer air before reaching the ailerons.

g. MACH Meter is an instrument designed to indicate MACH number. MACH indicating capability is incorporated into the airspeed indicator(s) of current generation turbine powered aircraft capable of MACH range speeds.

h. MACH number is a decimal number (M) representing the true airspeed (TAS) relationship to the local speed of sound (e.g., TAS 75 percent (0.75 M) of the speed of sound where 100 percent of the speed of sound is represented as MACH 1 (1.0 M)). The local speed of sound varies with changes in temperature.

i. MACH number (Critical) is the free stream MACH number at which local sonic flow such as buffet, airflow separation, and shock waves becomes evident. These phenomena occur above the critical MACH number, often referred to as MACH crit. These phenomena are listed as follows:

SUBSONIC MACH Numbers below 0.75
TRANSONIC MACH Numbers from 0.75 to 1.20
SUPERSONIC MACH Numbers from 1.20 to 5.0
HYPERSONIC MACH Numbers above 5.0

j. MACH Speed is the ratio or percentage of the TAS to the speed of sound (e.g., 1,120 feet per second (660 Knots (K)) at MSL). This may be represented by MACH number.

k. MACH Tuck is the result of an aftward shift in the center of lift causing a nose down pitching moment.

l. M_{MO} (MACH, maximum operation) is an airplane's maximum certificated MACH number. Any excursion past M_{MO}, whether intentional or accidental, may cause induced flow separation of boundary layer air over the ailerons and elevators of an airplane and result in a loss of control surface authority and/or control surface buzz or snatch.

m. Q-Corner or Coffin Corner is a term used to describe operations at high altitudes where low indicated airspeeds yield high true airspeeds (MACH number) at high angles of attack. The high angle of attack results in flow separation which causes buffet. Turning maneuvers at these altitudes increase the angle of attack and result in stability deterioration with a decrease in control effectiveness. The relationship of stall speed to MACH crit narrows to a point where sudden increases in angle of attack, roll rates, and/or disturbances; e.g., clear air turbulence, cause the limits of the airspeed envelope to be exceeded. Coffin corner exists in the upper portion of the maneuvering envelope for a given gross weight and G-force.

n. V_{MO} (Velocity maximum operation) is an airplane's indicated airspeed limit. Exceeding V_{MO} may cause aerodynamic flutter and G-load limitations to become critical during the dive recovery.

6. DISCUSSION.

a. *FAR Part 61* prescribes the knowledge and skill requirements for the various airman certificates and ratings, including category, class, and type ratings authorized to be placed thereon. The civil aircraft fleet consists of numerous aircraft capable of flight in the high-altitude environment. Certain knowledge elements pertaining to high-altitude flight are essential for the pilots of these aircraft. Pilots who fly in this realm of flight must receive training in the critical factors relating to safe flight operations in the high-altitude environment. These critical factors include knowledge of the special physiological and/or aerodynamic considerations which should be given to high-performance aircraft operating in the high-altitude environment. The high-altitude environment has different effects on the human body than those experienced at the lower altitudes. The aerodynamic characteristics of an aircraft in high-altitude flight may differ significantly from those of aircraft operated at the lower altitudes.

b. *Pilots who are not familiar with operations in the high-speed environment* are encouraged to obtain thorough and comprehensive training and a checkout in complex high-performance aircraft before engaging in extensive high-speed flight in such aircraft, particularly at high altitudes. The training should enable the pilot to become thoroughly familiar with aircraft performance charts and aircraft systems and procedures. The more critical elements of high-altitude flight planning and operations should also be reviewed. The aircraft checkout should enable the pilot to demonstrate a comprehensive knowledge of the aircraft performance charts, systems, emergency procedures, and operating limitations, along with a high degree of proficiency in performing all flight maneuvers and in-flight emergency procedures. The attainment of such knowledge and skill requirements by a pilot of high-performance aircraft should enhance the pilot's preparedness to transition to the operation of a high-speed aircraft in the high-altitude environment safely and efficiently.

7. SUMMARY.
It is beyond the scope of this AC to provide a more definitive treatment of the subject matter discussed herein. Rather, this AC will have served its purpose if it aids pilots in becoming familiar with the basic phenomena associated with high-altitude and high-speed flight. Pilots should recognize that greater knowledge and skills are needed for the safe and efficient operation of state-of-the-art turbine-powered aircraft at high altitude. Pilots are strongly urged to pursue further study from the many excellent textbooks, charts, and other technical reference material available through industry sources, and to obtain a detailed understanding of both physiological and aerodynamic factors which relate to the safe and efficient operation of the broad variety of high-altitude aircraft available today and envisioned for the future.

Thomas C. Accardi
Acting Director, Flight Standards Service

Table of Contents

Chapter 1. Recommendations High-Altitude Training

Chapter 1. Recommedations High-Altitude Training

1. **PURPOSE.** This chapter presents an outline for recommended high-altitude training that meets the requirements of FAR § 61.31(f). The actual training, which may be derived from this outline, should include both ground and flight training in high-altitude operations. Upon completion of the ground and flight training, the flight instructor who conducted the training should provide an endorsement in the pilot's logbook or training record, certifying that training in high-altitude operations was given. A sample high-altitude endorsement is available in the most recent version of AC 61-65, Certification: Pilots and Flight Instructors.

   a. **Although FAR § 61.31(f)** applies only to pilots who fly pressurized airplanes with a service ceiling or maximum operating altitude, whichever is lower, above 25,000 feet MSL, this training is recommended for all pilots who fly at altitudes above 10,000 feet MSL.

      (1) A service ceiling is the maximum height above MSL at which an airplane can maintain a rate of climb of 100 feet per minute under normal conditions.

      (2) All pressurized airplanes have a specified maximum operating altitude above which operation is not permitted. This maximum operating altitude is determined by flight, structural, powerplant, functional, or equipment characteristics. An airplane's maximum operating altitude is limited to 25,000 feet or lower unless certain airworthiness standards are met.

      (3) Maximum operating altitudes and service ceilings are specified in the Airplane Flight Manual.

   b. **The training** outlined in this chapter is designed primarily for light twin engine airplanes that fly at high altitudes but do not require type ratings. The training should, however, be incorporated into type rating courses for aircraft that fly above 25,000 feet MSL if the pilot has not already received training in high-altitude flight.

The training in this chapter does not encompass high-speed flight factors such as acceleration, G-forces, MACH, and turbine systems that do not apply to reciprocating engine and turboprop aircraft. Information on high-speed flight can be found in Chapter 2 of this AC.

2. **OUTLINE.** Additional information should be used to complement the training provided herein. The training outlined below, and explained in further detail in the remainder of this chapter, covers the minimum information needed by pilots to operate safely at high altitudes.

   a. *Ground Training.*

      (1) *The High-Altitude Flight Environment.*

      (i) Airspace.

      (ii) FAR.

      (2) *Weather.*

      (i) The atmosphere.

      (iii) Clouds and thunderstorms.

      (iv) Icing.

      (3) *Flight Planning and Navigation.*

      (i) Flight planning.

      (ii) Weather charts.

      (iii) Navigation.

      (iv) Navaids.

      (4) *Physiological Training.*

      (i) Respiration.

      (ii) Hypoxia.

      (iii) Effects of prolonged oxygen use.

      (iv) Decompression sickness.

      (v) Vision

      (vi) Altitude chamber (optional).

(5) *High-Altitude Systems and Components.*

(i) Turbochargers.

(ii) Oxygen and oxygen equipment.

(iii) Pressurization systems.

(iv) High-altitude components.

(6) *Aerodynamics and Performance Factors.*

(7) *Emergencies.*

(i) Decompressions.

(ii) Turbocharger malfunction.

(iii) Inflight fire.

(iv) Flight into severe turbulence or thunderstorms.

b. Flight Training.

(1) *Preflight Briefing.*

(2) *Preflight Planning.*

(i) Weather briefing and considerations.

(ii) Course plotting.

(iii) Airplane Flight Manual review.

(iv) Flight plan.

(3) *Preflight Inspection.*

(4) *Runup, Takeoff, and Initial Climb.*

(5) *Climb to High-Altitude and Normal Cruise Operations While Operating Above 25,000 Feet MSL.*

(6) *Emergencies.*

(i) Simulated rapid decompression.

(ii) Emergency descent.

(7) *Planned Descents.*

(8) *Shutdown Procedures.*

(9) *Postflight Discussion.*

3. GROUND TRAINING. Thorough ground training should cover all aspects of high-altitude flight, including the flight environment, weather, flight planning and navigation, physiological aspects of high-altitude flight, systems and equipment, aerodynamics and performance, and high-altitude emergencies. The ground training should include the history and causes of some past accidents and incidents involving the topics included in paragraph 2. Accident reports are available from the NTSB and some aviation organizations.

4. THE HIGH-ALTITUDE FLIGHT ENVIRONMENT. For the purposes of FAR § 61.31(f), flight operations conducted above 25,000 feet are considered to be high altitude. However, the high-altitude environment itself begins below 25,000 feet. For example, flight levels (FL) are used at and above 18,000 feet (e.g., FL 180) to indicate levels of constant atmospheric pressure in relation to a reference datum of 29.92" Hg. Certain airspace designations and Federal Aviation Administration (FAA) requirements become effective at different altitudes. Pilots must be familiar with these elements before operating in each realm of flight.

a. Airspace. Pilots of high-altitude aircraft are subject to three principle types of airspace at altitudes above 10,000 feet MSL. These are the Positive Control Area (PCA), which extends from FL 180 to FL 600; the Continental Control Area, which covers the continental United States above 14,500 feet MSL; and control zones that do not underlie the Continental Control Area, which extend upward from the surface and have no upper limit. (Other control zones terminate at the base of the Continental Control Area.)

b. Federal Aviation Regulations. In addition to the training required by FAR § 61.31(f), pilots of high-altitude aircraft should be familiar with FAR Part 91 regulations that apply specifically to flight at high altitudes.

(1) FAR § 91.215 requires that all aircraft operating within the continental United States at and above 10,000 feet MSL be equipped with

an operable transponder with Mode C capability (unless operating at or below 2,500 feet above ground level (AGL), below the PCA).

(2) FAR § 91.211(a) requires that the minimum flightcrew on civil aircraft of U.S. registry be provided with and use supplemental oxygen at cabin pressure altitudes above 12,500 feet MSL up to and including 14,000 feet MSL for that portion of the flight that is at those altitudes for more than 30 minutes. The required minimum flightcrew must be provided with and use supplemental oxygen at all times when operating an aircraft above 14,000 feet MSL. At cabin pressure altitudes above 15,000 feet MSL, all occupants of the aircraft must be provided with supplemental oxygen.

(3) FAR § 91.211(b) requires pressurized aircraft to have at least a 10-minute additional supply of supplemental oxygen for each occupant at flight altitudes above FL 250 in the event of a decompression. At flight altitudes above FL 350, one pilot at the controls of the airplane must wear and use an oxygen mask that is secured and sealed. The oxygen mask must supply oxygen at all times or must automatically supply oxygen when the cabin pressure altitude of the airplane exceeds 14,000 feet MSL. An exception to this regulation exists for two pilot crews that operate at or below FL 410. One pilot does not need to wear and use an oxygen mask if both pilots are at the controls and each pilot has a quick donning type of oxygen mask that can be placed on the face with one hand from the ready position and be properly secured, sealed, and operational within 5 seconds. If one pilot of a two pilot crew is away from the controls, then the pilot that is at the controls must wear and use an oxygen mask that is secured and sealed.

(4) FAR § 91.121 requires that aircraft use an altimeter setting of 29.92 at all times when operating at or above FL 180.

(5) FAR § 91.135 requires that all flights within the PCA be conducted under instrument flight rules (IFR) in an aircraft equipped for IFR and flown by a pilot who is rated for instrument flight.

(6) FAR § 91.159 and § 91.179 specify cruising altitudes and flight levels for respectively. For VFR flights between FL 180 to FL 290 (except within the PCA where VFR flight is prohibited), odd flight levels plus 500 feet should be flown if the magnetic course is 0 to 179, and even flight levels plus 500 feet should be flown if the magnetic course is 180 to 359. VFR flights above FL 290 should be flown at 4,000 foot intervals beginning at FL 300 if the magnetic course is 0 to 179 and FL 320 if the magnetic course is 180 to 359. For IFR flights in uncontrolled airspace between FL 180 and FL 290, odd flight levels should be flown if the magnetic course is 0 to 179, and even flight levels should be flown if the magnetic course is 180 to 359. IFR flights in uncontrolled airspace at or above FL 290 should be flown at 4,000 foot intervals beginning at FL 290 if the magnetic course is 0 to 179 and FL 310 if the magnetic course is 180 to 359. When flying in the PCA, flight levels assigned by air traffic control (ATC) should be maintained.

5. **WEATHER.** Pilots should be aware of and recognize the meteorological phenomena associated with high altitudes and the effects of these phenomena on flight.

a. The Atmosphere. The atmosphere is a mixture of gases in constant motion. It is composed of approximately 78 percent nitrogen, 21 percent oxygen, and 1 percent other gases. Water vapor is constantly being absorbed and released in the atmosphere which causes changes in weather. The three levels of the atmosphere where high-altitude flight may occur are the troposphere, which can extend from sea level to approximately FL 350 around the poles and up to FL 650 around the equator; the tropopause, a thin layer at the top of the troposphere that traps water vapor in the lower level; and the stratosphere, which extends from the tropopause to approximately 22 miles. The stratosphere is characterized by lack of moisture and a constant temperature of -55° C, while the temperature in the troposphere decreases at a rate of 2°C per 1,000 feet. Condensation trails, or contrails, are com-

Continued

mon in the upper levels of the troposphere and in the stratosphere. These cloud-like streamers that are generated in the wake of aircraft flying in clear, cold, humid air, form by water vapor from aircraft exhaust gases being added to the atmosphere causing saturation or supersaturation of the air. Contrails can also form aerodynamically by the pressure reduction around airfoils, engine nacelles, and propellers cooling the air to saturation.

b. Atmospheric density. Atmospheric density in the troposphere decreases 50 percent at 18,000 feet. This means that at FL 180, the air contains only one-half the oxygen molecules as at sea level. Because the human body requires a certain amount of oxygen for survival, aircraft that fly at high altitudes must be equipped with some means of creating an artificial atmosphere, such as cabin pressurization.

c. Winds.

(1) The jet stream is a narrow band of high-altitude winds, near or in the tropopause, that results from large temperature contrasts over a short distance (typically along fronts) creating large pressure gradients aloft. The jet stream usually travels in an easterly direction between 50 and 200 K. The speed of the jet stream is greater in the winter than in the summer months because of greater temperature differences. It generally drops more rapidly on the polar side than on the equatorial side. In the mid-latitudes, the polar front jet stream is found in association with the polar front. This jet stream has a variable path, sometimes flowing almost due north and south.

(2) Because of its meandering path, the polar front jet stream is not found on most circulation charts. One almost permanent jet is a westerly jet found over the subtropics at 25° latitude about 8 miles above the surface. Low pressure systems usually form to the south of the jet stream and move northward until they become occluded lows which move north of the jet stream. Horizontal windshear and turbulence are frequently found on the northern side of the jet stream.

d. Clear Air Turbulence (CAT). CAT is a meteorological phenomenon associated with high-altitude winds. This high-level turbulence occurs where no clouds are present and can take place at any altitude (normally above 15,000 feet AGL), although it usually develops in or near the jet stream where there is a rapid change in temperature. CAT is generally stronger on the polar side of the jet and is greatest during the winter months. CAT can be caused by windshear, convective currents, mountain waves, strong low pressures aloft, or other obstructions to normal wind flow. CAT is difficult to forecast because it gives no visual warning of its presence and winds can carry it far from its point of origin.

e. Clouds and Thunderstorms.

(1) Cirrus and cirriform clouds are high-altitude clouds that are composed of ice crystals. Cirrus clouds are found in stable air above 30,000 feet in patches or narrow bands. Cirriform clouds, such as the white clouds in long bands against a blue background known as cirrostratus clouds, generally indicate some type of system below. Cirrostratus clouds form in stable air as a result of shallow convective currents and also may produce light turbulence. Clouds with extensive vertical development (e.g., towering cumulus and cumulonimbus clouds) indicate a deep layer of unstable air and contain moderate to heavy turbulence with icing. The bases of these clouds are found at altitudes associated with low to middle clouds but their tops can extend up to 60,000 feet or more.

(2) Cumulonimbus clouds are thunderstorm clouds that present a particularly severe hazard to pilots and should be circumnavigated if possible. Hazards associated with cumulonimbus clouds include embedded thunderstorms, severe or extreme turbulence, lightning, icing, and dangerously strong winds and updrafts.

f. Icing. Icing at high altitudes is not as common or extreme as it can be at low altitudes. When it does occur, the rate of accumulation at high altitudes is generally slower than at low altitudes. Rime ice is generally more common at high altitudes than clear ice, although clear ice is possible. Despite the composition of cirrus clouds, severe icing is generally not a problem although it can occur in some detached cirrus. It is more common in tops of tall cumulus buildups, anvils, and over mountainous regions. Many airplanes that operate above 25,000 feet are equipped with deice or anti-ice systems, reducing even further the dangers of icing.

6. FLIGHT PLANNING AND NAVIGATION.

a. Flight Planning.

(1) Careful flight planning is critical to safe high-altitude flight. Consideration must be given to power settings, particularly on takeoff, climb, and descent to assure operation in accordance with the manufacturer's recommendations. Fuel management, reporting points, weather briefings (not only thunderstorms, the freezing level, and icing at altitude but at all levels and destinations, including alternates, that may affect the flight), direction of flight, airplane performance charts, high-speed winds aloft, and oxygen duration charts must also be considered. When possible, additional oxygen should be provided to allow for emergency situations. Breathing rates increase under stress and extra oxygen could be necessary.

(2) Flight planning should take into consideration factors associated with altitudes that will be transited while climbing to or descending from the high altitudes (e.g., airspeed limitations below 10,000 feet MSL, airspace, and minimum altitudes). Westward flights should generally be made away from the jet stream to avoid the strong headwind, and eastward flights should be made in the jet stream when possible to increase groundspeed. Groundspeed checks are particularly important in high-altitude flight. If fuel runs low because of headwinds or poor flight planning, a decision to fly to an alternate airport should be made as early as possible to allow time to replan descents and advise ATC.

b. Knowledge of Aircraft. Complete familiarity with the aircraft systems and limitations is extremely important. For example, many high-

altitude airplanes feed from only one fuel tank at a time. If this is the case, it is important to know the fuel consumption rate to know when to change tanks. This knowledge should be made part of the preflight planning and its accuracy confirmed regularly during the flight.

c. Gradual Descents. Gradual descents from high altitudes should be planned in advance to prevent excessive engine cooling and provide passenger comfort. The manufacturer's recommendations found in the Airplane Flight Manual should be complied with, especially regarding descent power settings to avoid stress on the engines. Although most jets can descend rapidly at idle power, many turboprop and light twin airplanes require some power to avoid excessive engine cooling, cold shock, and metal fatigue. ATC does not always take aircraft type into consideration when issuing descent instructions. It is the pilot's responsibility to fly the airplane in the safest manner possible. Cabin rates of descent are particularly important and should generally not exceed 500 or 600 feet per minute. Before landing, cabin pressure should be equal to ambient pressure or inner ear injury can result. If delays occur enroute, descents should be adjusted accordingly.

d. Weather Charts. Before beginning a high-altitude flight, all weather charts should be consulted, including those designed for low levels. Although high-altitude flight may allow a pilot to overfly adverse weather, low altitudes must be transited on arrival, departure, and in an emergency situation that may require landing at any point enroute.

e. Types of Weather Charts. Weather charts that provide information on high-altitude weather include Constant Pressure Charts, which provide information on pressure systems, temperature, winds, and temperature/dewpoint spread at the 850 millibar (mb), 700 mb, 500 mb, 300 mb, and 200 mb levels (5 charts are issued every 12 hours). Prognostic Charts forecast winds, temperature, and expected movement of weather over the 6 hour valid time of the chart. Observed

Continued

Tropopause Charts provide jet stream, turbulence, and temperature-wind-pressure reportings at the tropopause over each station. Tropopause Wind Prognostic Charts and Tropopause Height Vertical Windshear Charts are helpful in determining jet stream patterns and the presence of CAT and windshear.

f. Windshear. Windshear is indicated by dashed lines on Tropopause Height Vertical Windshear Charts. Horizontal wind changes of 40 K within 150 NM, or vertical windshear of 6 K or greater per 1,000 feet usually indicate moderate to severe turbulence and should be avoided. Pilot reports (PIREPs) are one of the best methods of receiving timely and accurate reports on icing and turbulence at high altitudes.

g. Navigation. Specific charts have been designed for flight at FL 180 and above. Enroute high-altitude charts delineate the jet route system, which consists of routes established from FL 180 up to and including FL 450. The VOR airways established below FL 180 found on low-altitude charts must not be used at FL 180 and above. High-altitude jet routes are an independent matrix of airways, and pilots must have the appropriate enroute high-altitude charts before transitioning to the flight levels.

h. Jet Routes. Jet routes in the U.S. are predicated solely on VOR or VORTAC navigation facilities, except in Alaska where some are based on L/MF navigation aids. All jet routes are identified by the letter "J" and followed by the airway number.

i. Reporting Points. Reporting points are designated for jet route systems and must be used by flights using the jet route unless otherwise advised by ATC. Flights above FL 450 may be conducted on a point-to-point basis, using the facilities depicted on the enroute high-altitude chart as navigational guidance. Random and fixed Area Navigation (RNAV) Routes are also used for direct navigation at high-altitudes and are based on area navigation capability between waypoints defined in terms of latitude/longitude coordinates, degree-distance fixes, or offsets from established routes or airways at a specified distance and direction. Radar monitoring by ATC is required on all random RNAV routes.

j. Point-to-Point Navigation. In addition to RNAV, many high-altitude airplanes are equipped with point-to-point navigation systems for high-altitude enroute flight. These include LORAN-C, OMEGA, Inertial Navigation System, and Doppler Radar. Further information about these and additional navigation systems are available in the Airman's Information Manual.

k. Navaids. VOR, DME, and TACAN depicted on high-altitude charts are designated as class H navaids, signifying that their standard service volume is from 1,000 feet AGL up to and including 14,500 AGL at radial distances out to 40 NM; from 14,500 feet AGL up to and including 60,000 feet AGL at radial distances out to 100 NM; and from 18,000 feet AGL up to and including 45,000 feet AGL at radial distances out to 130 NM. Ranges of NDB service volumes are the same at all altitudes.

7. **PHYSIOLOGICAL TRAINING.** To ensure safe flights at high altitudes, pilots of high-altitude aircraft must understand the physiological effects of high-altitude flight. Additional physiological training information, including locations and application procedures for attending an altitude chamber, can be found in paragraph 8 of this chapter. Although not required, altitude chamber training is highly recommended for all pilots.

a. Respiration is the exchange of gases between the organism and its environment. In humans, external respiration is the intake of oxygen from the atmosphere by the lungs and the elimination of some carbon dioxide from the body into the surrounding atmosphere. Each breath intake is comprised of approximately 21 percent oxygen, which is absorbed into the bloodstream and carried by the blood throughout the body to burn food material and to produce heat and kinetic energy. The partial pressure of oxygen forces oxygen through air sacs (alveoli), located at the end of each of the smaller tubes that branches out from the bronchial tubes and lungs, into the bloodstream. Other gases contained in the lungs reduce the partial pressure of oxygen entering the air sacs to about 102 mm Hg at ground level, which is approximately 21 percent of the total atmospheric pressure.

b. **The human body** functions normally in the atmospheric area extending from sea level to 12,000 feet MSL. In this range, brain oxygen saturation is at a level that allows for normal functioning. (Optimal functioning is 96 percent saturation. At 12,000 feet, brain oxygen saturation is approximately 87 percent which begins to approach a level that could affect human performance. Although oxygen is not required below 12,500 feet MSL, its use is recommended when flying above 10,000 feet MSL during the day and above 5,000 feet MSL at night when the eyes become more sensitive to oxygen deprivation.)

c. **Although minor physiological problems,** such as middle ear and sinus trapped gas difficulties, can occur when flying below 12,000 feet, shortness of breath, dizziness, and headaches will result when an individual ascends to an altitude higher than that to which his or her body is acclimated. From 12,000 to 50,000 feet MSL, atmospheric pressure drops by 396 mm Hg. This area contains less partial pressure of oxygen which can result in problems such as trapped or evolved gases within the body. Flight at and above 50,000 feet MSL requires sealed cabins or pressure suits.

d. **Hypoxia** is a lack of sufficient oxygen in the body cells or tissues caused by an inadequate supply of oxygen, inadequate transportation of oxygen, or inability of the body tissues to use oxygen. A common misconception among many pilots who are inexperienced in high-altitude flight operations and who have not been exposed to physiological training is that it is possible to recognize the symptoms of hypoxia and to take corrective action before becoming seriously impaired. While this concept may be appealing in theory, it is both misleading and dangerous

for an untrained crewmember. Symptoms of hypoxia vary from pilot to pilot, but one of the earliest effects of hypoxia is impairment of judgement. Other symptoms can include one or more of the following:

(1) Behavioral changes (e.g., a sense of euphoria).

(2) Poor coordination.

(3) Discoloration at the fingernail beds (cyanosis).

(4) Sweating.

(5) Increased breathing rate, headache, sleepiness, or fatigue.

(6) Loss or deterioration of vision.

(7) Light-headedness or dizzy sensations and listlessness.

(8) Tingling or warm sensations.

e. **While other significant effects of hypoxia** usually do not occur in a healthy pilot in an unpressurized aircraft below 12,000 feet, there is no assurance that this will always be the case. The onset of hypoxic symptoms may seriously affect the safety of flight and may well occur even in short periods of exposure to altitudes from 12,000 to 15,000 feet. The ability to take corrective measures may be totally lost in 5 minutes at 22,000 feet. However, that time would be reduced to only 18 seconds at 40,000 feet and the crewmember may suffer total loss of consciousness soon thereafter. A description of the four major hypoxia groups and the recommended methods to combat each follows.

(1) **Hypoxic (Altitude) Hypoxia.** Altitude hypoxia poses the greatest potential physiological hazard to a flight crewmember while flying in the high-altitude environment. This type of hypoxia is caused by an insufficient partial pressure of oxygen in the inhaled air resulting from reduced oxygen pressure in the atmosphere at altitude. If a person is able to recognize the onset of hypoxic symptoms, immediate use of

Continued

supplemental oxygen will combat hypoxic hypoxia within seconds. Oxygen systems should be checked periodically to ensure that there is an adequate supply of oxygen and that the system is functioning properly. This check should be performed frequently with increasing altitude. If supplemental oxygen is not available, an emergency descent to an altitude below 10,000 feet should be initiated.

(2) *Histotoxic Hypoxia.* This is the inability of the body cells to use oxygen because of impaired cellular respiration. This type of hypoxia, caused by alcohol or drug use, cannot be corrected by using supplemental oxygen because the uptake of oxygen is impaired at the tissue level. The only method of avoiding this type of hypoxia is to abstain, before flight, from alcohol or drugs that are not approved by a flight surgeon or an aviation medical examiner.

(3) *Hypemic (Anemic) Hypoxia.* This type of hypoxia is defined as a reduction in the oxygen carrying capacity of the blood. Hypemic hypoxia is caused by a reduction in circulating red blood cells (hemoglobin) or contamination of blood with gases other than oxygen as a result of anemia, carbon monoxide poisoning, or excessive smoking. Pilots should take into consideration the effect of smoking on altitude tolerance when determining appropriate cabin pressures. If heavy smokers are among the crew or passengers, a lower cabin altitude should be set because apparent altitudes for smokers are generally much higher than actual altitudes. For example, a smoker's apparent altitude at sea level is approximately 7,000 feet. Twenty thousand feet actual altitude for a nonsmoker would be equivalent to an apparent altitude of 22,000 feet for a smoker. The smoker is thus more susceptible to hypoxia at lower altitudes than the nonsmoker. Hypemic hypoxia is corrected by locating and eliminating the source of the contaminating gases. A careful preflight of heating systems and exhaust manifold equipment is mandatory. Also, cutting down on smoking would minimize the onset of this type of hypoxia. If symptoms are recognized, initiate use of supplemental oxygen and/or descend to an alti-

tude below 10,000 feet. If symptoms persist, ventilate the cabin and land as soon as possible because the symptoms may be indicative of carbon monoxide poisoning and medical attention should be sought.

(4) *Stagnant Hypoxia.* This is an oxygen deficiency in the body resulting from poor circulation of the blood because of a failure of the circulatory system to pump blood (and oxygen) to the tissues. Evidence of coronary artery disease is grounds for immediate denial or revocation of a medical certificate. In flight, this type of hypoxia can sometimes be caused by positive pressure breathing for long periods of time or excessive G-forces.

f. Effective Performance Time (EPT) or Time of Useful Consciousness (TUC) is the amount of time in which a person is able to effectively or adequately perform flight duties with an insufficient supply of oxygen. EPT decreases with altitude, until eventually coinciding with the time it takes for blood to circulate from the lungs to the head usually at an altitude above 35,000 feet. Table 1 shows the TUC (shown as average TUC) at various altitudes.

Table 1. Times Of Useful Consciousness At Various Altitudes

Altitude (Feet)	Sitting Quietly	Moderate Activity
22,000	10 minutes	5 minutes
25,000	5 minutes	3 minutes
30,000	1 minute	45 seconds
35,000	45 seconds	30 seconds
40,000	25 seconds	18 seconds

g. Other factors that determine EPT are the rate of ascent (faster rates of ascent result in shorter EPTs), physical activities (exercise decreases EPTs), and day-to-day factors such as physical fitness, diet, rest, prescription drugs, smoking, and illness. Altitude chamber experiments found a significantly longer TUC for nonsmoker pilots who exercise and watch their diet than for pilots who smoke and are not physically fit.

h. Prolonged oxygen use can also be harmful to human health. One hundred percent aviation oxygen can produce toxic symptoms if used for extended periods of time. The symptoms can consist of bronchial cough, fever, vomiting, nervousness, irregular heart beat, and lowered energy. These symptoms appeared on the second day of breathing 90 percent oxygen during controlled experiments. It is unlikely that oxygen would be used long enough to produce the most severe of these symptoms in any aviation incidence. However, prolonged flights at high altitudes using a high concentration of oxygen can produce some symptoms of oxygen poisoning such as infection or bronchial irritation. The sudden supply of pure oxygen following a decompression can often aggravate the symptoms of hypoxia. Therefore, oxygen should be taken gradually, particularly when the body is already suffering from lack of oxygen, to build up the supply in small doses. If symptoms of oxygen poisoning develop, high concentrations of oxygen should be avoided until the symptoms completely disappear.

i. When nitrogen is inhaled, it dilutes the air we breathe. While most nitrogen is exhaled from the lungs along with carbon dioxide, some nitrogen is absorbed by the body. The nitrogen absorbed into the body tissues does not normally present any problem because it is carried in a liquid state. If the ambient surrounding atmospheric pressure lowers drastically, this nitrogen could change from a liquid and return to its gaseous state in the form of bubbles. These evolving and expanding gases in the body are known as decompression sickness and are divided into two groups.

(1) *Trapped Gas.* Expanding or contracting gas in certain body cavities during altitude changes can result in abdominal pain, toothache, or pain in ears and sinuses if the person is unable to equalize the pressure changes. Above 25,000 feet, distention can produce particularly severe gastrointestinal pain.

(2) *Evolved Gas.* When the pressure on the body drops sufficiently, nitrogen comes out of solution and forms bubbles which can have adverse effects on some body tissues. Fatty tissue contains more nitrogen than other tissue; thus making overweight people more susceptible to evolved gas decompression sicknesses.

(i) SCUBA diving will compound this problem because of the compressed air used in the breathing tanks. After SCUBA diving, a person who flies in an aircraft to an altitude of 8,000 feet would experience the same effects as a nondiver flying at 40,000 feet unpressurized. The recommended waiting period before going to flight altitudes of 8,000 feet is at least 12 hours after nondecompression stop diving (diving which does not require a controlled ascent), and 24 hours after decompression stop diving (diving which requires a controlled ascent). For flight altitudes above 8,000 feet, the recommended waiting time is at least 24 hours after any SCUBA diving.

(ii) The bends, also known as caisson disease, is one type of evolved gas decompression sickness and is characterized by pain in and around the joints. The term bends is used because the resultant pain is eased by bending the joints. The pain gradually becomes more severe, can eventually become temporarily incapacitating, and can result in collapse. The chokes refers to a decompression sickness that manifests itself through chest pains and burning sensations, a desire to cough, possible cyanosis, a sensation of suffocation, progressively shallower breathing and, if a descent is not made immediately, collapse and unconsciousness. Paresthesia is a third type of decompression sickness, characterized by tingling, itching, a red rash, and cold and warm sensations, probably resulting from bubbles in the central nervous system (CNS). CNS disturbances can result in visual deficiencies such as illusionary lines or spots, or a blurred field of vision. Some other effects of CNS disturbances are temporary partial paralysis, sensory disorders, slurred speech, and seizures.

j. **Shock** can often result from decompression sicknesses as a form of body protest to disrupted circulation. Shock can cause nausea, fainting, dizziness, sweating, and/or loss of consciousness. The best treatment for decompression sickness is descent to a lower altitude and landing. If conditions persist after landing, recompression chambers can be located through an aviation medical examiner.

k. **Vision** has a tendency to deteriorate with altitude. A reversal of light distribution at high altitudes (bright clouds below the airplane and darker, blue sky above) can cause a glare inside the cockpit. Glare effects and deteriorated vision are enhanced at night when the body becomes more susceptible to hypoxia. Night vision can begin to deteriorate at cabin pressure altitudes as low as 5,000 feet. In addition, the empty visual field caused by cloudless, blue skies during the day can cause inaccuracies when judging the speed, size, and distance of other aircraft. Sunglasses are recommended to minimize the intensity of the sun's ultraviolet rays at high altitudes.

8. **ADDITIONAL PHYSIOLOGICAL TRAINING.** There are no specific requirements in FAR Part 91 or Part 125 for physiological training. However, in addition to the high-altitude training required by FAR § 61.31(f), which should include the physiological training outlined in this chapter, FAR Parts 121 and 135 require flight crewmembers that serve in operations above 25,000 feet to receive training in specified subjects of aviation physiology. None of the requirements includes altitude chamber training. The U.S. military services require its flight crewmembers to complete both initial and refresher physiological training, including instruction in basic aviation physiology and altitude chamber training. Other U.S. Government agencies, such as the National Aviation and Space Administration and FAA, also require their flight personnel who operate pressurized aircraft in the high-altitude flight environment to complete similar training. Although most of the subject material normally covered in physiological training concerns problems associated with reduced atmospheric pressure at high-flight altitudes, other equally important subjects are covered as well. Such subjects of aviation physiology as vision, disorientation, physical fitness, stress, and survival affect flight safety and are normally presented in a good training program.

a. **Physiological training programs** are offered at locations across the United States (Table 2) for pilots who are interested in learning to recognize and overcome vertigo, hypoxia, hyperventilation, etc., during flight. Trainees who attend these programs will be given classroom lectures, a high-altitude "flight" in an altitude chamber, and time in a jet aircraft cockpit spatial disorientation training device at some of the military bases that offer the course.

b. **Persons who wish to take this training** must be at least 18 years of age, hold a current FAA Airman Medical Certificate, and must not have a cold or any other significant health problem when enrolling for the course.

c. **Applications for physiological training** may be obtained at any FAA Flight Standards District Office. Persons who wish to enroll should send a completed application and payment (minimal fee for the course is $20) to the Mike Monroney Aeronautical Center, General Accounting Branch, AAC-23B, Box 25082, Oklahoma City, Oklahoma 73125.

d. **Within 30 to 60 days,** the applicant will be notified of the time and place of training.

Table 2. List of Training Locations

Aeronautical Center, OK	Fairchild AFB, WA	Peterson AFB, CO
Andrews AFB, MD	Jacksonville NAS, FL	Point Mugu NMC, CA
Barbers Point NAS, HI	Laughlin AFB, TX	Reese AFB, TX
Beale AFB, TX	Lemoore NAS, CA	San Diego NAS, CA
Brooks AFB, TX	Little Rock AFB, AR	Sheppard AFB, TX
Brunswick NAS, ME	MacDill AFB, CA	Vance AFB, OK
Cherry Point MCAS, NC	Mather AFB, CA	Whidbey Island NAS, WA
Columbus AFB, MS	NASA Johnson Space Center, TX	Williams AFB, AZ
Edwards AFB, CA	Norfolk NAS, VA	Wright AFB, AZ
Ellsworth AFB, CA	Patuxent River NAS, MD	Wright-Patterson AFB, OH
El Toro MCAS, CA	Pease AFB, NH	

9. **HIGH-ALTITUDE SYSTEMS AND EQUIP-MENT.** Several systems and equipment are unique to aircraft that fly at high altitudes, and pilots should be familiar with their operation before using them. Before any flight, a pilot should be familiar with all the systems on the aircraft to be flown.

a. Turbochargers. Most light piston engine airplanes that fly above 25,000 feet MSL are turbocharged. Turbochargers compress air in the carburetor or cylinder intake by using exhaust gases from an engine-driven turbine wheel. The increased air density provides greater power and improved performance. Light aircraft use one of two types of turbocharging systems. The first is the normalizer system, which allows the engine to develop sea level pressure from approximately 29 inches of manifold pressure up to a critical altitude (generally between 14,000 – 16,000 feet MSL). The supercharger system is a more powerful system which allows the engine to develop higher than sea level pressure (up to 60 inches of manifold pressure) up to a critical altitude. To prevent overboosting at altitudes below the critical altitude, a waste gate is installed in the turbocompressor system to release unnecessary gases. The waste gate is a damper-like device that controls the amount of exhaust that strikes the turbine rotor. As the waste gate closes with altitude, it sends more gases through the turbine compressor, causing the rotor to spin faster. This allows the engine to function as if it were maintaining sea level or, in the case of a supercharger, above sea level manifold pressure. The three principle types of waste gate operations are manual, fixed, and automatic.

(1) *Manual Waste Gate.* Manual waste gate systems are common in older aircraft but have been discontinued due to the additional burden on the pilot. Waste gates were often left closed on takeoff or open on landing, resulting in an overboost that could harm the engine.

(2) *Fixed Waste Gate.* Fixed waste gates pose less of a burden on the pilot, but the pilot must still be careful not to overboost the engine, especially on takeoff, initial climb, and on cold days when the air is especially dense. This type of waste gate remains in the same position during all engine operations, but it splits the exhaust flow allowing only partial exhaust access to the turbine. The pilot simply controls manifold pressure with smooth, slow application of the throttle to control against overboost. If overboost does occur, a relief valve on the intake manifold protects the engine from damage. This is not a favorable system due to fluctuations in manifold pressure and limited additional power from the restricted control over the exhaust flow. In addition, the compressor can produce excessive pressure and cause overheating.

(3) *Automatic Waste Gate.* Automatic waste gates operate on internal pressure. When internal pressure builds towards an overboost, the waste gate opens to relieve pressure, keeping the engine within normal operating limits regardless of the air density.

(i) The pressure-reference automatic waste gate system maintains the manifold pressure set by the throttle. Engine oil pressure moves the waste gate to maintain the appropriate manifold pressure, thus reducing the pilot's workload and eliminating the possibility of overboost. If the airplane engine is started up and followed by an immediate takeoff, cold oil may cause a higher than intended manifold pressure. Allow the oil to warm up and circulate throughout the system before takeoff.

(ii) The density-reference waste gate system is controlled by compressor discharge air. A density controller holds a given density of air by automatically adjusting manifold pressure as airspeed, ambient pressure, temperature, altitude, and other variables change.

b. Turbocharged engines are particularly temperature sensitive. Manufacturers often recommend increasing the fuel flow during climbs to prevent overheating. It is also important to cool the engine after landing. Allowing the engine to idle for approximately 1 minute before shutting it down permits engine oil to flow through the system, cooling the engine while simultaneously cooling and lubricating the turbocharger.

c. Most high-altitude airplanes come equipped with some type of fixed oxygen installation. If the airplane does not have a fixed installation, portable oxygen equipment must be readily accessible during flight. The portable equipment usually consists of a container, regulator, mask outlet, and pressure gauge. A typical 22 cubic foot portable container will allow four people enough oxygen to last approximately 1.5 hours at 18,000 feet MSL. Aircraft oxygen is usually stored in high-pressure system containers of 1,800 - 2,200 pounds per square inch (PSI). The container should be fastened securely in the aircraft before flight. When the ambient temperature surrounding an oxygen cylinder decreases, pressure within that cylinder will decrease because pressure varies directly with temperature if the volume of a gas remains constant. Therefore, if a drop in indicated pressure on a supplemental oxygen cylinder is noted, there is no rea-

son to suspect depletion of the oxygen supply, which has simply been compacted due to storage of the containers in an unheated area of the aircraft. High-pressure oxygen containers should be marked with the PSI tolerance (i.e., 1,800 PSI) before filling the container to that pressure. The containers should be supplied with aviation oxygen only, which is 100 percent pure oxygen. Industrial oxygen is not intended for breathing and may contain impurities, and medical oxygen contains water vapor that can freeze in the regulator when exposed to cold temperatures. To assure safety, oxygen system periodic inspection and servicing should be done at FAA certificated stations found at some fixed base operations and terminal complexes.

d. Regulators and masks work on continuous flow, diluter demand, or on pressure demand systems. The continuous flow system supplies oxygen at a rate that may either be controlled by the user or controlled automatically on some regulators. The mask is designed so the oxygen can be diluted with ambient air by allowing the user to exhale around the face piece, and comes with a rebreather bag which allows the individual to reuse part of the exhaled oxygen. The pilots' masks sometimes allow greater oxygen flow than passengers' masks, so it is important that the pilots use the masks that are indicated for them. Although certificated up to 41,000 feet, very careful attention to system capabilities is required when using continuous flow oxygen systems above 25,000 feet.

e. Diluter demand and pressure demand systems supply oxygen only when the user inhales through the mask. An automix lever allows the regulators to automatically mix cabin air and oxygen or supply 100 percent oxygen, depending on the altitude. The demand mask provides a tight seal over the face to prevent dilution with outside air and can be used safely up to 40,000 feet. Pilots who fly at those altitudes should not have beards and moustaches because air can easily seep in through the border of the mask. Pressure demand regulators also create airtight and oxygentight seals but they also provide a positive pressure application of oxygen to the mask face piece which allows the user's lungs to be pressurized with oxygen. This feature makes pressure demand regulators safe at altitudes above 40,000 feet.

f. Pilots should be aware of the danger of fire when using oxygen. Materials that are nearly fireproof in ordinary air may be susceptible to burning in oxygen. Oils and greases may catch fire if exposed to oxygen and, therefore, cannot be used for sealing the valves and fittings of oxygen equipment. Smoking during any kind of oxygen equipment use must also be strictly forbidden.

g. Surplus oxygen equipment must be inspected and approved by a certified FAA inspection station before being used. Before each flight, the pilot should thoroughly inspect and test all oxygen equipment. The inspection should be accomplished with clean hands and should include a visual inspection of the mask and tubing for tears, cracks, or deterioration; the regulator for valve and lever condition and positions; oxygen quantity; and the location and functioning of oxygen pressure gauges, flow indicators and connections. The mask should be donned and the system should be tested. After any oxygen use, verify that all components and valves are shut off.

h. Cabin pressurization is the compression of air in the aircraft cabin to maintain a cabin altitude lower than the actual flight altitude. Because of the ever present possibility of decompression, supplemental oxygen is still required. Pressurized aircraft meeting specific requirements of FAR Part 23 or Part 25 have cabin altitude warning systems which are activated at 10,000 feet. Pressurized aircraft meeting the still more stringent requirements of FAR Part 25 have automatic passenger oxygen mask dispensing devices which activate before exceeding 15,000 feet cabin altitude.

i. Pressurization in most light aircraft is sent to the cabin from the turbocharger's compressor or from an engine-driven pneumatic pump. The flow of compressed air into the cabin is regulated by an outflow valve which keeps the pressure constant by releasing excess pressure into the atmosphere. The cabin altitude can be manually selected and is monitored by a gauge which indicates the pressure difference between the cabin and ambient altitudes. The rate of change between these two pressures is automatically controlled with a manual backup control.

j. Each pressurized aircraft has a determined maximum pressure differential, which is the maximum differential between cabin and ambient altitudes that the pressurized section of the aircraft can support. The pilot must be familiar with these limitations, as well as the manifold pressure settings recommended for various pressure differentials. Some aircraft have a negative pressure relief valve to equalize pressure in the event of a sudden decompression or rapid descent to prevent the cabin pressure from becoming higher than the ambient pressure.

k. Reducing exposure to low barometric pressure lowers the occurrence of decompression sickness and the need for an oxygen mask is eliminated as a full time oxygen source above certain altitudes. Many airplanes are equipped with automatic visual and aural warning systems that indicate an unintentional loss of pressure.

l. Technology is continuously improving flight at high altitudes through the development of new devices and the improvement of existing systems. One such example is the pressurized magneto. Thin air at high altitudes makes the unpressurized magneto susceptible to crossfiring. The high tension pressurized system is composed of sealed caps and plugs that keep the electrodes contained within the body. A pressure line extends directly from the turbodischarger to the magneto. Pressurized magnetos perform better at high altitudes where low pressure and cold atmosphere have a detrimental effect on electrical conductivity. Flight above 14,000 feet with an unpressurized magneto should be avoided because of its higher susceptibility to arcing.

m. Another airplane component recommended for flight at high altitudes is the dry vacuum pump. Engine driven wet vacuum pumps cannot create sufficient vacuum to drive the gyros in the low density found at high altitudes. Furthermore, gyros and rubber deicing boots can be ruined by oil contamination from the wet pump system, which uses engine oil for lubrication and cooling. Dry vacuum pumps are lightweight, self-lubricating systems that eliminate oil contamination and cooling problems. These pumps can power either a vacuum or pressure pneumatic system, allowing them to drive the gyros, deice boots, and pressurize the door seals.

10. **AERODYNAMICS AND PERFORMANCE FACTORS.** Thinner air at high altitudes has a significant impact on an airplane's flying characteristics because surface control effects, lift, drag, and horsepower are all functions of air density.

a. The reduced weight of air moving over control surfaces at high altitudes decreases their effectiveness. As the airplane approaches its absolute altitude, the controls become sluggish, making altitude and heading difficult to maintain. For this reason, most airplanes that fly at above 25,000 feet are equipped with an autopilot.

b. A determined weight of air is used by the engine for producing an identified amount of horsepower through internal combustion. For a given decrease of air density, horsepower decreases at a higher rate which is approximately 1.3 times that of the corresponding decrease in air density.

c. For an airplane to maintain level flight, drag and thrust must be equal. Because density is always greatest at sea level, the velocity at altitude given the same angle of attack will be greater than at sea level, although the indicated air speed (IAS) will not change. Therefore, an airplane's TAS increases with altitude while its IAS remains constant. In addition, an airplane's rate of climb will decrease with altitude.

11. **EMERGENCIES AND IRREGULARITIES AT HIGH ALTITUDES.** All emergency procedures in the Airplane Flight Manual should be reviewed before flying any airplane, and that manual should be readily accessible during every flight. A description of some of the most significant high-altitude emergencies and remedial action for each follows.

a. Decompression is defined as the inability of the aircraft's pressurization system to maintain its designed pressure schedule. Decompression can be caused by a malfunction of the system itself or by structural damage to the aircraft. A decompression will often result in cabin fog because of the rapid drop in temperature and the change in relative humidity. A decompression will also affect the human body. Air will escape from the lungs through the nose and mouth because of a sudden lower pressure outside of the lungs. Differential air pressure on either side of the eardrum should clear automatically. Exposure to windblast and extremely cold temperatures are other hazards the human body may face with a decompression.

b. Decompression of a small cabin volume pressurized aircraft is more critical than a large one, given the same size hole or conditions, primarily because of the difference in cabin volumes. Table 3 is a comparison of cabin volume ratios between several large transport airplanes and some of the more popular general aviation turbojet airplanes in current use. Table 3 shows that, under the same conditions, a typical small pressurized aircraft can be expected to decompress on the order of 10 to 200 times as fast as a large aircraft. The B-747/Learjet comparison is an extreme example in that the human response, TUC, and the protective equipment necessary are the same. Actual decompression times are difficult to calculate due to many variables involved (e.g., the type of failure, differential pressure, cabin volume, etc.). However, it is more probable that the crew of the small aircraft will have less time in which to take life-saving actions.

Table 3. Aircraft Cabin Volume Ratios

Aircraft Type	Cabin Volumes in Cubic Feet	Ratio
DC-9 vs CE-650	5,840 vs 576	10:1
B-737 vs LR-55	8,010 vs 502	16:1
B-727 vs NA-265	9,045 vs 430	21:1
L-1011 vs G-1159	35,000 vs 1,850	19:1
B-747 vs Learjet	59,000 vs 265	223:1

Data Source: Physiological Considerations and Limitations in the High-Altitude Operation of Small Volume Pressurized Aircraft. E. B. McFadden and D. de Steigner, Federal Aviation Administration (FAA) Civil Aeromedical Institute (CAMI).

(1) An explosive decompression is a change in cabin pressure faster than the lungs can decompress. Most authorities consider any decompression which occurs in less than 0.5 seconds as explosive and potentially dangerous. This type of decompression is more likely to occur in small volume pressurized aircraft than in large pressurized aircraft and often results in lung damage. To avoid potentially dangerous flying debris in the event of an explosive decompression, all loose items such as baggage and oxygen cylinders should be properly secured.

(2) A rapid decompression is a change in cabin pressure where the lungs can decompress faster than the cabin. The risk of lung damage is significantly reduced in this decompression as compared with an explosive decompression.

(3) Gradual or slow decompression is dangerous because it may not be detected. Automatic visual and aural warning systems generally provide an indication of a slow decompression.

(4) Recovery from all types of decompression is similar. Oxygen masks should be donned, and a rapid descent initiated as soon as possible to avoid the onset of hypoxia. Although top priority in such a situation is reaching a safe altitude, pilots should be aware that cold shock in piston engines can result from a high-altitude rapid descent, causing cracked cylinders or other engine damage. The time allowed to make a recovery to a safe altitude before loss of useful consciousness is, of course, much less with an explosive than with a gradual decompression.

c. Increased oil temperature, decreased oil pressure, and a drop in manifold pressure could indicate a turbocharger malfunction or a partial or complete turbocharger failure. The consequences of such a malfunction or failure are twofold. The airplane would not be capable of sustaining altitude without the additional power supplied by the turbocharging system. The loss in altitude in itself would not create a significant problem, weather and terrain permitting, but ATC must be notified of the descent. A more serious problem associated with a failed turbocharger would be loss of cabin pressurization if the pressurization system is dependent on the turbocharger compressor. Careful monitoring of pressurization levels is essential during the descent to avoid the onset of hypoxia from a slow decompression.

d. Another potential problem associated with turbochargers is fuel vaporization. Engine driven pumps that pull fuel into the intake manifold are susceptible to vapor lock at high altitudes. Most high-altitude aircraft are equipped with tank-mounted boost pumps to feed fuel to the engine-driven pump under positive pressure. These pumps should be turned on if fuel starvation occurs as a result of vapor lock.

e. Because of the highly combustible composition of oxygen, an immediate descent to an altitude where oxygen is not required should be initiated if a fire breaks out during a flight at high altitude. The procedures in the Airplane Flight Manual should be closely adhered to.

f. Flight through thunderstorm activity or known severe turbulence should be avoided, if possible. When flight through severe turbulence is anticipated and/or unavoidable, the following procedures are highly recommended:

(1) Airspeed is critical for any type of turbulent air penetration. Use the Airplane Flight Manual recommended turbulence penetration target speed or, if unknown, an airspeed below maneuvering speed. Use of high airspeeds can result in structural damage and injury to passengers and crewmembers. Severe gusts may cause large and rapid variations in indicated airspeed. Do not chase airspeed.

(2) Penetration should be at an altitude that provides adequate maneuvering margins in case severe turbulence is encountered to avoid the potential for catastrophic upset.

(3) If severe turbulence is penetrated with the autopilot on, the altitude hold mode should be off. If the autopilot has an attitude hold mode, it should be engaged. The autopilot attitude hold mode can usually maintain attitude more successfully than a pilot under stress. With the autopilot off, the yaw damper should be engaged. Controllability of the aircraft in turbulence becomes more difficult with the yaw damper off. Rudder controls should be centered before engaging the yaw damper.

(4) When flight through a thunderstorm cannot be avoided, turn up the intensity of panel and cabin lights so lightning does not cause temporary blindness. White lighting in the cockpit is better than red lighting during thunderstorms.

(5) Keep wings level and maintain the desired pitch attitude and approximate heading. Do not attempt to turn around and fly out of the storm because the speed associated with thunderstorms usually makes such attempts unsuccessful. Use smooth, moderate control movements to resist changes in attitude. If large attitude changes occur, avoid abrupt or large control inputs. Avoid, as much as possible, use of the stabilizer trim in controlling pitch attitudes. Do not chase altitude.

12. **FLIGHT TRAINING.** Flight training required to comply with FAR § 61.31(f) may be conducted in a high-altitude airplane or a simulator that meets the requirements of FAR § 121.407. The simulator should be representative of an airplane that has a service ceiling or maximum operating altitude, whichever is lower, above 25,000 feet MSL. The training should consist of as many flights as necessary to cover the following procedures and maneuvers. Each flight should consist of a preflight briefing, flight planning, a preflight inspection (if an airplane is being used), demonstrations by the instructor of certain maneuvers or procedures when necessary, and a postflight briefing and discussion.

a. Preflight Briefing. The instructor should verbally cover the material that will be introduced during the flight. If more than one flight is required, previous flights should be reviewed at this time. The preflight briefing is a good time to go over any questions the trainee may have regarding operations at high altitudes or about the aircraft itself. Questions by the trainee should be encouraged during all portions of the flight training.

b. Preflight Planning. A thorough flight plan should be completed for a predetermined route. The flight plan should include a complete weather briefing. If possible, a trip to a Flight Service Station (FSS) is encouraged rather than a telephone briefing so the trainee can use actual weather charts. Winds, pilot reports, the freezing level and other meteorological information obtained from the briefing should be used to determine the best altitude for the flight. The information should be retained for future calculations.

(1) The course should be plotted on a high-altitude navigation chart noting the appropriate jet routes and required reporting points on a navigation log. Low-altitude charts should be available for planning departures and arrivals to comply with airspace and airspeed requirements. Alternate airports should also be identified and noted.

(2) The Airplane Flight Manual should be reviewed with particular attention to weight and balance, performance charts, and emergency procedures. Oxygen requirements, airspeeds, groundspeeds, time enroute, and fuel burn should be calculated using the Airplane Flight Manual and weather data, when applicable. Fuel management and descents should also be planned at this time. The Airplane Flight Manual should be readily accessible in the cabin in the event of an emergency.

(3) A flight plan should be completed using appropriate jet routes from the enroute high-altitude chart. The flight plan should be filed with the local FSS.

c. Preflight Inspection. The aircraft checklist should be followed carefully. Particular attention should be given to the aircraft's fuselage, windshields, window panels, and canopies to identify any cracks or damage that could rupture under the stress of cabin pressurization. The inspection should include a thorough examination of the aircraft oxygen equipment, including available supply, an operational check of the system, and assurance that the supplemental oxygen is in a readily accessible location.

d. Runup, Takeoff and Initial Climb. Procedures in the Airplane Flight Manual should be followed, particularly the manufacturer's recommended power settings and airspeeds to avoid overboosting the engine. Standard call-out procedures are highly recommended and should be used for each phase of flight where the airplane crew consists of more than one crewmember.

e. Climb to high-altitude and normal cruise operations while operating above 25,000 feet MSL. The transition from low to high altitude should be performed repeatedly to assure familiarity with appropriate procedures. Specific oxygen requirements should be met when climbing above 12,500 feet and pressurization should be adjusted with altitude. When passing through FL 180, the altimeter should be set to 29.92 and left untouched until descending below that altitude. Reporting points should be complied with, as should appropriate altitude selection for direc-

tion of flight. Throughout the entire climb and cruise above 25,000 feet, emphasis should be given to monitoring cabin pressurization.

f. Simulated Emergencies. Training should include at least one simulated rapid decompression and emergency descent. Do not actually depressurize the airplane for this or any other training. Actual decompression of an airplane can be extremely dangerous and should never be done intentionally for training purposes. The decompression should be simulated by donning the oxygen masks, turning on the supplemental oxygen controls, configuring the airplane for an emergency descent, and performing the emergency descent as soon as possible. This maneuver can be practiced at any altitude.

g. Descents. Gradual descents from altitude should be practiced to provide passenger comfort and compliance with procedures for transitioning out of the high-altitude realm of flight. The airplane manufacturer's recommendations should be followed with regard to descent power settings to avoid stress on the engine and excessive cooling. Particular emphasis should be given to cabin pressurization and procedures for equalizing cabin and ambient pressures before landing. Emphasis should also be given to changing to low-altitude charts when transitioning through FL 180, obtaining altimeter settings below FL 180, and complying with airspace and airspeed restrictions at appropriate altitudes.

h. Engine Shutdown. Allow the turbocharged engine to cool for at least 1 minute and assure that all shutdown procedures in the Airplane Flight Manual are followed. Before exiting the airplane, always check that all oxygen equipment has been turned off and that the valves on that equipment are closed.

i. Postflight Discussion. The instructor should review the flight and answer any questions the trainee may have. If additional flights are necessary to ensure thorough understanding of high-altitude operations, the material for the next flight should be previewed during the postflight discussion.

Chapter 2. MACH Flight at High Altitudes

13. PURPOSE. To present certain factors involved in the high-speed flight environment at high altitudes. It is the lack of understanding of many of these factors involving the laws of aerodynamics, performance, and MACH speeds that has produced a somewhat higher accident rate in some types of turbojet aircraft.

14. CRITICAL ASPECTS OF MACH FLIGHT. In recent years, a number of corporate jet airplanes have been involved in catastrophic loss of control during high-altitude/high-speed flight. A significant causal factor in these accidents may well have been a lack of knowledge by the pilot regarding critical aspects of high-altitude/MACH flight.

a. Maximum operating altitudes of general aviation turbojet airplanes have now reached 51,000 feet. It is, therefore, logical to expect these types of accidents to continue unless pilots learn to respect the more critical aspects of high-altitude/high-speed flight and gain as much knowledge as possible about the specific make and model of aircraft to be flown and its unique limitations.

b. From the pilot's viewpoint, MACH is the ratio of the aircraft's true airspeed to the local speed of sound. At sea level, on a standard day (59°F/15°C) the speed of sound equals approximately 660 K or 1,120 feet per second. MACH 0.75 at sea level is equivalent to a TAS of approximately 498 K (0.75 x 660 K) or 840 feet per second. The temperature of the atmosphere normally decreases with an increase in altitude. The speed of sound is directly related only to temperature. The result is a decrease in the speed of sound up to about 36,000 feet.

c. The sleek design of some turbojet airplanes has caused some operators to ignore critical airspeed and MACH limitations. There are known cases in which corporate turbojet airplanes have been modified by disabling the airspeed and MACH warning systems to permit intentional excursions beyond the FAA certificated V_{MO}/M_{MO} limit for the specific airplane. Such action may critically jeopardize the safety of the airplane by setting the stage for potentially hazardous occurrences.

d. The compulsion to go faster may result in the onset of aerodynamic flutter, which in itself can be disastrous, excessive G-loading in maneuvering, and induced flow separation over the ailerons and elevators. This may be closely followed by a loss of control surface authority and aileron buzz or snatch, coupled with yet another dangerous phenomenon called MACH-tuck, leading to catastrophic loss of the airplane and the persons onboard.

e. MACH-tuck is caused principally by two basic factors:

(1) Shock wave induced flow separation, which normally begins near the wing root, causes a decrease in the downwash velocity over the elevator and produces a tendency for the aircraft to nose down.

(2) Aftward movement of the center of pressure, which tends to unbalance the equilibrium of the aircraft in relation to its center of gravity (CG) in subsonic flight.

f. The airplane's CG is now farther ahead of the aircraft's aerodynamic center than it was in slower flight. This dramatically increases the tendency of the airplane to pitch more nosedown.

g. Pressure disturbances in the air, caused by an airfoil in high-altitude/high-speed flight, result from molecular collisions. These molecular collisions are the result of air that moves over an airfoil faster than the air it is overtaking can dissipate. When the disturbance reaches a point at which its propagation achieves the local speed of sound, MACH 1 is attained. One hundred percent, (100%) of the speed of sound at MSL with a temperature of 15°C is 760 statute or 660

Continued

nautical miles per hour. This speed is affected by temperature of the atmosphere at altitude. Thus, optimum thrust, fuel, and range considerations are significant factors in the design of most general aviation turbine powered airplanes which cruise at some percentage of MACH 1.

h. Because of the critical aspects of high-altitude/high-MACH flight, most turbojet airplanes capable of operating in the MACH speed ranges are designed with some form of trim and autopilot MACH compensating device (stick puller) to alert the pilot to inadvertent excursions beyond its certificated M_{MO}. This stick puller should never be disabled during normal flight operations in the aircraft.

i. If for any reason there is a malfunction that requires disabling the stick puller, the aircraft must be operated at speeds well below M_{MO} as prescribed in the applicable Airplane Flight Manual procedures for the aircraft.

j. An airplane's IAS decreases in relation to TAS as altitude increases. As the IAS decreases with altitude, it progressively merges with the low speed buffet boundary where prestall buffet occurs for the airplane at a load factor of 1.0 G. The point where high-speed MACH, IAS, and low speed buffet boundary IAS merge is the airplane's absolute or aerodynamic ceiling. Once an aircraft has reached its aerodynamic ceiling, which is higher than the altitude limit stipulated in the Airplane Flight Manual, the aircraft can neither be made to go faster without activating the design stick puller at MACH limit nor can it be made to go slower without activating the stick shaker or pusher. This critical area of the aircraft's flight envelope is known as coffin corner.

k. MACH buffet occurs as a result of supersonic airflow on the wing. Stall buffet occurs at angles of attack that produce airflow disturbances (burbling) over the upper surface of the wing which decreases lift. As density altitude increases, the angle of attack that is required to produce an airflow disturbance over the top of the wing is reduced until a density altitude is reached where MACH buffet and stall buffet converge (described in introductory paragraph 5m as coffin corner). When this phenomenon is encountered, serious consequences may result causing loss of control of the aircraft.

l. Increasing either gross weight or load factor (G-factor) will increase the low-speed buffet and decrease MACH buffet speeds. A typical turbojet airplane flying at 51,000 feet altitude at 1.0 G may encounter MACH buffet slightly above the airplane's Mmo (0.82 MACH) and low speed buffet at 0.60 MACH. However, only 1.4 G (an increase of only 0.4 G) may bring on buffet at the optimum speed of 0.73 MACH and any change in airspeed, bank angle, or gust loading may reduce this straight and level flight 1.4 G protection to no protection. Consequently, a maximum cruising flight altitude must be selected which will allow sufficient buffet margin for the maneuvering necessary and for gust conditions likely to be encountered. Therefore, it is important for pilots to be familiar with the use of charts showing cruise maneuvering and buffet limits. Flightcrews operating airplanes at high speeds must be adequately trained to operate them safely. This training cannot be complete until pilots are thoroughly educated in the critical aspect of aerodynamic factors described herein pertinent to MACH flight at high altitudes.

15. **AIRCRAFT AERODYNAMICS AND PERFORMANCE.** Pilots who operate aircraft at high speeds and high altitudes are concerned with the forces affecting aircraft performance caused by the interaction of air on the aircraft. With an understanding of these forces, the pilot will have a sound basis for predicting how the aircraft will respond to control inputs. The importance of these aerodynamic forces and their direct application to performance and the execution of aircraft maneuvers and procedures at altitude will be evident. The basic aerodynamics definitions that apply to high-altitude flight are contained in paragraph 5 of the introduction to this AC.

a. Wing Design.

(1) The wing of an airplane is an airfoil or aircraft surface designed to obtain the desired reaction from the air through which it moves.

The profile of an aircraft wing is an excellent example of an efficient airfoil. The difference in curvature between the upper and lower surfaces of the wing generates a lifting force. Air passing over the upper wing surface moves at a higher velocity than the air passing beneath the wing because of the greater distance it must travel over the upper surface. This increased velocity results in a decrease in pressure on the upper surface. The pressure differential created between the upper and lower surfaces of the wing lifts the wing upward in the direction of the lowered pressure. This lifting force is known as induced lift. Induced lift may be increased, within limits, by:

(i)   Increasing the angle of attack of the wing or changing the shape of the airfoil, changing the geometry, e.g., aspect ratio.

(ii) Increasing the wing area.

(iii) Increasing the free stream velocity.

(iv) A change in air density.

(2)   The pilot may have only varying degrees of control over these factors. Thus, the pilot must keep firmly in mind that an aircraft will obey the laws of physics just as precisely at its high-speed limits as it does during a slower routine flight, and that regardless of wing shape or design, MACH range flight requires precise control of a high volume of potential energy without exceeding the critical MACH number or MACH crit.

(3)   MACH crit is important to high-speed aerodynamics because it is the speed at which the flow of air over a specific airfoil design reaches MACH 1, but the most important effect is formation of a shock wave and drag divergence.

(4)   Sweeping the wings of an airplane is one method used by aircraft designers to delay the adverse effects of high-MACH flight and bring about economical cruise with an increase in the critical MACH number. Sweep allows a faster airfoil speed before critical MACH is reached when compared to an equal straight wing. This occurs because the airflow now travels over a different cross section (camber) of the airfoil. This new cross section has less effective camber which results in a reduced acceleration of airflow over the wing, thus allowing a higher speed before critical MACH is reached. Sweep may be designed either forward or rearward; the overall effect is the same. However, rearward sweep appears to be somewhat more desirable, since it has presented fewer problems to manufacturers of models of general aviation aircraft in terms of unwanted design side effects. In effect, the wing is flying slower than the airspeed indicator indicates and, similarly, it is developing less drag than the airspeed indicator would suggest. Since less drag is being developed for a given indicated airspeed, less thrust is required to sustain the aircraft at cruise flight.

(5)   There is a penalty, however, on the low speed end of the spectrum. Sweeping the wings of an aircraft increases the landing/stall speed which, in turn, means higher touchdown speed, with proportionally longer runway requirements and more tire and brake wear as opposed to a straight-wing design. A well-stabilized approach with precise control of critical "V" speeds is necessary. In other words, to achieve a safe margin airspeed on the wing that will not result in a stalled condition with the wingtips stalling prior to the rest of the wing and possibly rolling uncontrollably to the right or left, the swept-wing aircraft must be flown at a higher actual airspeed than a straight-wing aircraft.

(6)   Drag curves are approximately the reverse of the lift curves, in that a rapid increase in drag component may be expected with an increase of angle of attack with the swept wing; the amount being directly related to the degree of sweep or reduction of aspect ratio.

(7)   The extension of trailing edge flaps and leading edge devices may, in effect, further reduce the aspect ratio of the swept wing by increasing the wing chord. This interplay of forces should be well understood by the pilot of the swept wing aircraft, since raising the nose of the

Continued

aircraft to compensate for a mild undershoot during a landing approach at normal approach speeds will produce little lift, but may instead lead to a rapid decay in airspeed, thus rapidly and critically compromising the margin of safety.

(8) Another method of increasing the critical MACH number of an aircraft wing is through the use of a high-speed laminar airflow airfoil in which a small leading edge radius is combined with a reduced thickness ratio. This type of wing design is more tapered with its maximum thickness further aft, thus distributing pressures and boundary layer air more evenly along the chord of the wing. This tends to reduce the local flow velocities at high MACH numbers and improve aircraft control qualities.

(9) Several modern straight wing, turbojet aircraft make use of the design method described in paragraph 14h. To delay the onset of MACH buzz and obtain a higher M_{MO}, these aircraft designs may incorporate the use of both vortex generators and small triangular upper wing strips as boundary layer energizers. Both systems seem to work equally well, although the boundary layer energizers generally produce less drag. Vortex generators are small vanes affixed to the upper wing surface, extending approximately 1 to 2 inches in height. This arrangement permits these vanes to protrude through the boundary layer air. The vortex generators deflect the higher energy airstream downward over the trailing edge of the wing and accelerate the boundary layer aft of the shock wave. This tends to delay shock-induced flow separation of the boundary layer air which causes aileron buzz, and thus permits a higher M_{MO}. The lift characteristics of straight wing and swept-wing airplanes related to changes in angle of attack are more favorable for swept-wing airplanes. An increase in the angle of attack of the straight-wing airplane produces a substantial and constantly increasing lift vector up to its maximum coefficient of lift and, soon thereafter, flow separation (stall) occurs with a rapid deterioration of lift.

(10) By contrast, the swept wing produces a much more gradual buildup of lift with no well-defined maximum coefficient, the ability to fly well beyond this point, and no pronounced stall break. The lift curve of the short, low-aspect ratio (short span, long chord) wing used on present-day military fighter aircraft compares favorably with that of the swept wing, and that of other wing designs which may be even more shallow and gentle in profile.

(11) Regardless of the method used to increase the critical MACH number, airflow over the wing is normally smooth. However, as airspeed increases, the smooth flow becomes disturbed. The speed at which this disturbance is usually encountered is determined by the shape of the wing and the degree of sweep.

(12) When the aircraft accelerates, the airflow over the surface of the wing also accelerates until, at some point on the wing, it becomes sonic. The indicated airspeed at which this occurs is the critical MACH number (MACH crit) for that wing.

b. Jet Engine Efficiency.

(1) The efficiency of the jet engine at high altitudes is the primary reason for operating in the high-altitude environment. The specific fuel consumption of jet engines decreases as the outside air temperature decreases for constant revolutions per minute (RPM) and TAS. Thus, by flying at a high altitude, the pilot is able to operate at flight levels where fuel economy is best and with the most advantageous cruise speed. For efficiency, jet aircraft are typically operated at high altitudes where cruise is usually very close to RPM or exhaust gas temperature limits. At high altitudes, little excess thrust may be available for maneuvering. Therefore, it is often impossible for the jet aircraft to climb and turn simultaneously, and all maneuvering must be accomplished within the limits of available thrust and without sacrificing stability and controllability.

(2) Compressibility also is a significant factor in high-altitude flight. The low temperatures that make jet engines more efficient at high altitudes also decrease the speed of sound. Thus, for a given TAS, the MACH number will be significantly higher at high altitude than at sea level. This compressibility effect due to supersonic airflow will be encountered at slower speeds at high altitude than when at low altitude.

c. Controllability Factors.

(1) Static stability is the inherent flight characteristic of an aircraft to return to equilibrium after being disturbed by an unbalanced force or movement.

(2) Controllability is the ability of an aircraft to respond positively to control surface displacement, and to achieve the desired condition of flight.

(3) At high-flight altitudes, aircraft stability and control may be greatly reduced. Thus, while high-altitude flight may result in high TAS and high MACH numbers, calibrated airspeed is much slower because of reduced air density. This reduction in density means that the angle of attack must be increased to maintain the same coefficient of lift with increased altitude. Consequently, jet aircraft operating at high altitudes and high MACH numbers may simultaneously experience problems associated with slow speed flight such as Dutch roll, adverse yaw, and stall. In addition, the reduced air density reduces aerodynamic damping, overall stability, and control of the aircraft in flight.

(i) Dutch roll is a coupled oscillation in roll and yaw that becomes objectionable when roll, or lateral stability is reduced in comparison with yaw or directional stability. A stability augmentation system is required to be installed on the aircraft to dampen the Dutch roll tendency when it is determined to be objectionable, or when it adversely affects the control stability requirements for certification. The yaw damper is a gyro-operated autocontrol system installed to provide rudder input and aid in canceling out yaw tendencies such as those in Dutch roll.

(ii) Adverse yaw is a phenomenon in which the airplane heading changes in a direction opposite to that commanded by a roll control input. It is the result of unequal lift and drag characteristics of the down-going and up-going wings. The phenomena are alleviated by tailoring the control design by use of spoilers, yaw dampers, and interconnected rudder and aileron systems.

(4) Supersonic flow over the wing is responsible for:

(i) The formation of shock waves on the wing which result in drag rise.

(ii) An aft shift in the center of lift resulting in a nosedown pitching moment called MACH tuck.

(iii) Airflow separation behind the shock waves resulting in MACH buffet.

(5) Swept wing and airfoil design alone, with boundary layer energizers such as the vortex generators described earlier, has reduced the hazardous effect of the problems described above. However, these problems are still encountered to some extent by the modern turbojet airplane in high-altitude flight.

(6) In general, this discussion has been confined to normal level, unaccelerated 1.0 G flight. When turning or maneuvering about the pitch axis, however, acceleration of G-forces can occur while maintaining a constant airspeed. As G-forces increase, both the aircraft's aerodynamic weight and angle of attack increase. The margin over low-speed stall buffet decreases, as well as the margin below MACH buffet, because of the increased velocity of the air over the wing resulting from the higher angle of attack. This, in effect, could lower the aerodynamic ceiling for a given gross-weight. Increased G-loading can also occur in nonmaneuvering flight because of atmospheric turbulence or the lack of fine touch skill by the pilot. Pilots flying at high altitudes in areas where turbulence may be expected must carefully consider acceptable safety margins nec-

Continued

essary to accommodate the sudden and unexpected vertical accelerations which may be encountered with little or no warning. How wide is the safety margin between low-speed and high-speed buffet boundaries for an altitude and weight in a 30° bank? The answer may be easily determined by reference to the Cruise Maneuver/Buffet Limit Chart for a particular aircraft. For example, in a typical jet aircraft, the 1.0 G buffet-free margin at FL 350 is 135 K; at FL 450 this speed is reduced to a mere 26 K. Thus, the safety margin in airspeed spread diminishes rapidly as the aircraft climbs and leaves little room for safety in the event of a air turbulence encounter or accidental thunderstorm penetration.

(7) If a thunderstorm cannot be avoided, follow high-altitude thunderstorm penetration procedures and avoid over-action of thrust levers. When excessive airspeed buildup occurs, pilots may wish to use speed brakes. The use of aerodynamic speed brakes, when they are part of the lateral control system, may change the roll rate any time there is a lateral control input.

(8) For detailed information concerning the operation of specific turbojet aircraft, refer to the aircraft's Airplane Flight Manual.

FAA-P-8740-11 — Stepping Up to a Complex Aircraft

Date: **9/78**   Initiated by: **AFS-800**

Stepping Up to a Complex Airplane Involves Three Basic Systems:
- The Propeller
- The Engine
- The Landing Gear

Propeller
- Controls the engine RPM.

- Works like a car's transmission: low gears (low pitch angles) for high RPMs and more power for take-off and initial climb. Higher gears (large pitch angles) for lower RPMs and greater efficiency (more miles per gallon) in cruise.

- Familiarize yourself with the recommended climb and cruise power settings before you start your engine. For some engines, under certain conditions, the "square rule" may be used during initial climb, i.e., manifold pressure in inches of mercury equals engine RPMs in hundreds.

- Take off and land with the propeller control in the high RPM position.

Engine
- Throttle controls manifold pressure.

- Changes in power control settings should be made as follows:

  —To INCREASE power: mixture, prop, then throttle. *Then readjust the mixture.*

  —To DECREASE power: throttle, prop, *then* mixture.

- Carburetor induction is a simple system but is icing sensitive.

- Fuel injection is more complex, more efficient, and less icing prone. Still susceptible to induction filter icing.

- Turbocharging is an exhaust-driven system capable of providing sea level or higher induction system pressure at altitude.

- Different systems require different procedures: KNOW YOURS.

Landing Gear
Classified by type of retraction mechanism: electrical, hydraulic, or mechanical (each not covered here).

- Electrical gear circuits protected by fuses and/or circuit breakers.

  —Emergency extension possible with hand crank.

  —Disable the landing gear electrical circuit before using the emergency system.

- Hydraulic gear system mechanically less complicated.

  —Typical emergency hydraulic gear extension accomplished with hand pump, CO_2, or gravity freefall, or any combination of these systems.

- Once down, do not attempt to retract the gear using the emergency system.

- Landing gear position indicator lights can typically be checked with a "press-to-test" feature.

- "Squat switches" are *not* fool proof. Be sure your gear switch is in the DOWN position before turning on the electrical power.

- DO NOT RETRACT THE GEAR until

  —Aircraft is positively airborne, and

  —Insufficient runway remains for landing.

- KNOW your gear operating speeds.

- Unusual pitch and yaw indications can be used to verify suspected gear malfunctions.

- After landing, taxi clear of the active runway before operating cockpit controls. PAY ATTENTION. It's easier to taxi with the flaps down than with the gear up!

- When temperatures are near freezing, use caution to prevent slush and water from splashing onto the gear mechanism. If you have to takeoff in slushy conditions, cycle the gear several times to prevent ice from adhering to movable gear parts.

In General

- Know your airplane—ALL of its systems. The key to transitioning any airplane is your *Pilot's Operating Handbook*—KNOW IT COLD.

- Don't over extend your experience. Take it one step at a time. Complexity compounds itself.

- Use your checklist! Double check before landing with a final GUMP check: Gas, Undercarriage, Mixture, and Propeller.

- Get a complete checkout by a competent instructor pilot who is familiar with your specific make and model.

- Take frequent check rides. "Practice makes better—and sometimes 'perfect'."

FAA-P-8740-19 — Flying Light Twins Safely

Date: **9/78**   Initiated by: **AFS-800**

Introduction

The major difference between flying a twin engine and a single engine airplane is knowing how to manage the flight if one engine loses power for any reason. Safe flight with one engine-out requires an understanding of the basic aerodynamics involved—as well as proficiency in engine-out procedures.

Loss of Power on One Side

Loss of power from one engine affects both climb performance and controllability of any light twin.

Climb Performance

Climb performance depends on an excess of power over that required for level flight. Loss of power from one engine obviously represents a 50% loss of power but, in virtually all light twins, climb performance is reduced by at least 80%. (*See* Figure 1)

The amount of power required for level flight depends on how much drag must be "overcome" to sustain level flight. It's obvious, that if drag is increased because the gear and flaps are down and the prop windmilling, more power will be required. Not so obvious, however, is the fact that drag also increases as the square of the airspeed while power required to maintain that speed increases as the cube of the airspeed. (*See* Figure 2).

Thus, climb performance depends on four factors:

- Airspeed—too little or too much will decrease climb performance.

- Drag—gear, flaps, cowl flaps, prop and speed.

- Power—amount available in excess of that needed for level flight.

- Weight—passengers, baggage and fuel load greatly affect climb performance.

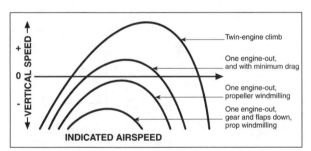

Figure 1. Effect of one engine-out and airplane configuration on vertical speed

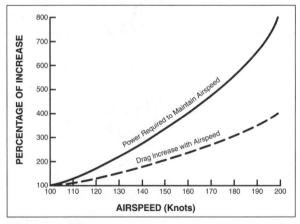

Figure 2. Effect of airspeed on drag — and power required to maintain that airspeed while in level flight

Yaw

Loss of power on one engine also creates yaw due to asymmetrical thrust. Yaw forces must be balanced with the rudder. (*See* Figure 3)

Roll

Loss of power on one engine reduces prop wash over the wing. Yaw also affects the lift distribution over the wing causing a roll toward the "dead" engine. (*See* Figure 4) These roll forces may be balanced by banking into the operating engine.

Critical Engine

The critical engine is that engine whose failure would most adversely affect the performance or handling qualities of the airplane. The critical engine on most U.S. light twins is the left engine as its failure requires the most rudder force to overcome yaw. At cruise, the thrust line of each engine is through the propeller hub.

But, at low airspeeds and at high angles of attack, the effective thrust centerline shifts to the right on each engine because the descending propeller blades produce more thrust than the ascending blades (P-factor). Thus, the right engine produces the greatest mechanical yawing moment and requires the most rudder to counterbalance the yaw.

Key Airspeed for Single Engine Operations

Airspeed is the key to safe single engine operations. For most light twins there is an:

- airspeed below which directional control cannot be maintained.
  V_{MCA}

- airspeed below which an intentional engine cut should never be made.
  V_{SSE}

- airspeed that will give the best single engine rate of climb (or the slowest loss of altitude).
  V_{YSE}

- airspeed that will give the steepest angle of climb with one engine-out.
  V_{XSE}

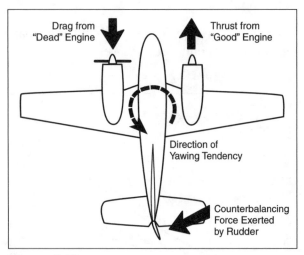

Figure 3. Yaw

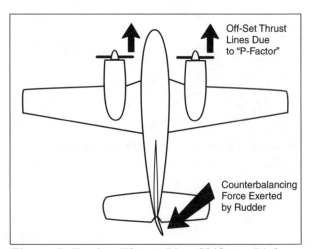

Figure 5. Engine Thrust Line Shifts to Right at Low Airspeeds and at High Angles of Attack

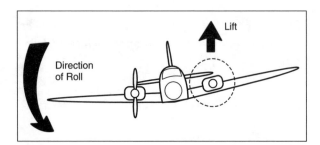

Figure 4. Roll

Minimum Control Speed Airborne (V$_{MCA}$)

V$_{MCA}$ is designated by the red radial on the airspeed indicator and indicates the minimum control speed, airborne at sea level. V$_{MCA}$ is determined by the manufacturer as the minimum airspeed at which it's possible to recover directional control of the airplane within 20 degrees heading change and, thereafter, maintain straight flight, with not more than 5 degrees of bank if one engine fails suddenly with:

• Takeoff power on both engines,

• Rearmost allowable center of gravity,

• Flaps in takeoff position,

• Landing gear retracted,

• Propeller windmilling in takeoff pitch configuration (or feathered if automatically featherable).

However, sudden engine failures rarely occur with all of the factors listed above and, therefore, the actual V$_{MCA}$ under any particular situation may be a little slower than the red radial on the airspeed indicator. However, most airplanes will not maintain level flight at speeds at or near V$_{MCA}$. Consequently, it is not advisable to fly at speeds approaching V$_{MCA}$ except in training situations or during flight tests.

Intentional One Engine Inoperative Speed (V$_{SSE}$)

V$_{SSE}$, is specified by the airplane manufacturer in new Handbooks and is the minimum speed at which to perform intentional engine cuts. Use of V$_{SSE}$ is intended to reduce the accident potential from loss of control after engine cuts at or near minimum control speed. V$_{SSE}$ demonstrations are necessary in training but should only be made at a safe altitude above the terrain and with the power reduction on one engine made at or above V$_{SSE}$. Power on the operating (good) engine should then be set at the position for maximum continuous operation. Airspeed is reduced slowly (one knot per second) until directional control can no longer be maintained or the first indication of a stall obtained. (*See* Figure 7)

Recovery from flight below V$_{MCA}$ is made by reducing power to idle on the operating (good) engine, decreasing the angle of attack by dropping the nose, accelerating through V$_{MCA}$, and then returning power to the operating engine and accelerating to V$_{YSE}$, the blue radial speed.

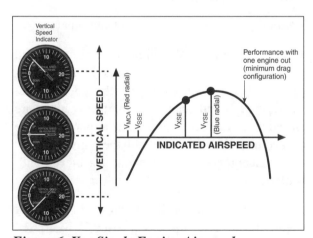

Figure 6. Key Single Engine Airspeeds

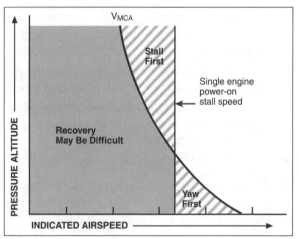

Figure 7. Relationship Between Stall Speed and V$_{MCA}$ for Aircraft with Normally Aspirated Engines

Best Single Engine Rate of Climb Speed (V_{YSE})

V_{YSE} is designated by the blue radial on the airspeed indicator. V_{YSE} delivers the greatest gain in altitude in the shortest possible time, and is based on the following criteria:

- critical engine inoperative, and its propeller in the minimum drag position.

- operating engine set at not more than maximum continuous power.

- landing gear retracted.

- wing flaps in the most favorable (i.e., best lift/drag) ratio position.

- cowl flaps as required for engine cooling.

- airplane flown at recommended bank angle.

Drag caused by a windmilling propeller, extended landing gear, or flaps in the landing position will severely degrade or destroy single engine climb performance. Single engine climb performance varies widely with type of airplane, weight, temperature, altitude and airplane configuration. The climb gradient (altitude gain or loss per mile) may be marginal or even negative—under some conditions. Study the Pilot's Operating Handbook for your specific airplane and know what performance to expect with one engine out. Remember, the Federal Aviation Regulations do not require any single engine climb performance for light twins that weigh 6000 pounds or less and that have a stall speed of 61 knots or less.

Best Single Engine Angle of Climb Airspeed (V_{XSE})

V_{XSE} is used only to clear obstructions during initial climbout as it gives the greatest altitude gain per unit of horizontal distance. It provides less engine cooling and requires more rudder control than V_{XSE}.

Single Engine Service Ceiling

The single engine service ceiling is the maximum altitude at which an airplane will climb, at a rate of at least 50 feet per minute in smooth air, with one engine feathered. New Handbooks show service ceiling as a function of weight, pressure altitude and temperature while the old Flight Manuals frequently use density altitude.

The single engine service ceiling chart should be used during flight planning to determine whether the airplane, as loaded, can maintain the Minimum Enroute Altitude (MEA) if IFR, or terrain clearance if VFR, following an engine failure.

Basic Single Engine Procedures

Know and follow, to the letter, the single engine emergency procedures specified in your Pilot's Operating Handbook for your specific make and model airplane. However, the basic fundamentals of all the procedures are as follows:

- Maintain aircraft control and airspeed at all times. This is cardinal rule No. 1.

- Usually, apply maximum power to the operating engine. However, if the engine failure occurs during cruise or in a steep turn, you may elect to use only enough power to maintain a safe speed and altitude. If the failure occurs on final approach, use power only as necessary to complete the landing.

- Reduce drag to an absolute minimum.

- Secure the failed engine and related subsystems.

The first three steps should be done promptly and from memory. The check list should then be consulted to be sure that the inoperative engine is secured properly and that the appropriate switches are placed in the correct position. The airplane must be banked into the live engine with the "slip/skid" ball out of center toward the live engine to achieve Handbook performance.

Another note of caution: Be sure to identify the dead engine, positively, before feathering it. Many red faced pilots—both students and veterans alike have feathered the wrong engine. Don't let it happen to you. Remember: First, identify the suspected engine (i.e., "Dead foot means dead engine"); second, verify with cautious throttle movement; then feather. But be sure it is dead and not just sick.

Engine Failure on Takeoff

If an engine fails before attaining liftoff speed, the only proper action is to discontinue the takeoff. If the engine fails after liftoff with the landing gear still down, the takeoff should still be discontinued if touchdown and rollout on the remaining runway is still possible.

If you do find yourself in a position of not being able to climb, it's much better to pull the power on the good engine and land straight ahead than try to force a climb and lose control.

Pilot's Operating Handbooks have charts that are used in calculating the runway length required if the engine fails before reaching liftoff speed and may have charts showing performance after liftoff such as:

- Accelerate-Stop Distance. That's the distance required to accelerate to liftoff speed and, assuming failure to engine at the instant that liftoff speed is attained, to bring the airplane to a full stop.

- Accelerate-Go Distance. That's the distance required to accelerate to liftoff speed and, assuming failure of an engine at the instant liftoff speed is attained, to continue the takeoff on the remaining engine to a height of 50 feet.

Study your accelerate-go charts carefully. No airplane is capable of climbing out on one engine under all weight, pressure altitude and temperature conditions. Know, before you take the actual runway, whether you can maintain control and climbout if you lose an engine while the gear is still down. It may be necessary to off-load some weight, or wait for more favorable temperature or wind conditions.

When to Fly V_X, V_Y, V_{XSE}, and V_{YSE}

During normal two engine operations, always fly V_Y (or V_X if necessary for obstacle clearance) on initial climbout. Then, accelerate to your cruise climb airspeed, which may be V_Y plus 10 to 15 knots after you have obtained a safe altitude. Use of cruise climb airspeed will give you better engine cooling, increased inflight visibility and better fuel economy. However, at the first indication of an engine failure during climbout, or while on approach, establish V_{YSE} or V_{XSE}, whichever is appropriate. (Consult your Handbook or Flight Manual for specifics).

Summary

Know the key airspeeds for your airplane and when to use them:

V_{MC} (Red Radial)—never fly at or near this airspeed except in training or during flight test situations.

V_{SSE} never intentionally cut an engine below this airspeed.

V_{YSE} (Blue Radial)—always fly this airspeed during a single engine emergency during climbout (except when necessary to clear an obstacle after takeoff) and on final approach until committed for landing.

V_{XSE}—Fly V_{XSE} to clear obstacles, then accelerate to V_{YSE}.

Know the performance limitations of your airplane, including its:

- accelerate-stop distances,

- accelerate-go distances,

- single engine service ceiling, and

- maximum weight for which single engine climb is possible.

Know the basic single engine emergency procedures:

- Maintain control of the airplane by flying at the proper airspeed.

- Apply maximum power, if appropriate.

- Reduce drag (includes feathering).

- Complete engine-out checklist.

And finally, put your knowledge into practice with a qualified instructor pilot observing and assisting you. Engine failures can be handled competently and safely by proficient pilots. Keep your proficiency up and every flight in a multiengine airplane should be a safe one.

FAA-P-8740-29 — Meet Your Aircraft

Date: **6/80**   Initiated by: **AFS-800**

Acknowledgment

The material contained in this pamphlet originally appeared in a pamphlet published by the Insurance Company of North America. The Federal Aviation Administration appreciates the cooperation of INA in granting permission for use of their material in the Accident Prevention Program.

Purpose

This quiz is designed to aid a pilot in understanding the aircraft he flies. Although no attempt is made to cover in depth all information contained in the typical Owner's Manual, this booklet will provide a review of the basic information a pilot should know before taking off on a cross-country flight. Since the questions are designed to be answered in an open book fashion, no minimum passing score is set, although it is assumed that a pilot holding at least a private license would score high. It is suggested that, in addition to the review provided by this booklet, a thorough, periodic review be made of the Owner's Manual.

Instructions

Since this is an open book test, you may use any book which will provide you with a correct answer. The Owner's Manual for the aircraft you plan to use is required, and the Airman's Information Manual is suggested. All answers concerning aircraft performance and limitations should be obtained from the Owner's Manual for the aircraft you plan to fly. If you find a question not applicable to this aircraft, simply omit it. If you are unable to locate the answer to a given question, we suggest you discuss it and any questions answered improperly with your flight instructor.

Name _____ **Date** _____

Make _____ **Model** _____ **Airman's certificate** _____

Ratings _____ **Medical certificate type-expiration date** _____

Total time _____ **Last 90 days** _____ **Time in make & model** _____

Date of latest biannual flight review _____

1. What is the normal climb-out speed?

_____

2. What is the best rate of climb speed?

_____

3. What is the best angle of climb speed?

_____

4. What is the maximum flap-down speed?

_____

5. What is the maximum gear-down speed?

_____

6. What is the stall speed in a normal landing configuration?

_____

7. What is the clean-stall speed?

_____

8. What is the approach to landing speed?

_____

9. What is the maneuvering speed?

_____

10. What is the red-line speed?

_____

11. What engine off glide speed will give you the maximum range?

_____

12. (Multi-engine only) What is the VMC?

_____

13. What is the make and horsepower of the engine(s)?

_____ Hp.

14. What is the estimated TAS at 5,000 ft. and 65% power?

_____

15. What RPM or combination of RPM and Manifold Pressure yields 65% power at 5000' MSL?

_____ RPM &

_____ MP

16. How many gallons of fuel are used per hour at 65% power at 5000' MSL?

_____

17. How many *Usable* gallons of fuel can you carry?

_____

18. Where are the fuel tanks located, and what are their capacities?

Main tank _____

gallons _____

Left tank _____

gallons _____

Right tank _____

gallons _____

Rear tank _____

gallons _____

Auxiliary tank #1 _____

gallons _____

Auxiliary tank #2 _____

gallons _____

19. (Multi-engine only) In the event an engine fails, can all on-board fuel be fed to the running engine?_____

    If yes, explain how:

    _____

    _____

    _____

    _____

20. With full fuel load at 65% power, at 5,000 ft, allowing a 45 minute reserve, what is the maximum duration (in hours)?

    _____

21. What speed will give you the best glide ratio?

    _____

22. What is the octane rating of the fuel used by this aircraft?

    _____

23. How do you drain the fuel sumps?

    _____

24. What weight of oil is being used?

    _____

25. Is the landing gear fixed, manual, hydraulic, or electric? If retractable, what is the back-up system for lowering the gear?

    _____

    _____

26. What is the maximum allowable crosswind component for the aircraft?

    _____

27. How many people will this aircraft carry safely with a full fuel load?

    _____

28. What is the maximum allowable weight the aircraft can carry in the baggage compartment(s)?

    Rear _____ lbs.

    Front _____ lbs.

    Belly _____ lbs.

    Left engine nacelle _____ lbs.

    Right engine nacelle _____ lbs.

    Total _____ lbs.

29. What take-off distance is required to clear a 50 ft obstacle at maximum gross weight at a pressure altitude of 5,000 ft. and 75 degrees (F)? (Assume no wind and a hard surface runway.)

    _____ ft.

30. What would the answer to number 29 be if the take-off were made from a sea-level pressure altitude?

    _____

31. Would high humidity increase or decrease this distance?

    _____

32. How do you find pressure altitude?

    _____

33. What is your maximum allowable useful load? (Check the weight and balance data in the aircraft, not the Owner's Manual.)

    _____ lbs.

34. Solve the weight and balance problem for the flight you plan to make. If you plan to fly solo, solve for a 170 pound passenger in each seat.

    Does your load fall within the weight and balance envelope? _____

    What is your gross weight? _____ lbs.

    If you solved the problem contemplating 170 lb. passengers in each seat, how much fuel could you carry? _____

    Where? _____

    If you carry full fuel how much baggage could you carry? _____ lbs.

    Where? _____

35. Where can you find an FSS phone number?

    _____

36. List two frequencies you can use to contact the FSS:

Transmit	**Receive**
1. _____	_____
2. _____	_____

37. What is the emergency frequency?

    _____

38. To operate a fixed wing aircraft in a Group 1 TCA, the aircraft must have the following equipment:

    1. _____

    2. An operable two-way radio capable of communicating with the appropriate ATC facility.

    _____

    3. An operable coded radar beacon transponder having automatic pressure altitude reporting capability.

    _____

39. What are the minimum FAR requirements for a pilot to legally carry passengers?

    _____

40. What is the present ceiling and surface wind at YTR? _____
    YTR SA2200 50SCT 100BKN 250BKN 12 128/ 23/16/2304/991

41. On the weather sequence reports the wind speed is given in knots; how is visibility measured, in nautical miles or statute miles?

    _____

42. Assuming the aircraft shown below is tuned to the VOR pictured and the VOR receiver OBS is set on 45 degrees, is the To-From readout reading To or From?

    _____

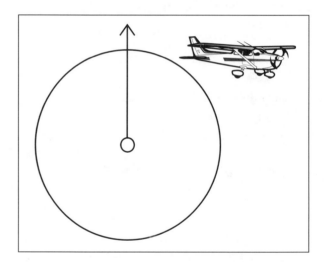

43. Fill in the blanks below, indicating cloud clearances and visibility required by the Federal Air Regulations (a) within and (b) outside controlled airspace, and (c) more than 1200 ft above the surface and over 10,000 MSL.

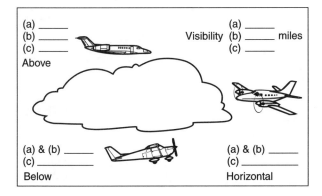

(a) _____
(b) _____
(c) _____
Above

Visibility (a) _____
         (b) _____ miles
         (c) _____

(a) & (b) _____
(c) _____
Below

(a) & (b) _____
(c) _____
Horizontal

Use the drawing below for the next two questions.

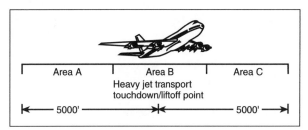

Area A   Area B   Area C
         Heavy jet transport
         touchdown/liftoff point
|← 5000' →|←→|← 5000' →|

44. If you must take off following a departing jet transport on the same runway, in what area should you plan your lift off?

A ☐   B ☐   C ☐

45. If you must land behind a landing jet transport, where should you aim for touchdown?

A ☐   B ☐   C ☐

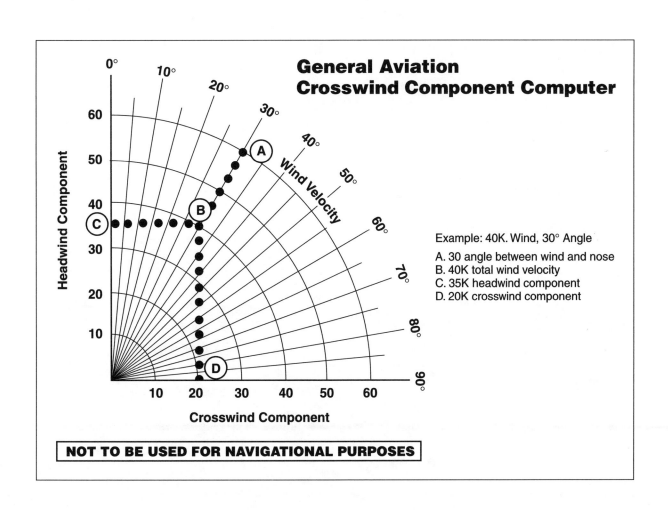

General Aviation Crosswind Component Computer

0° 10° 20° 30° 40° 50° 60° 70° 80° 90°
Wind Velocity

Headwind Component
60 50 40 30 20 10

A
B
C
D

Example: 40K. Wind, 30° Angle

A. 30 angle between wind and nose
B. 40K total wind velocity
C. 35K headwind component
D. 20K crosswind component

Crosswind Component
10 20 30 40 50 60

NOT TO BE USED FOR NAVIGATIONAL PURPOSES

Glossary

absolute ceiling. The altitude at which the airplane will no longer climb with maximum available power applied under standard atmospheric conditions.

accelerate-go distance. The takeoff roll distance required to accelerate to V_1 (V_{YSE} for piston twins) and continue the takeoff if an engine fails at that speed. This is not provided by all manufacturers, which is a tacit admission the airplane in question cannot accomplish this.

accelerate-stop distance. The runway distance required for an airplane to accelerate to V_1 (V_{YSE} for piston twins), lose an engine at that speed, and slow the airplane to a speed no greater than 35 mph.

accessory case. Usually found at the rear of the engine, this is where the drives for the magnetos, engine-driven pumps, etc., are located.

accumulator, unfeathering. A system which will drive a feathered propeller toward the unfeathered position, without having to use the starter or diving in an attempt to windmill the propeller.

best angle-of-climb speed (V_X). The speed that results in the greatest altitude gained per unit of distance.

best rate-of-climb speed (V_Y). The speed that results in the greatest altitude gained per unit of time.

blue line airspeed. Best rate of climb with an engine out (V_{YSE}), marked by a blue radial line on the airspeed indicator.

cabin altitude. In a pressurized airplane, the altitude equivalent experienced by the passengers as a result of air being pumped into the cabin; usually 8,000 feet or less.

cabin rate of climb/descent. The rate at which the pressure in the cabin is changed by the pressurization system; usually 500 feet per minute or less.

coarse pitch. The low-RPM setting of the propeller control. Cruise settings are relatively coarse.

constant-speed propeller. Also called a variable-pitch propeller. Blade angle is changed by a governor in order to maintain a constant rotational speed selected by the pilot.

counter-rotating propellers. To eliminate the "critical" engine, the right propeller on some airplanes rotates counterclockwise while the left engine's propeller rotates clockwise. Thus the moment arm for both propeller discs is close to the fuselage.

cowl flaps. Adjustable doors on the bottom of the engine nacelle which admit additional cooling air when needed.

critical altitude. The altitude at which the turbocharger waste gate is fully closed, providing maximum boost. Above this altitude, engine power will diminish.

critical engine. The engine on a multi-engine airplane that would cause the most difficulty in maintaining control of the airplane if it failed in a critical condition of flight, such as takeoff.

crossfeed. An arrangement of fuel system plumbing on multi-engine aircraft that allows any of the engines to operate from any of the fuel tanks.

drift down. Descent to the absolute ceiling with an engine out.

empennage. The horizontal stabilizer, elevator rudder, and vertical fin, or any combination thereof, for controlling the airplane in pitch and bank.

excess horsepower. Power in excess of that necessary to sustain the airplane in level flight.

feathered. A propeller blade turned with its leading edge 90° to the relative wind, to minimize drag, is said to be feathered.

flat pitch. The propeller pitch position which results in high RPM—the takeoff and short-final setting of the propeller control. Occasionally referred to as "fine pitch."

flat plate drag. Drag developed by the propeller disc when the propeller is driving the engine (or windmilling).

heavy twin. A multi-engine airplane that weighs between 6,000 and 12,500 pounds for takeoff.

induced drag. Drag that is the inevitable result of lift generation. Induced drag increases with increased angle of attack and is greatest at the low speeds, which require large angles of attack.

intercooler. A heat exchanger. Air heated in the turbocharger's compressor stage passes through the intercooler on its way to the intake manifold, and is cooled as outside air is directed over the intercooler's surface.

ISA. International Standard Atmosphere. The standard pressure and temperature used to determine performance. Its application at sea level is the most familiar—29.92" Hg and 59°F.

light twin. A multi-engine airplane with a maximum gross takeoff weight of less than 6,000 pounds; or, one that stalls at less than 61 knots. This is not to be confused with the distinction between a small airplane and a large airplane, where the cut-off is 12,500 pounds. A Duchess is a light twin; a Navajo is a heavy twin.

manifold pressure. The absolute pressure in the induction system of a piston engine. In a normally aspirated engine, manifold pressure at full throttle will be almost equal to the pressure outside the airplane, making it (at one inch of manifold pressure equals 1,000 feet of altitude) a rudimentary altimeter in an emergency.

minimum controllable airspeed (V_{MC}). Lowest speed at which the airplane is controllable with one engine developing takeoff power and the other engine's propeller windmilling. Marked by a red radial line on the airspeed indicator.

normally aspirated. An engine that breathes by sucking in air. The descending piston does the same thing for the cylinder that your diaphragm does for your lungs.

P-factor. The force exerted by the downward-moving propeller blade. P-factor increases as the angle of attack of the propeller blade increases.

parasite drag. Drag caused by skin friction and the aircraft structure itself. Engine cooling air accounts for the largest percentage of parasite drag. Because total parasite drag is a function of airspeed, it is least at low speeds and greatest at high speeds.

power loading. The ratio found by dividing the maximum weight of the aircraft by the brake horsepower produced by all the engines.

propeller disc. The invisible disc formed by a rotating propeller. Visualizing the propeller disc helps you understand the effects of airflow over the portion of the wing behind the disc and on the empennage. Keep all parts of your body outside of the propeller disc.

service ceiling. The altitude at which an aircraft can maintain a steady rate of climb of 100 feet per minute.

single-engine service ceiling. The highest altitude at which a multi-engine airplane with one propeller feathered can maintain level flight.

V-speeds

V_A. Design maneuvering speed.

V_{EF}. Speed at which the critical engine is assumed to fail during takeoff.

V_F. Design flap speed.

V_{FE}. Maximum flaps extended speed.

V_{LE}. Maximum speed with landing gear extended.

V_{LO}. Landing gear operating speed.

V_{MC}. Minimum control speed with the critical engine inoperative.

V_{NE}. Never-exceed speed.

V_{NO}. Maximum structural cruising speed.

V_R. Rotation speed; the speed at which the first control input to lift the airplane off the surface is made.

V_{SO}. Stall speed in the landing configuration.

V_{S1}. Stall speed in a specific configuration (usually gear and flaps up).

V_X. All-engine best angle-of-climb speed.

V_{XSE}. Engine-out best angle-of-climb speed.

V_Y. All-engine best rate-of-climb speed.

V_{YSE}. Engine-out best rate-of-climb speed.

waste gate. A controllable butterfly valve in the exhaust pipe of a reciprocating engine equipped with an exhaust-driven turbosupercharger. When the waste gate opens, exhaust gases leave the engine through the exhaust pipe. But when the waste gate closes, the gases must pass through the turbine that drives the supercharger compressor. By controlling the amount the waste gate is open, the speed of the turbosupercharger can be controlled. This speed determines the manifold pressure in the engine.

windmilling. An unfeathered propeller on a failed engine will "windmill," or be rotated by the relative wind, creating as much drag as a flat plate equal in diameter to the propeller disc.

yaw. Left-right rotation of the airplane around the vertical axis, seen from the cockpit as left-right motion of the nose of the airplane.

zero fuel weight. The maximum weight of the airplane before any fuel is loaded into the wing tanks. If your airplane has a fuselage tank, its contents are included in the zero fuel weight.

zero thrust. An experimentally-derived power setting that simulates operations with one propeller feathered, while keeping the engine ready for use.

Index